MONTGOMERY COLLEGE LIBRARY
GERMANTOWN CAMPUS

HISTORICAL EVOLUTION
OF
MODERN NATIONALISM

THE HISTORICAL EVOLUTION OF MODERN NATIONALISM

By
CARLTON J. H. HAYES
Professor of History in Columbia University

NEW YORK / RUSSELL & RUSSELL

COPYRIGHT, 1931, BY CARLTON J. H. HAYES
COPYRIGHT RENEWED, 1959, BY C. J. H. HAYES
REISSUED, 1968, BY RUSSELL & RUSSELL
A DIVISION OF ATHENEUM PUBLISHERS, INC.
BY ARRANGEMENT WITH EVELYN CARROLL HAYES
L. C. CATALOG CARD NO: 68-15128
ISBN: 0-8462-1147-5
PRINTED IN THE UNITED STATES OF AMERICA

PREFACE

FIVE years ago I published a volume of *Essays on Nationalism* which dealt primarily with the extreme militant type of contemporary nationalism, its nature, its historical rise, and its inherent dangers for the future. I was quite aware then that this kind of nationalism, though most in evidence during and after the World War, was only one of several kinds which had been advocated at various times and by various persons. In the present volume I am seeking to supplement the *Essays* with an account of the different major types of nationalism which have been evolved in Europe within the last two centuries. For there is need, I believe, of emphasizing the fact that nationalism is plural rather than singular.

In discussing the historical evolution of modern nationalism, it is not my purpose to describe the historical development of those social and economic forces which more or less blindly and yet with seeming inevitability have served to transform petty principalities and huge empires into a new political order based on the principle of nationality. Nor is it my purpose to explain, except quite incidentally, the practical operation of those agencies, military, literary, or educational, by means of which the masses of mankind have latterly been inspired with national patriotism. In other words, I do not propose in the following pages to treat of nationalism either as a social

PREFACE

process or as a popular movement, though of course such treatments would be entirely legitimate. Rather, I propose to treat of nationalism as an "ism," as a body of doctrines, as a political philosophy, and to discuss the successive schools of nationalist thought which have had important popular followings. It is the apostles and not the disciples on whom attention is centered.

It should be said that four of the following chapters are revised versions of lectures which I gave at Hyannis, Massachusetts, in the summer of 1929 under the auspices of the World Unity Institute and that the whole volume has profited from reports and discussions of mature students in the seminar which I have conducted at Columbia University during the past five years.

CARLTON J. H. HAYES

Afton, New York,
January 18, 1931.

CONTENTS

CHAPTER	PAGE
PREFACE	v

I. INTRODUCTION: NATIONALISM AND INTERNATIONALISM . . . 1
   1. To Grotius: Old Style 1
   2. From Grotius to Bentham: New Style . . 6

II. HUMANITARIAN NATIONALISM 13
   1. The "Enlightenment" 13
   2. Bolingbroke 17
   3. Rousseau 22
   4. Herder 27
   5. Humanitarianism and the French Revolution 33
   6. Humanitarianism and National Self-Determination 37

III. JACOBIN NATIONALISM 43
   1. The "Jacobins" 43
   2. General Characteristics 50
   3. The New Agencies 57
   4. "Secularization" 69
   5. Under Napoleon 79

IV. TRADITIONAL NATIONALISM 84
   1. The "Reaction" 84
   2. Burke 88
   3. Bonald 95
   4. Schlegel 101
   5. General Characteristics 109
   6. Under Metternich 114

CONTENTS

CHAPTER	PAGE
V. LIBERAL NATIONALISM	120
1. Bentham	120
2. General Characteristics and Post-Benthamite Evolution	133
3. Guizot	139
4. Welcker	147
5. Mazzini	151
6. In Wars of National Liberation	158
VI. INTEGRAL NATIONALISM	164
1. "Integral," the Word and the Thing	164
2. Comte	168
3. Taine	173
4. Barrès	184
5. Maurras	202
6. Pioneers of Fascism	212
7. Perversion of Liberal Nationalism	224
VII. ECONOMIC FACTORS IN NATIONALISM	232
1. The "Industrial Revolution"	232
2. Economic Liberalism	241
3. Socialism	249
4. National Economists: Fichte, List, Rodbertus, and the Historical School	262
5. Economic Nationalism	277
VIII. CONCLUSION: SOME QUESTIONS CONCERNING NATIONALISM	288
1. Why the Vogue?	288
2. An Inevitable and Circuitous Evolution?	303
3. War or Peace?	311
INDEX OF NAMES	323

CHAPTER I

INTRODUCTION: NATIONALISM AND INTERNATIONALISM

[§ 1]

MAN is a social animal, not so much in that he is indiscriminately social with all men as in that he is peculiarly social with particular groups of men. He seems always to have been drawn naturally to some special group and to have displayed a marked loyalty to it.

Among primitive men the preëminent group is normally the tribe, a relatively small and homogeneous group of great cohesive strength. Each tribe has a distinctive pattern of life and culture, a distinctive dialect, a distinctive social and political organization, a distinctive system of religious beliefs and magical practices, a distinctive set of customary laws and ceremonies and art-forms. Each tribe works and wars as a unit and indoctrinates its members with supreme loyalty to it.

Now if we designate the tribe by the word "nation," as many ancient writers did, we can readily perceive that "nationalism" is an attribute of primitive society. It becomes clear to us that the prehistoric world was peopled with nationalists and that the tribesmen described by Homer or by the authors of the Old Testament or by Tacitus or by discoverers of America or explorers of Africa were devoted to nationalism. To be sure, this primitive tribalism was a small-scale nationalism, and, so far as we know, it was not theorized about. But it was universally accepted as a fact and it was as vitally influential as it was natural.

This, however, does not tell the whole story. For, while man's most striking loyalty has been to the group, he has always been able to detect and in measure to respect a similar human nature in other men. The member of a primitive tribe usually combines with deep devotion to his own "nation" a curious interest in, and even admiration of, other tribes, other "nations," so that with his "nationalism" he joins, perhaps paradoxically, a regard for foreigners which may be termed "internationalism." On occasion he finds it convenient and not at all impossible to favor confederation of his group with others and to expand his "national" loyalty into something approaching "international" loyalty. Even among the most backward peoples of the world there is no absolute antithesis between "nationalism" and "internationalism."

Indeed, throughout much the greater span of historic civilization—the long period in which man has lived a settled life and supplied us with written records—there is observable a pronounced tendency toward the diffusion of foreign influence ("internationalism") and the weakening of tribalism ("nationalism"). Inventions or discoveries by particular tribes in particular regions, such as the use of bronze or iron or the employment of the camel or the horse or the manufacture of paper or the elaboration of the alphabet, soon spread and provided common cultural patterns for numerous tribes over wide areas. Military conquest and commercial intercourse led to the coalescence of tribal states into extensive empires—Egyptian, Assyrian,

INTRODUCTION

Chinese, Persian, Hellenic, Roman, etc.—and to the gradual subordination of tribal or urban loyalty to imperial loyalty. Certain religions appeared—Buddhism, Christianity, Islam, etc.—which speedily overflowed tribal barriers and superimposed on "national" loyalties an "international" loyalty. For many centuries, from the earliest century of Egyptian hieroglyphs to at least the sixteenth century Anno Domini, civilized human beings were reconciling their natural group sociability with a possibly more artificial sociability in larger groupings. "Nations" continued to exist, but they seemed to be progressively less compelling than international religions and international empires.

In Europe, prior to the sixteenth century, men's minds had long entertained the idea that the best and highest form of political organization was a far flung empire which should draw various tribes and peoples together in common bonds of law and allegiance, and actually there had long been a Roman Empire or a Holy Roman Empire which was, or pretended to be, much larger and greater than any "nation." For more than a thousand years, moreover, there had been a Christian Church which claimed to be catholic and which really dictated common manners and morals to most inhabitants of the Empire and of many other states too.

In the sixteenth and seventeenth centuries—at the dawn of our modern age—the traditional internationalism of civilized Europe crumbled. The Catholic Church was wrecked by the rise of Protestantism, and its international sway was forcibly broken. Each political ruler proceeded to determine what the religion of his own subjects should be, more or less in disregard of the thunders of the universal pontiff on the banks of the Tiber. At the same time the Holy Roman Empire, already racked by medieval conflicts with the Church, was rent by new tumults, partially religious and partially political and economic, and thereby it lost whatever international place and prestige it had formerly enjoyed. And from the ruins of Empire and the wreckage of Church emerged the modern state system of Europe.

The states which composed this new system were very different from the "nations" of primitive tribesmen. They were much larger and much looser. They were more in the nature of agglomerations of peoples with diverse languages and dialects and with divergent traditions and institutions. In most of them a particular people, a particular nationality, constituted the core and furnished the governing class and the official language, and in all of them minority as well as majority nationalities usually evinced a high degree of loyalty to a common monarch or "sovereign." They were referred to, in contradistinction to the older comprehensive Empire, as "nations" or "national states," and popular loyalty to their sovereigns has sometimes been described as "nationalism." But it must rigidly be borne in mind that they were not "nations" in the primitive tribal sense and that their "nationalism" had other foundation than that of present-day nationalism. The European "nations" of the sixteenth century were more akin to small empires than to large tribes.

Among these new "nations" developed a new type of "internationalism." The internationalism of primitive tribesmen had consisted of a recognition of the naturalness of tribalism for all men and of occasional formal negotiations between tribes. The internationalism of civilized Europeans for centuries prior to the sixteenth had meant the subjection of local group feeling to the claims of a great empire or the demands of an inclusive church. Now, in the sixteenth century, with the firm establishment of a considerable number of independent sovereignties, "internationalism" came to signify primarily a fixed formal relationship among them. It was at this time that regular international diplomacy began on a large scale, that permanent ambassadors and envoys were despatched from one sovereign to another and instructed to uphold the political independence and economic interest of the "nations" they severally represented. It was in the early part of the following century—the seventeenth—that Hugo Grotius gave classical expression to the principles of the new "internationalism," holding that "nations" are free, sovereign, equal states, and telling how they should behave toward one another in war and in peace.

So arose the formal internationalism of modern times, with its peculiar "international law." This phrase was not yet coined. To denote the rules and precepts which should be observed by sovereigns in their mutual dealings, Grotius used the same words—"jus gentium" ("law of nations")—as had been employed by ancient and medieval jurists to describe the special privileges of tribes who had been incorporated in the old Empire. It was not until the eighteenth century, and then by Jeremy Bentham, that the words "international law" and "internationalism" were invented. But the things described, if not the words accurately describing them, existed in vigor from the middle of the seventeenth century.

[§ 2]

The kind of internationalism which arose in Europe in the sixteenth and seventeenth centuries was not based on what today we call "nationalism." For this nationalism—the paramount devotion of human beings to fairly large nationalities and the conscious founding of a political "nation" on linguistic and cultural nationality—was not widely preached or seriously acted upon until the eighteenth century.

There had long been, of course, some consciousness of nationality among European peoples. Englishmen and Frenchmen and other groups with distinctive languages and traditions had long appreciated and boasted that they were English or French or some other brand of superior beings, as the case might be. There had been, moreover, for a very long time—certainly ever since the beginning of recorded history—some patriotism, and at times some very robust patriotism. But only exceptionally, after the waning of tribalism and before the eighteenth century A.D., had patriotism been fused with the consciousness of nationality to produce genuine nationalism.

For centuries, ever since the rise of the oriental empires of antiquity, it had been the exception, rather than the rule, for an independent state to embrace one and only one nationality. The individual had normally been patriotic about his city, his locality, his ruler, or his empire, but not about his nationality. The ancient Greek had been

INTRODUCTION

supremely patriotic about Athens or Sparta, but not about Greece. The ancient Latin-speaking Roman had bestowed the utmost patriotic devotion upon the city-state of Rome or upon the whole heterogeneous Roman Empire, but not upon the Latin nationality as such. The medieval European had been vastly more patriotic about his town or his county, or about Christendom as a whole, than about any particular national state. Even in early modern times, when the new internationalism was emerging, the Britisher was devoted to a government which ruled indifferently over Irishmen, Welshmen, and some Frenchmen, as well as over Englishmen, and which, as late as the reign of Good Queen Bess, employed French as an official language. Frenchmen, also, in early modern times were less devoted to the French nationality than to particular regions and to a royal dynasty which ruled over Germans, Flemings, Bretons, and other "foreign" nationalities, as well as over Frenchmen. And it should be recalled that other European states of the sixteenth and seventeenth centuries were even less nationalist than England or France.

The kind of "internationalism" which immediately preceded the advent of modern nationalism and which Grotius defined was, then, not concerned with relations between nationalities or strictly national states, but rather with relations between actually existing states and their dynastic rulers. Few states were yet based primarily on any principle of linguistic or cultural nationality, and consequently the relations among them might be described more accurately as inter-state than as inter-national.

Moreover, the inter-state, or international, relations of

the sixteenth, seventeenth, and early eighteenth centuries had to do less with attempts to build up homogeneous nationalities and to serve nationalist ends than to increase the wealth and prestige of reigning families or favored classes within a community; and they were characterized by diplomatic trickery and chicanery and accompanied by dynastic and commercial wars. European peoples were bartered from one reigning family to another like so many cattle, sometimes as a marriage-dowry, sometimes as the booty of conquest. Overseas peoples were exploited by rival sets of European tradesmen and soldiers. There were great dynastic wars to decide what foreign family should sit upon the throne of Spain or Austria or Poland. There were great commercial wars to determine whether natives of America, Asia, and Africa should be subject to the privileged classes of Spain, Holland, France, or England. The masses in the several European countries were not usually compelled to fight in these wars; the fighting was done by professional soldiers. But the masses suffered indirect losses: they had no say about the making of war or of peace; they perceived no profits for themselves; and in last analysis they had to pay the costs. Under the new internationalism of early modern times, national self-determination was not a recognized right.

No sooner did this new kind of internationalism seem to be firmly established and extensively practiced, however, than the new nationalism appeared, questioning it, assailing it, and threatening to subvert it. The new nationalism appeared clearly and unmistakably in Europe in the eighteenth century, a century which was far more critical and self-searching than any earlier period of like

INTRODUCTION

duration in recorded history, a century which was peculiarly revolutionary.

It was in the eighteenth century that fault-finding became the vocation of most intellectuals and middle-class persons in England, France, Italy, Germany, and many another country of Christendom. They found fault with illogical, illiberal, crazy institutions and conditions which they had inherited from the past. They found fault with existing society, with existing religion, with existing economics, with existing politics. Many of them found fault with those commercial and dynastic wars which had attended the immediately antecedent rise of "internationalism" and whose consequences to the masses were now so painfully evident. The eighteenth-century fault-finders may not have been quite so realistic as they imagined themselves to be, but the sweep and the frankness and the vigor of their criticism were most refreshing and, as events proved, were provocative of revolutionary action. The century to which they gave tone and character was destined to mark the inauguration of much of our distinctively contemporary civilization.

The critical spirit of the eighteenth century was not merely destructive. It was also constructive. It was applied to the building up of two particular concepts and programmes of action which have special concern for us here. One was the stressing of the idea that man is a social animal not only within a relatively small group but also in respect of his whole kind and species, that all men are brothers, and that the welfare of each is or should be the responsibility of all. Not since the days of the early Christians and the Stoical Marcus Aurelius had there been so much preaching of the principle of cosmopolitanism and so much counselling of one's fellows to transcend narrow local and group-loyalties and to become "citizens of the world," devoted to the progress of humanity at large.

At the same time, as immediate means to the ultimate end, a second concept and programme of action received emphatic endorsement. It was nationalism. For most eighteenth-century critics, it must be borne in mind, were nationalists as well as humanitarians. They were enormously interested not only in humanity at large but in special "primitive" manifestations of it, which they perceived in the savage tribes of America, in the curious peoples of the Orient, as well as in the more or less fanciful aborigines of the "civilized" nationalities of Europe. Whence they fell to speculating on the similarities and contrasts between "peoples," between what essentially are nationalities; and the more they speculated, the more they convinced themselves that nationalities are fundamental units of human society and the most natural agencies for undertaking needful reforms and for promoting human progress. Without being fully aware of what they were doing, they were invoking a revival of tribalism.

Some of the new nationalism was cultural, without direct political implications. But some of it, and a rapidly growing proportion, was definitely political. This nationalism involved the revolutionary recognition of the right of national self-determination, the right of individuals to determine the sovereign state to which they would belong and the form of government under which they would

INTRODUCTION

live. It was argued that, if this right were fully established, not only would local and group loyalties be merged in a higher, more inclusive, and more rational loyalty to the nation, but each sovereign nation, becoming truly a "national state," would be emancipated from the dynastic and class bonds which hitherto had weighed upon it and distressed it and would be enabled to care equally for all its citizens and thereby to confer inestimable benefits upon mankind.

With the emergence of the new nationalism (the new tribalism), "internationalism" underwent some change in popular meaning. Internationalism should not signify merely a formal relationship between any sovereign states, but rather any relationship, formal or otherwise, between national states, and even between nationalities, whether these possessed sovereign states or not. Moreover, the humanitarian impulses of eighteenth-century nationalists led them to believe most staunchly that individuals of one nationality should have a high regard for the interests and sentiments of individuals of other nationalities, and that the supreme purpose of international diplomacy as well as of nationalism was the assurance of orderly, reasonable, pacific progress to the whole world. As Hugo Grotius's *Law of War and Peace*, published in 1625, may be taken as the interpretation of "internationalism" just before the rise of nationalism, so Jeremy Bentham's *Principles of International Law*, published in 1843, is excellent evidence of the changed connotation of the word which eighteenth-century nationalism effected.

Internationalism is now a relationship between states which presumably are national and nationalist and also it is a movement for sympathetic understanding, mutual comity, and universal peace among the several self-conscious nations. It is generally in this twofold sense that we shall employ the word "internationalism" in the ensuing pages. In this sense, internationalism presupposes nationalism.

Modern nationalism signifies a more or less purposeful effort to revive primitive tribalism on an enlarged and more artificial scale. The first definite doctrines to such effect were put forth in the eighteenth century. To the exposition of what they were and to an account of their evolution, let us now give closer attention.

CHAPTER II

HUMANITARIAN NATIONALISM

[§ 1]

IN THE eighteenth century, rather suddenly, emerged a philosophy of nationalism. It emerged in the midst of dynastic and colonial wars and of the popular unrest occasioned by them. It emerged also in the midst of the curious intellectual developments that were equally characteristic of that century. It promised a way of escape from the crazy evils of the time to a logical millennium of the near future, and faith in just such a millennium was a marked trait of eighteenth-century thought.

The eighteenth century was *par excellence* the century of "serious thinkers." It was the century when every person who thought at all thought himself an intellectual and termed himself "enlightened." "Enlightenment" was conceived of, indeed, as the goal of all human effort. Monarchs, the despots of the age, were "enlightened." Philosophers were "enlightened." Professors, preachers, and priests, even business men and gentlemen farmers, were "enlightened."

Eighteenth-century "enlightenment" was a fourfold concept. First, it involved the substitution of the natural for the supernatural, of science for theology, and the assumption that the whole universe of matter and mind is guided and controlled by ineluctable *natural law*. Secondly, it exalted and almost deified human *reason*, which could and should be utilized by the individual to discover the laws of nature and to enable him to conform his life to them. Thirdly, assuming that man would use his reason and obey the natural law, it promised the *progress* and perfectibility of the human race. Fourthly, it included a tender regard for the natural rights of the individual and a predilection for the social blessings of an enlightened *humanitarianism*.

In the light of these concepts, a great deal of criticism was indulged in, much of it destructive and some of it constructive. Institutions and practices which through age had acquired any degree of popular veneration in the domains of religion, politics, and society were now ruthlessly dissected by the "enlightened" in order to discover if they were rational, if they were in harmony with natural law, if they promoted human progress, guaranteed individual rights, and conferred immediate benefits on humanity. In the domain of religion, for example, it seemed easy to prove, and a host of enlightened philosophers proved to their own satisfaction, that no revealed or supernatural religion could be reasonable or in accordance with the obvious requirements of nature and that in particular historic Christianity, whether Catholic or Protestant, was but a tissue of myths and superstitions and the church an infamous sham. The true religion, these same enlightened philosophers contended, must be natural Theism or Deism, a simple faith in a God who had been the First Cause of Natural Law and the Original Giver of Reason, Natural Rights, and the Impulse to Progress.

He had acted once in the grand manner and thenceforth, enslaved by the very Law which He had decreed for human beings and for the stars, He had become a helpless supernumerary of the universe, incapable of any real service and entitled only to be called creator, with a small c. But if faith was simplified and minimized in the new dispensation of the enlightenment, good works were magnified. These, however, were not so much the traditional good works of medieval theologians—whom the enlightened philosophers of the eighteenth century held in supreme contempt—as the imputed virtues of the pristine natural man, the *bon sauvage*, and the reputed virtues of the antique rational Stoic, the republican Greek or Roman.

To political institutions of the age, the enlightened philosophers applied their criticism also. They found here, too, very much that was merely traditional and quite contrary to the dictates of reason, nature, and republican virtue. They inveighed against inequalities and injustices, against tyranny and arbitrariness. They begged governors to be enlightened and to adopt the ideal forms of government which they themselves prodigally deduced from their own reflections on natural law and natural rights. They were especially insistent that all government must be "for the good of the governed" and that the prince is but the "first servant of his people." Incidentally, many of their ideal schemes contained fertile germs of the doctrine of popular sovereignty and of the devices of political democracy.

Through wide ranges of human society the enlightened minds of the eighteenth century played as freely as reason permitted. A new individualism, based on natural law and natural rights, was to be established. The individual was to be free to do anything and everything which did not directly impair the like freedom of his fellows; he should be free to speak, to write, to publish, to worship, to attend meetings, and to join associations. One noteworthy group of enlightened philosophers—the so-called "Economists," or "Physiocrats"—claimed that the individual should be free to possess property, to follow any profession, to engage in any trade, to make any contract, unhampered by the regulation of the state or the privilege of any legal monopoly. Against "privilege," indeed, the whole band of serious thinkers in the eighteenth century declaimed as against the unpardonable sin, for "privilege" was not only irrational but anti-humanitarian. And in the name of humanity and with the zeal of humanitarians, the "enlightened" set in motion a multitude of reform movements. There was a movement to reform the laws. There was a movement to reform the prisons. There were movements against slavery, against serfdom, and against intolerance. All the reforms, it was argued, were demanded by reason and rendered feasible by progress.

It was in this intellectual milieu of the eighteenth century that the first systematic doctrines of nationalism were expounded, and though they differed from each other in certain details, as their several authors were differently circumstanced, they all were infused with the spirit of the Enlightenment. They were based on natural law. They were evolved by more or less pure reason. They were presented as inevitable and therefore desirable steps in human progress. In object they were strictly humanitarian. They were urged, in truth, with motives so obviously humanitarian—with so kindly an eye to the well-being of the whole human race, with so touching a regard for the rights of other nationalities, and with so resentful an attitude toward jingoism and intolerance—that they may justly be described as variant specimens of a single humanitarian nationalism.

Humanitarian nationalism was the earliest and for some time the only kind of formal nationalism. It arose and flourished in the eighteenth century, and its essential unity, as well as some of its detailed variations, can perhaps best be made clear by brief analyses of the nationalist doctrines of three philosophers of the Enlightenment: an Englishman, Henry St. John, Viscount Bolingbroke; a Frenchman, Jean Jacques Rousseau; and a German, Johann Gottfried von Herder.

[§ 2]

Bolingbroke (1678-1751), though a Tory politician and a nominal member of the Church of England, though an ambitious aristocrat and a dashing fellow with the ladies, was very "enlightened" and wished above all to be remembered by a grateful posterity as a great philosopher.[1] Thrown out of high public office at an age when most men are taking the first steps in politics, he had ample leisure and means, in the midst of inveterately unsuccessful efforts to regain political preferment, to indite a con-

[1] The present author has treated of Bolingbroke's nationalism at some length in an essay entitled "The Philosopher Turned Patriot" and published in *Essays in Intellectual History, Dedicated to James Harvey Robinson* (New York, Harper, 1929), pp. 189-206.

siderable mass of philosophical writings. The most bulky, which are now the least read, dealt with religion, denouncing the supernatural, the miraculous, and the metaphysical, tradition, the Bible, and all ecclesiastical authority, and extolling natural rights and natural law, reason, and humanitarianism. Bolingbroke was one of the first Englishmen to attempt a blasting of the Christian Rock of Ages and he was a pioneer in the chaste religion of nature and reason—the religion which he called Theism.

The Theism of Bolingbroke, like the new natural religion of most eighteenth-century philosophers, was somewhat chilly. Their God of Reason was very remote, very impersonal, very scientific, and veritably enchained by eternal laws of decorum and orderliness. They did not usually spell Him with capital letters. They could not get excited about him or feel impelled by him to hold revival meetings. They discussed his attributes—his bigness and his helplessness—with solemnity and in finely balanced sentences which pleased the mind but which only mildly titillated the sentiments. They had to have other outlets for emotional enthusiasm and heart-felt worship; other cults they had to seek for personal devotion. Some turned to pure humanitarianism and its multitudinous good works; others, including Bolingbroke, turned to humanitarian nationalism.

Bolingbroke's philosophy of nationalism is contained chiefly in four of his briefer writings: *The Idea of a Patriot King, On the Spirit of Patriotism, Remarks on the History of England,* and *A Dissertation upon Parties;* but there are pertinent passages in his longer *Fragments* or *Minutes of Essays*.[1] The thing itself, according to Bolingbroke, though he did not use the word "nationalism," is derived directly from the First Cause of All Things, the God of Nature and Reason. This God had created nationalities on Earth, or at any rate He had implanted in human nature the irresistible impulse to form nationalities, marked off from one another by differences of geography, climate, language, character, and government, and He had promulgated two great natural laws for their guidance. One of these, "the universal law of reason," is the same to all and obligatory alike on all. The other, "the particular law or constitution of laws by which every distinct community has chosen to be governed," is germane and peculiar to each nationality. Through reason both these laws have been revealed to men, and by nature both are binding on men. The one safeguards humanity; the other protects nationality; both are compatible with each other.

The God of Nature and Reason intended, according to Bolingbroke, that national government "should be good." Its form is immaterial, provided it corresponds with the spirit of the particular nationality, but the "legal reverence" which, under the second great natural law, a nationality owes to a king or any other government is "national, not personal." And it is the prime business of every national government to further national interests, not dynastic or class interests; and true national interests, under the first great natural law, require a foreign policy

[1] The best complete edition of *The Works of Bolingbroke* is in eight volumes (London, 1809).

of peace and a reasoned respect for the rights and interests of other nationalities.

What, in essence, Bolingbroke did was to rear a new edifice of nationalism in place of the old fanes of ecclesiasticism. Skeptical about the old, he was credulous about the new. While denying that "traditional Christianity" was derived from a supernatural God, he affirmed that nationality came directly from the God of Nature. Authority, which he denounced as tyrannical in the Christian church, he acclaimed as reasonable and divine in the national state. He actually replaced old Gods with new. He played John the Baptist to the nationalist gospel and fashioned a sacred ark for the new covenant of nationalism.

Bolingbroke, while providing a philosophical basis for generic nationalism in all countries, was especially concerned with its proper manifestations in England. He believed that the British—or at any rate the English—were a distinctive nationality with a special "genius," and that the British Constitution, with its guaranties of "British liberties," with its limited monarch (as "God is a monarch, yet not an arbitrary but a limited monarch"), with its national church, and with its privileged landed nobility, was the divinely ordained national expression of the British genius. Consequently every Britisher owed patriotic duty and service to the British Constitution, and Bolingbroke himself so far subordinated his customary philosophic calm to the exigencies of patriotic ardor as to write most glowingly of the wonderful deeds of Queen Elizabeth and other glorious English sovereigns and to pen some of the stanzas for *Rule Britannia,* the earliest of national anthems.

Of course, if the British Constitution were really to serve national interests it was vitally necessary that the king should be a patriot, that the church should be Deistic and strictly subordinate to the civil power,[1] that the privileged nobility should be "enlightened" and should aid the "moneyed interests" by encouraging trade and commerce, and by maintaining British supremacy on the seas and in the colonies, and that the mass of the people should be actuated entirely and solely by the spirit of national patriotism, spurning devisive parties or factions, rallying to one national party, intent upon the pursuit of national interests, vigorous in defense of national honor.

The nationalism of Bolingbroke was political, and palpably aristocratic. To pursue true national interests and to defend fine national honor, any form of national government, particularly the British, must contain a strongly aristocratic element. For the "Author of Nature has thought fit to mingle" in every nationality "a few, and but a few, of those on whom He is graciously pleased to bestow a larger proportion of the ethereal spirit than is given in the course of His providence to the sons of men. These are they who engross almost the whole reason of the species: who are born to instruct, to guide, and to preserve." The "herd of mankind" have only to obey.

[1] Bolingbroke seems to have imagined that the Church of England, as it was in his day, might conveniently embody his religion of nationalism: it was decent and decorous; it was perhaps not too Christian; and it was national. He was willing to tolerate all religions, but he pleaded, in behalf of a national religion, that "all other religions must be kept too low to become the rivals of it."

Above all, however, the aristocratic political nationalism of Bolingbroke was humanitarian. Every nationality had a "genius," and every nationality was entitled to a polity consonant with its genius. Bolingbroke, for all his British patriotism, was a good deal of a cosmopolite. He lived much abroad. He knew French as well as he knew English. He conversed or corresponded with a large number of the "enlightened" on the Continent as well as in England. Like other intellectuals of his age, he felt an aversion to persecution and intolerance, a repugnance to war and cruelty. Not once in all his voluminous writings did he assail foreigners or belittle any alien nationality; never did he preach or imply jingoism. He regarded nationalism as the most natural and reasonable means not only of forwarding legitimate national interests but also of assuring the highest type of internationalism and the best fruits of humanitarianism.

[§ 3]

Rousseau (1712-1778), that harassed, half-crazed genius who knew so little how to order his own life and yet exercised a commanding influence on the lives of others, is seldom thought of as a philosopher of nationalism. He certainly wrote nothing systematic or explicit on the subject. But just as certainly his general political philosophy is implicit with ideas favorable to a well-rounded doctrine of humanitarian nationalism.

Rousseau's most famous little tract—*Le Contrat Social*—set forth the central doctrine that government is the outcome of a contract freely made, a consent voluntarily given, by "the people," and that it may be changed at any time as the "general will" of the people shall dictate. Here clearly was the principle of popular sovereignty, the foundation of political democracy. The doctrine was hardly new; it had been enunciated, at least in large part, by such Englishmen as Locke and Milton, by a group of Spanish Jesuits, and by several medieval schoolmen. But Rousseau's was a brilliant literary synthesis, and it was published at the right psychological moment, when all manner of European intellectuals, especially French, were searching for a formula by which they might logically effect a reformation of existing government and society. Rousseau was sufficiently utopian in phrase and content to appeal to the "pure" rationalists of his age; besides, he employed the whole jargon of the Enlightenment—the state of nature and natural rights, liberty and equality, individualism and humanitarianism,—and by repudiating the theocratic or ecclesiastical tendencies of many of his predecessors and directing his own synthesis toward a frankly secular society and government, he won the esteem of an age which abhorred the metaphysical and the theological.

Rousseau did not explain precisely what he meant by "the people." "The people" presumably might be any aggregate of human beings living in any given territory or under any given government. They might, or might not, be a linguistic and cultural nationality. Yet despite the obscurity on this point in Rousseau's theory, it was to become quite clear as soon as the theory was put into practice that only "the people" who shared a community of language and historic traditions would have the means and the inclination to assert the principle of popular sovereignty and to insure the operation of political democracy. Certain forms of nationalism were to arise without the support of political democracy, but political democracy was to be a mighty prop for the most popular brands of nationalism. Just as Rousseau's doctrine provided directly for a determination of the form of government by "the people," so it involved indirectly the national self-determination of peoples. Furthermore, from his doctrine could be deduced quite logically the idea that a people—a nation—consists not of unequal classes but of individuals equal in rights and duties, and also the idea that a popular or national state is strictly secular and absolutely sovereign.

In *Le Contrat Social* and at greater length in *Émile*, Rousseau struck a note which would have been a bit out of harmony with the severely classical Enlightenment at the beginning of the eighteenth century, in the days of Bolingbroke, let us say, but which in the second half of the century merely added a rich overtone to the orchestration of the intellectuals. This note was the worshipful, indeed the romantic, attitude toward primitive nature. Let everyone get back to nature. Nature is lovely and adorable. Its beauties for the first time are observed in the icy crags of Switzerland, in the lapping Lake of Geneva, in the quiet pastures and leafy dells of rural France, in the majestic fiords of Norway, in the dense trackless forests of America. The solid virtues which it implants are detected and idolized for the first time in savage breasts and primitive hearts. The American Indians become, almost overnight, the "good savages," the paragons of virtue, the living exemplars of the almost mystical simplicity and honesty and dignity which have ever characterized the natural man unspoiled by the artificialities of civilized society. And it is among the "common people," therefore, in every country, among the uneducated and the untutored, among those who are nearest to the state of nature, that the greatest virtue is to be found; they are the surest guaranty of the integrity of the republic. Hence the common people make the state; the state exalts the common people; and it is a concern of all that the education of the common people be natural and in primitive republican virtue. It was by such preachments that Rousseau communicated an emotional glow as well as an educational programme to the nationalism which was derived from his teachings.

In one of Rousseau's minor works—his *Considération sur le Gouvernement de Pologne*—which he wrote at the request of a Polish nobleman in 1772, when Poland was gravely threatened by the predatory ambitions of the neighboring dynasts of Russia, Prussia, and Austria, he gave some practical advice as to how a people, in this case the Polish nationality, might properly and helpfully become more nationalist. After relating how Moses welded the Jews "into a nation" by means of peculiar laws and religious rites that have kept them distinct from other peoples throughout the centuries, Rousseau affirms in general that "it is the national institutions which form the genius, the character, the tastes, and the customs of a people; which make one people and not another; which inspire the ardent love of country founded on habits impossible to trace back to their source." Then, addressing the Poles directly, "You do not know how to prevent the Russians from swallowing you. Fix it at least so that they cannot digest you. The virtue of your citizens, their patriotic zeal, the particular form which national institutions can give your spirits, these are the only ramparts which are always ready for your defense and which no army can force." As devices for quickening national sentiment, Rousseau mentions the award of special honors to meritorious patriots, the revival of national customs, the holding of national games, the presentation of national plays, and the observance of holidays which should "breathe patriotism." But of all such devices, education is the most important to give people "a national form." "A child in opening its eyes ought to see the fatherland," and until death the citizens should see no other; all should be educated in "the love of country, that is to say, in the love of liberty and the laws." "The national education is only procured by free men . . . ; it ought to be gratuitous, or, if this is impossible, it should be open to the poorest through scholarships." "In addition, each citizen ought to be a soldier from a sense of duty . . . ; such a national militia will cost the Republic little, will be always prepared to serve it, and will serve it well because each person defends his own goods better than another's."

In these counsels Rousseau outlined a whole programme of nationalist propaganda—a national army, a national education, a national theater, national customs and ceremonies—which, if not immediately utilized by the Poles, was very shortly to be adopted by a nationality much closer to his heart and much more affected by the Enlightenment and its attendant nationalism. Unlike the aristocratic nationalism of Bolingbroke, Rousseau's was democratic; instead of a king and a landed nobility, all the individual citizens, particularly the "common people," were to be the custodians of national patriotism. The latter would serve national interests the better.

But the democratic nationalism of Rousseau was quite as humanitarian in purpose and aim as the aristocratic nationalism of Bolingbroke. Rousseau had lived in many countries and entertained no great preference for any, unless perhaps it was for the little city-state of Geneva. He sought the aggrandizement of no nationality at the expense of others. The splendid sentimentalism of all his writings betrayed the depth of the humanitarianism within him. He was at bottom, despite his superficial volatility, an honest, warm-hearted, and humane creature. He was saddened to behold human beings about him "in chains," and he was sure that if they would but grasp the implements which he offered them—the state of nature, the social compact, liberty and equality, the general will, popular sovereignty, and the nationalism implicit in all his teachings,—they could break their chains and as free men exemplify to the whole world the fraternity within and among nations which must be the natural fruit of republican virtue.

[§ 4]

Herder (1744-1803) was in many respects a more typical product of eighteenth-century "enlightenment" than either Bolingbroke or Rousseau. He did not so much create it as express it. He himself was no aristocrat and no political philosopher. He was broadly interested in culture; he was preacher, teacher, scholar, scientist, poet, essayist, educator; and the myriad writings which flowed from his pen during four decades were stamped with his devotion to the laws and rights of nature, with his faith in human progress, and above all with his very real affection for humanity.

Born of poor and pious parents in East Prussia, the youthful Herder displayed such aptitude for study that a wealthy patron enabled him to attend the university of Königsberg, where he came under two principal intellectual influences, which he was to fuse in his later life. The one was the influence of Kant, and the other was the influence of the German Pietists. From the former he learned to reconcile his Protestant Christian faith with the rationalism of the age and also to admire the political and educational philosophy of Rousseau. From the German Pietists he derived a conviction that religion is less a matter of intellectual dogma than of inner feeling and likewise an appreciation of the importance of the common folk in the cultural, as well as in the political, domain, the importance of folk-language, folk-literature, folk-custom. He became, at Königsberg, an Evangelical Lutheran clergyman, and, after an apprenticeship in the Russo-German city of Riga and some travels abroad, he spent the major part of his life as court-preacher and minister of education in the service of the very "enlightened" Grand Duke of Saxe-Weimar. Herder's vocation, however, did not fire him with the bigoted zeal of a Martin Luther; rather, it afforded him the leisure, the independence, and the respectability necessary for the development and extension of his avocations.

Herder was interested only incidentally in politics. His absorbing interest was in culture. Indeed his greatest contribution was his conception of cultural nationalism, his exposition of what most basically distinguishes one nationality from another. Bolingbroke had assumed differences among nationalities and had founded his aristocratic nationalism on such an assumption. Rousseau had talked much about "the people," and frequently as if it were a nationality, but he had nowhere clearly defined it. Herder elaborated a whole philosophy of nationality and national differences. This philosophy is implied in most of his numerous writings; it is most systematically presented in his masterpiece, *Ideen zur Philosophie der Geschichte der Menschheit* (1784).[1]

Herder's eye—a good eighteenth-century eye—wandered far in time and space and saw nationality in every place and every age; there were nationalities (he still called them "nations" or "peoples") not only in Europe but in Asia, Africa, America, and the isles of the seas; not only in modern times, but in the middle ages and in remotest antiquity. The more he reflected on what he saw, the more convinced he was that nationalities are most natural divisions of the human race, set off from one another by immutable laws which the kindly providence of the God of Nature and Reason has implanted deep in human hearts. Specifically, according to Herder, an

[1] The present author has written more fully on this subject in an essay entitled "Some Contributions of Herder to the Doctrine of Nationalism," and published in the *American Historical Review*, Vol. XXXII (1927), pp. 719-736.

aggregate of human beings is first differentiated from another by peculiarities of geography and climate; then it develops distinctive historical traditions—an appropriate language, literature, education, manners, and customs; thereby it becomes a full-fledged nationality possessed of a "folk-character," a kind of "national soul," and a truly national culture. Thenceforth, individuals are marked by the "character" of their nationality, and so abiding is it that it remains with them for several generations after they have removed from one country to another. In Herder's own words: "As a mineral water derives its component parts, its operative powers, and its flavor from the soil through which it flows, so the ancient character of peoples arose from the family features, the climate, the way of life and education, the early actions and employments that were peculiar to them. The manners of the fathers took deep root and became the internal prototype of the race. . . . The more secluded they lived, nay frequently the more they were oppressed, the more their character was confirmed: so that if every one of these nations had remained in its place the Earth might have been considered as a garden, where in one plot one human national plant, and in another another, bloomed in its proper form and nature, where in this corner one kind of national animal, and in that corner another, pursued its course according to its instincts and character." He goes on to say that through various vicissitudes many peoples have been dispersed from their early habitats and have developed new habits in accordance with the necessities laid upon them by a new environment and a new series of

HUMANITARIAN NATIONALISM

outward events, but limited always by the original "folk-character."

National character being natural and reasonable, Herder would have everyone prize it and labor for its full realization. "The savage," he said, "who loves himself, his wife, and child with quiet joy and glows with activity for his tribe as for his own life, is in my opinion a more real being than that cultivated shadow who is enraptured with the shadow of his whole species. . . . The savage has room in his poor hut for every stranger. . . . The deluded heart of the idle cosmopolite is a home for no one." Herder would have the scientific spirit of his age brought to bear upon the comparative study of nationality. He appealed for a comparative "physiognomy" of the peoples of the world. Eloquently and at length he urged the scientific study of anthropology, philology, and comparative religion, and even more eloquently, at even greater length, he implored intellectuals to utilize the results of such scientific study to reëstablish in their pristine beauty and grandeur the several national languages, literatures, religions, customs, costumes, and all other precious attributes of cultural nationalism. He himself set an example by compiling and publishing anthologies of folk-poetry representing a great variety of nationalities.

Especially did Herder apply his principles to the German nationality. Self-respect was needed, he contended, by all peoples, and particularly in his time by the German people. German self-respect could be heightened by an educational reform, which would substitute the teaching of German for that of Latin and

French, and by a religious reform, which would restore to the Germans a national religion curiously compounded of the cult of ancient German paganism, the liberty of German Protestantism, and the humanitarianism of the Enlightenment. German self-respect could be further heightened by the sympathetic study of German archaeology and philology and by the writing and reading of German anthropologies and German histories. It could be carried to final fitting heights by a universal cherishing of the German language and of German poetry.

What Herder demanded for the Germans, he was sincerely willing and anxious to concede to all other nationalities. His view was world-wide, and his philosophy was intended to be universally applicable. Humanity was the goal of all his strivings and preachings. He constantly envisaged the world as a garden of separate flower beds, each beautiful and fragrant in its own distinctive manner, each deserving to be tended and tilled with loving care, and together constituting the multi-colored, multi-scented bouquet of perfect humanity. He dwelt upon and amplified his picture of the ideal nationality, conscious of the dignity of its own heritage, reverencing its past, laboring with informed ability toward the future consummation of the promise of the past, respecting the similar-dissimilar activities of other peoples, reaching out toward the object of a fulfilled humanity—the common end toward which each nationality came struggling up in its own way.

Herder was a bitter foe of imperialism. He denounced as criminal the effort of any nation to subject or interfere in any way with the natural development of another, and for a government to abridge or demean the culture of a people appeared to him as the worst manifestation of irrational despotism. He was as sensitive to the rights of Asiatic nationalities as to those of European peoples, and he repeatedly assailed the attempts of so-called Christian powers to Europeanize India and China and to blot out what was most distinctive and therefore most sacred to the nations of the East and of inestimable value to humanity at large. Though usually unconcerned with political nationalism, and seemingly indifferent to forms of government, Herder asserted on one occasion when he was inveighing against imperialism that "the most natural state is *one* people with *one* national character. . . . Nothing appears so directly opposed to the purpose of government as the unnatural enlargement of states, the wild mixture of breeds and nations under one sceptre." It was a convinced humanitarian who was speaking. For Herder's humanitarianism was even purer and more "enlightened" than Rousseau's or Bolingbroke's.

[§ 5]

Bolingbroke, Rousseau, and Herder—an Englishman, a Frenchman, and a German—have been selected as more or less typical examples of a considerable number of "enlightened" philosophers who, in the eighteenth century, prior to the great French Revolution, made significant contributions to a doctrine of humanitarian nationalism. The nationalism clear or implied in the teachings of Bolingbroke and Rousseau was primarily political: it demanded that each nationality should possess a national government which would pursue national ends; in the one case it was to be aristocratic, and in the other, democratic. On the other hand, the nationalism set forth in Herder's writings was almost wholly cultural: it insisted that each nationality should prize its national culture—its language, literature, and historical usages and traditions—which would strengthen national character.

Other philosophers and publicists of the time were similarly divided in the championship of aristocratic, democratic, or strictly cultural elements in the new nationalism. But all of them who championed any variety of nationalism were, like their prototypes Bolingbroke, Rousseau, and Herder, humanitarian in outlook and intent. Being eighteenth-century intellectuals, they were "enlightened"; and humanitarianism, let us repeat, was an essential part of the Enlightenment. They might differ about detail and emphasis, but they were one in stressing the humanitarian character of any and every nationalism. To them nationalism and humanitarianism did not seem incompatible. An "enlightened" person, they argued, could best serve humanity at large and the cause of internationalism by being a devoted and a reasonable nationalist. Let each nationality put its own house in order, sweep abuses out, dust superstitions away, repair and arrange the political or cultural furnishings; humanity would benefit, international peace would ensue, and human progress would proceed apace.

What such "intellectuals" of the eighteenth century so clearly expressed must have been at least latent in the minds of common people. At any rate, the doctrine of humanitarian nationalism was applied by a whole nation,

HUMANITARIAN NATIONALISM

rather suddenly, in the great French revolution from 1789 to 1793. It was stated, vaguely but substantially, in the *cahiers* or recommendations of the electoral assemblies which met all over France during the winter of 1788-1789 and which urged that the Estates-General should emphasize the unity of France and its national interests and likewise its international and humanitarian mission. And with the convening of the Estates-General and their transformation in June 1789 into the "National Constituent Assembly," humanitarian nationalism was in the ascendant in revolutionary France.

In those momentous years between 1789 and 1793 the French revolutionaries boldly proclaimed national unity. In their initial declaration "of the rights of man and of the citizen" they solemnly asserted that "the principle of all sovereignty resides essentially in the nation. No body or individual may exercise any authority which does not proceed directly from the nation." Boldly they set out to sweep away whatever they thought was irrational and inimical to national unity. They abolished class distinctions and special privileges. They dispossessed the nobility. They destroyed the guilds. They put an end to serfdom. They sheared the church of its property and independence. They erased the old provincial frontiers. They outlawed all languages but French. They levelled the classes down and the masses up to a common median of "citizens," and all "citizens" were equally to be "national," that is, French. All "citizens," moreover, were equally to be endowed with individual liberties and with national obligations. Government was to be by all and for all; it was to be democratic as well as national. For political democracy and humanitarian nationalism were born together in France; they were twins; they were different but simultaneous offspring of the same humanitarian parentage.

The new nationalism and the new democracy were ushered into France, not only with reasoned speeches of legislators, but also with much heart-warmth on the part of the people. In November 1789 some twelve thousand citizens from various towns and villages in the old provinces of Languedoc and Dauphiné more or less spontaneously assembled as national guardsmen at Étoile on the Rhône and swore to an oath which partook of the nature less of a legal document than of a profession of religious faith. "We, soldier-citizens of both banks of the Rhône, fraternally assembled for the public welfare, swear before high heaven, on our hearts and on our weapons, devoted to the defense of the state, that we will remain forever united. Abjuring every distinction of our several provinces, offering our arms and our wealth to the common fatherland, supporting the laws which come from the National Assembly, we swear to give all possible succor to each other to fulfill these sacred duties, and to fly to the help of our brothers of Paris or of any town of France which may be in danger, in the cause of liberty." In January 1790, at Pontivy, a similar demonstration was held and a similar oath taken by representatives of 150,000 national guardsmen of the provinces of Brittany and Anjou. In May, at Lyons, an even larger crowd, representing Burgundy, Franche-Comté, and Lyonnais, bound themselves even more enthusiastically to the sacred cause of national federation and fraternity. At

Paris on the Champs de Mars, on July 14, 1790, the "federation movement" reached its climax. In the presence of a seated audience of 150,000 and as many more standing, some fifty thousand popular delegates of all the provinces took the oath of national brotherhood; two hundred priests said Mass and blessed the assemblage; twelve hundred musicians played; forty cannons were fired.

All this was nationalist. But in the minds of most participants in the "federation movement" and certainly in the minds of the revolutionary leaders, at least in the early stages of the Revolution, it did not preclude attendant devotion, quite as sincere, to internationalism and humanity. Just as citizens of the various provinces of France should be united in a fraternity of the French nation, so the peoples of Europe and of the whole world should be federated in an international fraternity of liberty and equality, peace and progress. Just as the French were establishing national unity and sovereignty and getting rid of tyranny and privilege, so should other peoples assert the right of national self-determination and, imitating French example, strike off the shackles which bound them.

[§ 6]

National self-determination was a natural corollary alike to the doctrine of nationalism and to that of democracy. Both involved the recognition of the right of individuals in any region to determine not only under what government they would live but also to what state they would belong. If the people in a particular region, hitherto not a part of France, wished to be French, their wishes should be respected, regardless of what Grotius or any other exponent of the earlier internationalism had said. The wishes of the people of such a region could easily be ascertained by letting them vote, or, as the French revolutionaries styled it, by holding a plebiscite. Thus, when the inhabitants of the papal districts of Avignon and Venaissin voted by majority vote in July 1791 that they wished to join France and become members of the French nationality, the French Government, despite the protests of the pope, acceded to their wishes and incorporated them in the Fatherland, contending that it was thereby safeguarding the natural rights of human beings against the artificial "rights" of a despot. Similar plebiscites were held in Savoy in 1792 and at Nice in 1793, with results somewhat disadvantageous to their former suzerain, a lay despot, but highly favorable to France and the principle of national self-determination.

Foreign peoples did not have to join France. But in the interests of humanity they should exercise the right of national self-determination. They should destroy tyrants and freely choose to live under a government of their own making which would guarantee them the blessings of liberty, equality, and fraternity. Only thereby could international peace and universal brotherhood be secured.

French revolutionaries, being humanitarian as well as nationalist, were gradually led by the light of reason and faith to perceive that France, as the supremely humanitarian nation, must not labor for herself alone but for Europe and the world, that she must not limit her exertions to her own people but must inspire other peoples to follow her example. The French revolutionaries, with humanitarian heart-beats, welcomed to Paris and conferred honorary French citizenship on a considerable number of like-minded foreigners, including Thomas Paine, Jeremy Bentham, and that most singular of all cosmopolitan enthusiasts, Anacharsis Clootz, the self-styled "advocate of the human race" and the author of *The Universal Republic, or Address to Tyrannicides* dated "at the headquarters of the Globe in February of the Year IV." It was surely a sign of the humanitarianism of the French nationalists that Clootz was elected by French suffrages to membership in both the National Assembly and the National Convention.

Eventually, in April 1792, France went to war with Austria. But in the minds of the French revolutionaries it was a new kind of war. It was a war to make the world safe for democracy and nationalism. It was a war, not between dynasts or between peoples, but between despots and nationalities. It was a war, not for material gain, but for the welfare of humanity. Accompanying the formal declaration of hostilities was this remarkable proclamation: "The National Assembly proclaims that the French nation, faithful to the principles consecrated by its constitution, 'not to undertake any war with a view to conquest nor ever to employ its forces against the liberty of any people,' only takes up arms for the maintenance of its own liberty and independence; that the war which it is forced to prosecute is not a war of nation against nation, but the just defense of a free people against the unjust aggression of a king; that the French nation never confuses its brethren with its real enemies; that it will neglect nothing which may reduce the curse of war, spare and preserve property, and cause all the unhappiness inseparable from war to fall alone upon those who have conspired against its liberty; that it adopts in advance all foreigners who, abjuring the cause of its enemies, shall range themselves under its banners and consecrate their efforts to the defense of liberty, and it will promote by all means in its power their settlement in France. . . ."

In December of the same year, with the tide of battle turning in favor of France and with the revolutionaries thoroughly committed to the democracy and nationalism of Jean Jacques Rousseau and ready to decapitate their own late despot—Louis XVI, now "Citizen Capet"—the National Convention of the Republic stated the case in a more threatening manner; but from the French viewpoint it was still an humanitarian case. "The French nation declares that it will treat as enemies every people who, refusing liberty and equality or renouncing them, may wish to maintain, recall, or treat with the prince and the privileged classes; on the other hand, it engages not to subscribe to any treaty and not to lay down its arms until the sovereignty and independence of the people whose territory the troops of the Republic shall have entered shall be established, and until the people shall have adopted the principles of equality and founded a free and democratic government." Apparently other nationalities were to be free to exercise the right of self-determination, if they exercised it in accordance with French models, but not otherwise. To the French, the dictate still appeared to be at the behest of humanity and in its interests. But to many foreigners at the beginning of 1793 it seemed to be less in the cause of humanity than in that of fanatical French nationalism.

Was humanitarian nationalism already losing its soul and its essence? Certainly a Bolingbroke would have been scandalized by the "excesses" of the French Revolution, but he would have blamed them on the democratic, rather than on the humanitarian, element in nationalism; and the Englishmen who were soon to wield very real cudgels against the French revolutionaries were nationalist and aristocratic and in their sonorous professions most humanitarian. A Herder was as indifferent to the French Revolution as to other political happenings, such as those within the petty principalities of his own fatherland; he continued, while proclamations and declarations poured out from Paris, to peg away at Weimar on cultural nationalism, ever in benevolent humanitarian vein. In Germany and elsewhere on the Continent there were already some responsive stirrings, not as yet to the nationalism which was political, but to that which was cultural—and humanitarian.

Humanitarian nationalism was not destroyed by the French Revolution. The French Revolutionaries themselves professed to be actuated by it. Their most stubborn foes, the English, were also devotees of it. And many a neutral person explained his position by reason of it.

Yet humanitarian nationalism was undergoing a seasonal alteration. As the eighteenth century neared its end, new robes of thought became fashionable, and among the outmoded clothing was the gossamer cloak of humanitarianism. This cloak nationalism laid temporarily aside.

But nationalism, thus nakedly exposed, was not a single thing; it was aristocratic and democratic and neither. Each thing which it was, proceeded promptly to don a new dress. Democratic nationalism became "Jacobin"; aristocratic nationalism became "traditional"; nationalism which was neither democratic nor aristocratic became "liberal." Each of the new entities claimed to be the chief if not the sole heir to humanitarian nationalism, and each on occasion admired and boasted of the beautiful old cloak that had been laid aside. It is doubtful, however, if Bolingbroke or Herder or even Rousseau would have been altogether satisfied with the humanitarianism of the later nationalisms.

To the successors and in a sense the carriers of humanitarian nationalism we may now turn our attention. First and foremost, at the close of the eighteenth century, is the complex of doctrines and practices which may conveniently be labelled Jacobin nationalism.

CHAPTER III

JACOBIN NATIONALISM

[§ 1]

"JACOBIN" was originally the name of a Parisian monastery. When, during the French Revolution, one of the clubs which members of the National Constituent Assembly formed for social purposes, the Breton Club,[1] appropriated the hall of the monastery for its own meetings and headquarters, "Jacobin" became the popular designation of the Club itself. This Club speedily gained great and wide influence. It admitted members who were not members of the National Assembly; it held formal meetings and discussions to which the general public was admitted; it established some twelve hundred branches throughout the country and conducted a regular correspondence with them. Its power increased, until it became actually greater than that of the National Assembly. When the National Assembly finally adjourned in September 1791, the election of the Legislative Assembly was accomplished mainly under the guidance of the Jacobin Club. Many of the stirring events which followed in swift succession were determined by the voice of Jacobins, whose deliberations were regarded by the Parisian

[1] This was the original name of the Club. Subsequently, its official name was changed to "The Society of Friends of the Constitution."

masses with more interest than those of the Legislative Assembly. The Club reached the zenith of its power when the National Convention met in September 1792 and proclaimed France a Republic. The agitation for the death of the ex-king, the storm which destroyed the Girondist Party, the excitement of the lowest classes against the bourgeoisie, and the inauguration of the Reign of Terror over all France, were largely the work of the Jacobins.

The Jacobin Club received its death-warrant with the fall and execution of Robespierre in August 1794. It was finally closed by a law of November 1794; and shortly afterwards its place of meeting—the Jacobin monastery—was demolished. But the name had been too closely associated with fateful events, messianic to one multitude and satanic to another, to perish with a specific organization or a particular building. The whole course of events from 1791 to 1794 and the philosophy underlying them came to be described loosely as "Jacobin." What friends and apologists of the French Revolution lauded as beneficent or necessary steps in national progress and what its foes and critics denounced as "excesses" were comprehensively referred to as "Jacobinism," alike by friend and foe, regardless of whether any particular step or "excess" had been originated or sponsored by the Jacobin Club. In this way, "Jacobin" has passed into common parlance as a term designating persons in sympathy with the extreme actions and sentiments of the great French Revolution and including of course a considerable number who were not members of the Jacobin Club.

In those momentous years from 1791 to 1794 when

JACOBIN NATIONALISM

"Jacobinism" was in the ascendant in France, much was done or planned to perfect the doctrine of nationalism and to carry it into full effect. The nationalism which accordingly emerged may conveniently be described as Jacobin nationalism. It was based in theory on the humanitarian democratic nationalism of Jean Jacques Rousseau and was developed by a galaxy of revolutionary lights for the express purpose of safeguarding and extending the liberty, the equality, and the fraternity which had been asserted and partially established under severely humanitarian auspices in the early days of the Revolution.

Among the leading lights of "Jacobin" nationalism were several remarkable constellations. First, there was the so-called Girondist group, including Brissot, lawyer and journalist from Chartres; Pétion, another lawyer from Chartres; Vergniaud, lawyer from Limoges; Roland, manufacturer from Nantes, and his charming young wife, Madame Roland, whose salon at Paris was the rendezvous of the group. The members of this group were young enthusiasts and idealists. They were all in their thirties, except M. Roland, who was a kind of benevolent patron to them. They were all of the well-to-do, "enlightened" middle class, trained most punctiliously in the ancient classics and in oratory, and eager to avail themselves of every opportunity to pour out floods of eloquence in praise of the antique republican virtue of Greece and Rome. They were convinced apostles of republicanism and uncompromising opponents of monarchy. Above all, they were pure patriots in the ancient sense, believing that the institutions and practices of the small city-state of Sparta were quite applicable to the large national state of France. They were not very practical, and they had a penchant for well-intentioned but blundering intrigue. It was they who, in the hope of discrediting the monarchy and securing the republic, prevailed upon the Legislative Assembly to declare war against Austria. They succeeded in their immediate object, but the war they let loose proved to be a Pandora's box against whose escaping evils their own pure patriotism was not proof. Their eloquence was stilled by the guillotine during the ensuing Reign of Terror.

Secondly, there was the so-called Mountainist group, itself a congeries of factions, men of action as well as of words. There was, all by himself, Marat, the aging "enlightened" physician, the fierce editor of the *Ami du Peuple*, the whole-souled intolerant patriot, who stirred "the people" to hate their enemies and distrust their leaders, and who was martyred in his bathtub by a good Girondist girl. There were the Dantonists, headed by Danton himself, lawyer from Champagne and agitator in Paris, the strong-voiced, strong-willed advocate of patriotic "audacity" in the face of foreign and domestic enemies, a volcano of energy and perhaps the most statesmanlike of all extremists, eventually counselling moderation and dying bravely on the scaffold for such counsels, together with his friend and disciple Desmoulins, lawyer and journalist from Picardy. There were the Hébertists, including Hébert, lawyer and journalist from Alençon, and Chaumette, medical student in his twenties from Nevers, violently anti-Christian and fanatically devoted to the religion of reason and also, by an ironical trick of destiny, to the Reign of Terror, in which they themselves perished. There were Robespierre, lawyer from Artois, and Couthon, lawyer from Clermont-Ferrand, both in their thirties, and the particularly pure Saint-Just, son of a country gentleman in Nivernais and still in his twenties —puritanical doctrinaires who knew Rousseau better than they knew human nature, who bored their auditors with long-winded sermons, who perpetually paraded the faults of others and their own virtues, but who by reason of their seriousness and honesty and their very fanaticism acquired an influence and for a time a predominance over abler men; they too ended on the guillotine.

The Mountainists as a group were forceful nationalists; they were too intent upon the making of republican patriots, too busily engaged in breaking "traitors," real or fancied, to go much beyond Rousseau in the formulation of a theory of national patriotism. The nature and philosophy of their nationalism must be sought in their actions.

It is not wholly so in the case of two Jacobins who managed to steer a fortunate course between and among rival revolutionary factions, thereby escaping the guillotine, and who have left us memorials and memoirs of the faith within them and within many of their associates. One was Bertrand Barère (1755-1841), a lawyer from southern France, attractive in appearance, engaging in manners, whose social qualities, "enlightened" opinions, and gifts as essayist and orator earned him a substantial reputation in his native region and in National Assembly and National Convention, of both of which bodies he was a prominent member. At first, when the constitutional monarchists were dominant under such leaders as

Mirabeau and Siéyès, he was a moderate revolutionary, championing the popular cause of national unity, constitutional government, subordination of the church to the national state, abolition of serfdom and special privileges, and various other humanitarian reforms; and the journal which he founded at Paris, the *Point du Jour*, and which enhanced his prestige, was at first neither extreme nor intolerant.

Gradually, however, as the popular temper at Paris became more radical, and especially after the attempted flight of the King in June 1791 had discredited monarchy, Barère underwent conversion to republicanism and identified himself with the Girondists; his reward was membership from October 1791 to September 1792 in the newly instituted supreme court. Then, elected to the National Convention and keenly aware of the rapidly rising tide of extreme radicalism, he threw in his lot with the Mountainists. He voted for the death of "Citizen Capet," remarking that "the tree of liberty could not grow unless it were watered with the blood of kings." He became a member of the Committee of Public Safety, busying himself chiefly with the conduct of foreign affairs. He voted for the death of the Girondists, and by timely flatteries endeared himself temporarily to Robespierre. He urged on the Terror, and rendered the extremists great service by the telling phrases of his oratory, by his clear expositions of the problems of the day, and by his aptitude for practical achievement. When popular reaction set in, it was Barère who drew up the report outlawing Robespierre; and though imprisoned himself for his own complicity in the Terror, he escaped and after living in concealment for several years reappeared as a secret agent of Napoleon. He died a natural death, the last survivor of the Committee of Public Safety, and a pensioner of King Louis Philippe.

Superficially it must appear that Barère was thoroughly opportunist and unscrupulous. He certainly was a weathervane to the gusts of factional strife which stirred Jacobinism, but even as such he has considerable utility for us; his obvious veerings from moderation to extremism are an excellent index to highly significant aspects of Jacobin thought. However, one must come away from a painstaking study of Barère's writings and public activities with the conviction that the man, despite his political tergiversations, entertained from first to last a constant and fundamental devotion to France, a supreme nationalism, which was essentially religious and a bit intolerant. Barère's inmost philosophy, which alone gives some unity to his varied career, was Jacobin nationalism.

The other man—Lazare Carnot (1753-1823)—was far nobler. He was from northern France, an engineer and an army officer, always of high personal integrity and great practical ability. Thoroughly devoted to the revolutionary principles of liberty, equality, and fraternity, he served with distinction as a hard-working member of the Legislative Assembly and rose to a high position in the National Convention and on its Committee of Public Safety, honored and respected by each of the quarrelling factions. His most widely recognized fame was that of "organizer of victory," for he it was who organized, equipped, inspired, and directed the national republican armies of France for their sensational victories over the mounting coalition of foreign foes. For a time in 1800 he served anew as minister of war, helping incalculably, by his energy, skill, and enthusiasm, to achieve for Napoleon the brilliant military results of the Italian and Rhenish campaigns. As soon, however, as he understood Napoleon's imperial ambitions, he resigned office and retired to private life, reëmerging only toward the close of Napoleon's reign to offer his services in the time of French defeat and to defend Antwerp with heroism against the final attacks of the Allies. He died in exile, an unswerving Jacobin and patriot to the last. Indeed, it is as the purest and best of Jacobin nationalists that Carnot should be celebrated. Not alone in his military efforts, but in his daily life and counsels, in his set speeches in the National Convention, and in the memorials which he addressed to Napoleon and to Louis XVIII, he expressed with ever memorable dignity and persuasiveness the creed of his almost fanatical nationalism.

It may be not without interest to add that the Jacobin tradition was maintained in the Carnot family. Lazare's son edited the memoirs of Barère and was conspicuous in the Second French Republic. Lazare's grandson became President of the Third French Republic.

[§ 2]

From the more or less philosophical writings and speeches of Carnot and Barère and from the sayings and especially the doings of Girondists and Mountainists, it is possible to extract the various elements which, together, constitute Jacobin nationalism. In the first place, most if not all of the Jacobins started with Rousseau and with approval of the efforts of the National Assembly—so far as they went—to put his precepts into practice. The Jacobins, in general, admired or professed greatly to admire "the people," especially the "common people"; they believed in "popular sovereignty" and "natural law"; they accepted as "natural" individual liberty, social equality, and national fraternity. They were democrats, egalitarians, and nationalists—each, they thought, in Rousseau's sense. Also, in their own estimation, they were Rousseau-like humanitarians; they were conferring on humanity, not simply on France, the greatest benefits it had ever received.

But, starting with the theory of Rousseau, the Jacobins were impelled by a seemingly inexorable sequence of events to be clear where he was vague and to inaugurate a number of policies which were supplementary to, if not at variance with, the mind of the Master. Approving of the fundamental work of the National Assembly, they similarly felt obliged, in order to preserve it against its enemies, to build the great superstructure of the National Convention and the Terror. Rousseau had stressed liberty and had invoked patriotism as a servant of liberty. The Jacobins, starting with this ideal, ended by making national patriotism the master of liberty. Napoleon Bonaparte expressed the true inwardness of the Jacobin development when he asserted that the French people cared more for equality than for liberty and most of all for national glory.

It may well be that the blame for the Jacobin developments, if blame there be, rests not with the Jacobins themselves but with the selfish foes of the Revolution. Every Jacobin began with Rousseau and aspired to a democratic nationalism which was to be preëminently humanitarian. Hence Jacobin nationalism might have been but a concrete application of the humanitarian democratic nationalism which Rousseau, in the spirit of the eighteenth-century "enlightenment," had foreshadowed. The "might have been," however, has only an academic interest. In fact, there were Frenchmen who disagreed with the Jacobins and who mocked at Rousseau and intrigued against democracy; and, worse still, there were masses of foreigners who blindly followed their several kings and princes in violent attacks on everything which Rousseau had championed. If the Jacobins were ready for a trial of humanitarian democratic nationalism, most of humanity was not ready. In the circumstances, the Jacobins were faced with domestic rebellion and foreign war, and the immediate outcome was a democratic nationalism which was more factional than humanitarian.

Jacobin nationalism, as it developed in the midst of foreign war and domestic rebellion, acquired four characteristics. In the first place, it became suspicious and quite intolerant of internal dissent. It labored to root out and destroy any faction which appeared to be lacking in supreme loyalty not only to France in general but also to the particular France of Jacobin dreams—France, one and indivisible, democratic and republican, egalitarian and secular. It perceived a dangerous enemy in every person or tendency that might realize for France any other kind of dream. It fought regionalism and "federalism" and every tendency toward provincial autonomy and

JACOBIN NATIONALISM

away from the disciplined centralization of the state. It clamored against royalists and feudalists, guilds and classes, kings and aristocrats, priests and monks, against anyone who might mislead the "people" and restore "privilege." Its programme was nicely summarized by Barère: "Liberty and equality—these are our rights; unity and indivisibility—these are our maxims; the constitution and the laws—these are our blessings; the destruction of La Vendée, the punishment of traitors, the extirpation of royalism—these are our needs; the prompt reunion and use of all our forces against common enemies—these are our sacred duties."[1] With the Jacobins, the needs and duties bulked larger than the rights. Their nationalism created and throve in an atmosphere of suspicion; and for lapses, real or fancied, from a rigorous orthodoxy they invented and utilized the guillotine. The Terror was their work, and in their excess of suspicion and intolerance they slew not only "reactionaries" but groups of their own kind—Girondists, Dantonists, Hébertists, Robespierrists.

Secondly, Jacobin nationalism, to attain its ends, relied eventually on force and militarism. Against domestic dissenters, compulsion and violence were employed. Against foreign foes, all the resources of a new military spirit and machine were set in motion. "Liberty," as Barère explained, "has become the creditor of all citizens. Some owe her their industry, others their fortune; some their advice, others their arms; all owe her their blood. Thus, then, all French people of both sexes and of all ages are called upon by *la Patrie* to defend liberty. All moral and

---
[1] *Archives Parlemeñtaires*, Vol. LXX, p. 91.

physical faculties, all political and industrial talents belong to *la Patrie;* all metals and elements are its tributaries. Let everyone take his post in the national and military movement that is in preparation. The young men will fight; the married men will forge arms, transport baggage and artillery, and provide subsistence; the women will work at the soldiers' clothing, make tents, and become nurses in the hospitals for the wounded; the children will make lint out of old linen; and the old men, again performing the mission they had among the ancients, will be carried to the public squares, there to inflame the courage of the young warriors and propagate the hatred of kings and the idea of the unity of the republic. The houses of the nation shall be turned into barracks, the public squares into workshops, the cellars into factories of gunpowder; all saddle horses will be requisitioned for the cavalry, all carriage horses for the artillery." [1] It was done according to Barère's word. Carnot, at first the "organizer of defense," became the "organizer of victory." Jacobin nationalism ended by bringing to the nations of the world, not the peace which humanitarians had hoped, but a sword.

Thirdly, Jacobin nationalism became fanatically religious. Into the pure reason of the "Enlightenment" it infused the thrilling emotion of a novel and romantic religious experience. The symbols and ceremonies which it evolved—the national flag, the national anthem, the national holidays, the national shrines, the liberty caps, the altars to *la Patrie*, the graven tablets of the national law, the republican baptisms and funerals, the solemn

[1] *Moniteur*, April 4, 1793, p. 420.

parades and eulogies, the inscriptions of *Mort pour la Patrie*—were touching manifestations of the new religion of nationalism which the Jacobins substituted for the older Catholic faith; no Christian could regard sacrilege with greater aversion than did the Jacobin. Nor was the Jacobin faith merely one of externals: it possessed the heart and soul of many a Frenchman, and it produced fruits in abundance. As one of its devotees testified, "In 1794 we believed in no supernatural religion; our serious interior sentiments were all summed up in the one idea, how to be useful to the fatherland. Everything else,—raiment, food, advancement,—was in our eyes only trivial detail. . . . In the street our eyes filled with tears when we encountered on the wall an inscription in honor of the drummer-boy Barra [killed when he was thirteen, because, to prevent a surprise-attack, he would not stop beating his drum]. For us, who knew no other large assemblies, there were numerous fêtes and rites which nourished the dominant sentiment in our hearts. It was our only religion." [1]

Especially did the religion of Jacobin nationalism sway the military men. At one extreme, the son of a day-laborer, a young Jacobin soldier, who served continuously in the armies of the Republic from 1792 to 1796, wrote to his mother: "When *la Patrie* calls us for her defense, we should rush to her as I would run to a good meal. Our life, our goods, and our talents do not belong to us. It is to the nation, to *la Patrie*, to which everything belongs. I know indeed that you and some other inhabitants of our village do not share these sentiments. You and they

[1] Stendhal, *Vie de Napoléon* (1877), p. 2.

are insensible to the cries of this outraged fatherland. But as for me, who have been reared in liberty of conscience and of thought, who have always been a republican in my soul, though obliged to live under a monarchy, the principles of love for *la Patrie*, for liberty, for the republic, are not only engraved on my heart, but they are absorbed in it and they will remain in it so long as that Supreme Being who governs the universe may be pleased to maintain within me the breath of life."[1] At the other extreme, the great Carnot, in the midst of his herculean military labors, could be prayerful. "O France! O my Fatherland! O great people, truly great people! Receive this vow which I renew every day, which I address at this moment to all that Thou containest of virtuous and honest souls, to all those who preserve within themselves the sacred spark of liberty: May thy glory be immortal, may thy prosperity be constant."[2]

Fourthly, Jacobin nationalism was characterized by missionary zeal. Little of the earlier humanitarian nationalism had been zealously or fiercely missionary. Bolingbroke and Herder esteemed "sweet reasonableness," or any rate what they called the dictates of "enlightened reason," too highly, and they, as well as Rousseau, were too cosmopolitan, to indulge in sustained flights of passionate oratory or to design gigantic engines of propaganda in behalf of a particular nationalism. Besides, Bolingbroke's nationalism was aristocratic: its triumph depended

[1] F. X. Joliclerc, *Volontaire aux armées de la Révolution: ses Lettres 1793-1796*, ed. by Étienne Joliclerc (1905), Letter of Dec. 13, 1793, pp. 141-143.
[2] *Réponse de L. N. M. Carnot au Rapport fait sur la Conjuration du 18 fructidor an V, Conseil des Cinq-cents par J. Ch. Bailleul, au nom d'une commission spéciale* (London, n. d.), pp. 206-239.

on a patriotic king, a patriotic nobility, and a patriotic church; what use could there be of a systematic apostolate among the masses? And Herder's nationalism was strictly cultural: it was to be achieved by poets and scholars; why should it be complicated and perhaps thwarted by political agencies? But the nationalism of the Jacobins was different. It was more religious than rational, and what religion does not require proselytes? It was political as well as cultural, and it appropriately produced political instruments. It was democratic and republican, and, as has been said, highly intolerant; and its apostles quite naturally felt the need and the urge to employ every conceivable means to secure popular conformity. Abroad, its missionary zeal was evidenced by its armies and its wars. At home, it was displayed in the creation and functioning of numerous novel agencies of nationalist propaganda. It is these agencies which peculiarly distinguish Jacobin from humanitarian nationalism. To them we must give some special attention.

[§ 3]

A new type of army was created by the Jacobins and utilized for nationalist ends. For several centuries previously, the usual European army had comprised professional soldiers, led by aristocratic commanders and loyal to a monarch. Such had been the nature of the French army on the eve of the Revolution. At first, the revolutionaries had contented themselves with authorizing the enrollment of volunteers in an auxiliary "National Guard," with requiring all armed forces to take an oath of allegiance to the "nation," and with opening army offices to men of ability regardless of birth. But later, under Jacobin influence and in face of foreign war, the revolutionaries set forth a new ideal and established a new practice. The ideal, in Barère's words, was that "in France the soldier is a citizen, and the citizen a soldier." [1] It was the new modern ideal of "the nation in arms."

In July 1792, under the inspiring leadership of Carnot, the country was proclaimed "in danger"; all citizens capable of bearing arms were put "in a state of permanent activity"; every citizen, under pain of imprisonment, had to declare to republican officials his arms and ammunition; and the government might requisition any material or supplies for "national defense." In August 1793 was introduced a systematic and unsparing conscription—the most remarkable event that is recorded in the history of armies,—and within a few months the French Republic had a national army of 1,200,000 men, five times as many as Louis XIV, at the height of his power, had been able to enlist in his royal army. In 1798 conscription, hitherto regarded as an emergency-measure, was formally adopted as a permanent national policy. It was enacted that every able bodied young Frenchman was liable to conscripted military service for five years. It was a notable triumph for Jacobin nationalism. It took the French peasants who, only a few years earlier, used to hide in caves or forests like escaped slaves, and made soldiers of them. These same peasant-soldiers, as the event proved, were not to lay down their arms until they had conquered Europe.

[1] *Memoirs,* ed. by Hippolyte Carnot and P. J. David, Eng. trans. (1896), Vol. II, p. 28.

JACOBIN NATIONALISM

The new conscript armies of France were nationalist. They could not have been formed, the rank and file would not have submitted to them, if nationalist sentiment had not been widespread in the land, and especially if there had not been a popular fear of what the triumph of the enemy might mean to the country and its citizens. The enthusiasm with which volunteers and conscripts rallied to the national colors is well attested and indicates clearly the driving force of nationalist emotion in the masses. But this emotion was intensified and molded by the Jacobins, who perceived in the new militarism not only the indispensable means of removing the foreign menace but also a most effective agency for propagating their own nationalist principles within France. The Jacobins did not stop with the creation of a citizen army and with equipping and sending it for battle against the enemy. They identified civil with military patriotism; they labored for an intimate union between the army and the republic, between the army and the nation. By inducting recruits into military service with solemn rites and patriotic orations, they fired them with initial zeal. By mingling conscripts from widely separated regions in common service under the national tricolor and marching them to the stirring strains of the national *Marseillaise*, they impressed upon them the unity and indivisibility and the spiritual mission of the national state. By incessant appeals to the seemingly paradoxical motives of sacrifice and glory, they buoyed up the morale of the soldiers in the field and their relatives at home; and against the despondent or the fainthearted, as against outright traitors, they invoked the iron and blood of the Terror. The central government at Paris, the local officials, the "deputies on mission," the clubs, the newspapers, the tribunals, all were mobilized to make the army more thoroughly nationalist.

Believing that a military education "is the basis of the education of free men," the Jacobins, under the leadership of Carnot and Barère, founded in 1794, and "École de Mars" for the training of future army officers. According to Barère's plan, the 3000 students would be chosen among the children of *sansculottes* serving in the army; half of them would be children of less fortunate citizens, and the other half, children of volunteers who had been wounded in action. They would be taught in the same class-rooms and would eat together at the same table, under the watchful eyes of the representatives of the people. They would be instructed in the art of war at the expense of the state, and would acquire an imperishable hatred of kings and the most profound love for *la Patrie*.[1] The "École de Mars" was the Jacobin forerunner of the military school of St. Cyr which Napoleon Bonaparte founded in 1803 and which has remained a typical exponent of military nationalism.

The armies of the French Republic were infused with Jacobin nationalism, and they also became its special missionaries, both abroad and at home. At home they put down insurrection and suppressed dissent. Abroad they caused kings to tremble and aristocrats to despair. For years, and so long as other nationalist armies were not arrayed against them, they swept everything before them. They not only preserved the republic and Jacobin-

[1] *Moniteur*, June 3, 1794, pp. 1038-1039.

ism, but they obtained within four years what Louis XIV during his very long reign had failed to obtain, the "natural frontiers" of France—the Alps and the Rhine. Everywhere they propagated the principles and practices of Jacobin nationalism. Their success was a tremendous fact in human history, attributable less to any special technical improvement in the military art than to the novel morale which sustained them and which they confirmed in their compatriots.

The "nation in arms" was one Jacobin concept of great significance for nationalist propaganda. The "nation in public schools" was another. Previous to the French Revolution, it had long and generally been held that children belonged to their parents and that it was for parents to determine what schooling, if any, their children should have. If the parents wished and could afford to give their children a formal education, they provided them with tutors or sent them to schools which were maintained by the church. For centuries, in almost every country of Europe, education had been private and voluntary; it had been conducted by the church rather than by the state; it had been a privilege for some rather than a right of all; it had been directed toward the classics and Christian piety rather than toward the vernaculars and national patriotism. The French nationalists at the close of the eighteenth century sought to revolutionize all this. Mirabeau devised a scheme for the new education; and the Constitution of 1791 proclaimed: "There shall be created and organized a system of public instruction common to all the citizens and gratuitous in respect of those subjects of instruction which are indispensable to all men. Schools of various grades shall be supplied according to need. . . . Commemorative days shall be designated for the purpose of preserving the memory of the French Revolution, of developing the spirit of fraternity among all citizens, and of attaching them to the constitution, the fatherland, and its laws." Accordingly, Talleyrand presented a formal report to the National Assembly in September 1791, outlining a system of primary, secondary, and professional schools, headed by a "National Institute," which should be established and maintained by the state and which should promote "national culture." A second report was made by Condorcet to the Legislative Assembly in April 1792, recommending a similar system, headed by a "National Society of Arts and Sciences." These reports were not acted upon; other matters, particularly those relating to national defense, were soon too pressing. But the "nation in public schools" remained an ideal for the Jacobins.

The Jacobins declared in their abortive Constitution of 1793 that "Education is the need of all, and society owes it equally to all members." They talked much about the need for the new education, and they actually suppressed the old by dissolving the religious teaching orders and closing the church schools. They envisaged a system in which all French children would be obliged to attend state-supported and state-controlled schools, where they would be thoroughly grounded in the national language and revolutionary doctrines, in devotion to the republic and the fatherland. On Barère's motion, the National Convention in May 1793 decreed that in each place with a population of from 400 to 1500 there should be a public primary school for the training of children in citizenship and that the teachers should give instruction once a week to adult citizens.[1] That children belong to the nation, rather than to their parents, the same Barère declared the following year. "The principles that ought to guide parents are that children belong to the general family, to the republic, before they belong to particular families. ... The spirit of private families must disappear when the great family calls. The republic leaves to parents the guidance of your first years, but as soon as your intelligence forms itself the republic proudly claims the rights it holds over you. You are born for the republic and not for the pride or the despotism of families."[2]

The revolutionaries were clear as to the value and need of the new education for nationalist propaganda, but circumstances prevented them from devoting to it the attention and funds which they devoted to the new militarism. It remained for Napoleon—a Jacobin himself, in his own fashion—to take the first important steps toward the actual establishment of a complete system of national schools. Since his time, the almost universal adoption of the institutions of the new education and their utilization for patriotic purposes have been an outstanding productive legacy of Jacobin nationalism.

If the original Jacobins were sluggish in translating all their theories of education into action, they were prompt to recognize the significance of language as the basis of nationality and to try to compel all inhabitants of France to use the French language. They contended that success-

[1] *Moniteur*, May 31, 1793, p. 656.
[2] *Ibid.*, June 3, 1794, p. 1039.

ful rule by "the people" and united action by the nation were dependent, not only on a certain uniformity of habits and customs, but even more on an identity of ideas and ideals which could be effected by speeches, the printing press, and other instruments of education, provided that these employed one and the same language. Confronted with the historic fact that France was not a linguistic unit—that, in addition to widely variant dialects in different parts of the country, "foreign" languages were spoken in the west by Bretons, in the south by Provençals, Basques, and Corsicans, in the north by Flemings, and in the northeast by Alsatian Germans—they resolved to stamp out the dialects and the foreign languages and to force every French citizen to know and employ the French language. Otherwise, they argued, it was idle to carry on national propaganda among people who could not read even the Declaration of the Rights of Man and who constituted a danger to the republic because they could not appreciate the necessity for acting with it. The French Jacobins were the first, but by no means the last, who have sought systematically to destroy linguistic minorities in a country and to exalt and expand a dominant nationality by forcing its language upon all the citizens of a state.

"We have revolutionized," said Barère, "the government, the laws, the habits, the customs, commerce, and thought; let us also revolutionize the language which is their daily instrument." "Citizens!" he exclaimed in his report to the National Convention in behalf of the Committee on Public Safety in January 1794, "Citizens! the language of a free people ought to be one and the same

JACOBIN NATIONALISM

for all; . . . free men are all alike, and the vigorous accent of liberty and equality is the same whether it comes from the mouth of an inhabitant of the Alps, the Vosges, or the Pyrenees. . . . We have observed that the dialect called Bas-Breton, the Basque dialect, and the German and Italian languages have perpetuated the reign of fanaticism and superstition, secured the domination of priests and aristocrats, prevented the Revolution from penetrating nine départements, and favored the enemies of France. You have taken away from these stray fanatics the empire of saints by establishing the republican calendar; take away from them the empire of priests by teaching the French language. . . . It is treason to *la Patrie* to leave the citizens in ignorance of the national language."[1]

On the basis of Barère's report, it was decreed that teachers of French should be appointed by "the representatives of the people," on the nomination of popular patriotic societies, and sent to places where dissident dialects or languages were spoken. Such teachers would be paid five hundred livres a year from the national treasury and would be expected to teach the French language and the Declaration of the Rights of Man to children of both sexes and on the holidays of the republican calendar to read aloud in French to all the people "the laws of the republic, preferably those relating to agriculture and to the rights of citizens." By the same decree the patriotic societies were summoned to increase their local branches with a view to multiplying the means by which the French language should be made known "in the most

[1] *Ibid.*, January 28, 1794, pp. 519-520.

remote country villages."[1] Subsequently, in June 1794 the Convention, after listening to a long and perfervid discourse by Grégoire in support of linguistic uniformity, authorized the preparation and compulsory use of a new grammar and a new dictionary of the French language, "fit for the language of liberty."[2]

The rise of Jacobin nationalism synchronized with the rise of a new type of journalism—the sheet of news and editorial comment which was written in popular and sensational style, printed rapidly, sold cheaply, and read widely. Many of the Jacobin leaders were founders and editors of just such sheets, and the Jacobins in general believed ardently that if "the people" were to be democratic and patriotic, they must be provided with daily information and opinion and incitement. In theory, the Jacobins asserted the absolute freedom of the press; every citizen had the "natural right" to publish or read whatever he would, and logically this might cover a journalism that was pacifist and even anti-patriotic. In fact, however, the Jacobins were quick to paralyze the hands, by cutting off the heads, of such journalists as "misled" the people; and the new journalism became a most effective agency for the propagation of Jacobin nationalism.

It was likewise in respect of a new type of voluntary association which now appeared—the semi-private, semi-public propagandist society. Here, too, the Jacobins paid much lip-service to the freedom of association as a "natural right" of all men, but they actually forbade asso-

---
[1] *Collection Baudouin*, Pluviôse, l'an II, pp. 74-75.
[2] *Ibid.*, Prairial, l'an II, no. 609, p. 2.

ciations of workingmen and persecuted associations of clergymen, while fostering and lauding associations of patriots. The revolutionary clubs—the Jacobin, the Cordelier, and others—were the earliest examples of a kind of propagandist organization which is nowadays commonplace, the organization of private citizens in order to influence the opinion and activity of the government and the general public and employing as means to its end a national headquarters, branch societies, and more or less professional speakers, pamphleteers, and lobbyists. Such organizations exist today for very many different purposes, but their original prototype was militantly patriotic; it was at once a product and a propagator of Jacobin nationalism.

The new militarism, the new schooling, the new journalism, the new patriotic societies: these were intended, or at any rate served, to quicken the consciousness of common nationality among Frenchmen and to inspire them with supreme devotion to a nationalism which was democratic and republican, secular and egalitarian. But perhaps the agency by which the Jacobins set chief store was that of nationalist ritual. Rousseau had suggested the historic rôle of national ceremonies and customs in welding citizens together and attaching them to *la Patrie*. The Jacobins had the opportunity and the will to adopt his suggestion and to apply it, with almost infinite elaboration, to modern nationalism. "The French cock," said Barère, "will surpass the Roman eagle, and the inscription 'The French People' will be purer and far more democratic than the 'S. P. Q. R.' of ancient Rome."

Certainly in symbolism the national patriots of France surpassed the urban patriots of Rome.

"The Republic must penetrate the souls of citizens through all the senses."[1] Indeed, under Jacobin auspices, the citizens were enabled almost constantly to see the "glorious tricolor," to hear the *Marseillaise*, that "religious invocation," to smell and taste the gunpowder which was fired at solemn celebrations of national victory, and to touch the relics of civilian or military heroes. National fêtes were frequently celebrated at Paris and in the provinces. Altars and temples were dedicated to *la Patrie*.[2] Sculpture, painting, and all the other arts were pressed into the service of nationalist propaganda. Music, particularly, was utilized, for "it humanizes the violent and fanatical habits of the Italians; it tempers the hotheaded and impetuous inclinations of the French; it draws a smile from the melancholy Englishman . . . ; it makes the Spaniard more religious; it leads all the troops to battle, to victory, to death."[3]

"How are you to know a Republican?" asked Barère. You will know him when he speaks of "*la Patrie* with a religious sentiment" and of "the majesty of the people with religious devotion."[4] The Jacobin faith in the mystic power of words and formulas, ritual and symbols, was at bottom religious, and its exercise contributed immeasurably to the promotion and intensification of nationalism.

[1] Barère, in *Moniteur*, June 3, 1794, p. 1039.
[2] It was the Jacobins, for example, who made the Panthéon the rallying point for French patriots and foreign tourists which it is today.
[3] Barère, *De la Pensée du Gouvernement Républicain*, 2nd ed. (1797), p. 102.
[4] *Ibid.*, p. 140.

JACOBIN NATIONALISM

[§ 4]

The Jacobins rendered their nationalism much more exclusive and paramount than had been that nationalism which earlier Humanitarians had extolled. Perhaps it was because the Jacobins were essentially religious. Perhaps it was because they were fiercely democratic. Perhaps it was because they had to deal practically with conditions of war and terror which had not been foreseen in the theorizing of their "enlightened" predecessors. The fact remains, whatever its explanation may be, that to the Jacobins "the people" has become "the nation," a mystical entity, an absolute sovereign, a Moloch not only of classes but of individuals. It catechizes its own citizens, and by force it seeks to catechize the citizens of other nations. It conscripts youth for war or for schools and abrogates the historic rights of the father and the family. It can seize everything and destroy anything, for above it there is no law. The will of the nation is God. It feels itself immense and irresistible. It has a horror of divisions, schisms, minorities. It labors for unity, uniformity, concentration. It proudly proclaims personal liberty and boldly abridges particular liberties which appear to be at variance with national interests. Its vaunted liberty, in last analysis, is not for the individual but for the national state. The nation may do whatever it will; the individual may do only what the national state determines. Above all, the individual owes supreme loyalty and the devoutest worship to *la Patrie*, the *Great Mother*. "Citizens, it is I [the Great Mother, *la Patrie*] that undertakes to protect your personal safety, your peace, your property: What wilt thou give me in return for constant benefit? If it happens that I am in peril, if unnatural children torment my bosom, . . . wouldst thou abandon me in these stormy moments for the price of my invariable protection? . . . No! . . . There are times when I would command the sacrifice . . . even of thy life which I have so steadily protected." [1]

La Patrie, in Jacobin hearts, was a God, and a jealous God who would brook the worship of no other. Now it so happened that another God had for centuries been popularly worshipped in France—the Christian God— and many of His priests had also been intolerant of dissent from their organization, the Catholic Church. It was natural that the new religion of nationalism should come into conflict with the old religion of Catholicism. The way was paved, though somewhat unwittingly, on the eve of the French Revolution. French philosophers of the eighteenth century, in measure as they were "enlightened," made the Catholic Church the butt of sarcasm, ridicule, or pity. They denounced its supernatural claims, its "superstitious" practices, and its traditional privileges. They largely emancipated themselves from Christian worship. But most of them discovered some good in Catholic Christianity. They professed admiration for its moral teachings and its works of mercy. They recognized its utility in disciplining and keeping in order the "unenlightened" masses, and, as Voltaire expressed it, if there were no God they would have to make one for the common people. As humanitarians and, in a sense, cosmopolites, they were impressed by the supra-national,

---

[1] Barère in *Procès-Verbal de l'Assemblée Nationale*, no. 699, pp. 7-8.

catholic sway of the ecclesiastical organization. The very fact that a goodly number of French abbés and even some French bishops were numbered among the "enlightened" philosophers was an augury that the Catholic Church might be so reformed and "purified" as to become rationally tolerant of other religions, including that of nationalism. The augury was illusory.

It is true that in the early days of the French Revolution the issue between state and church, between nationalism and Catholicism, was not squarely joined. The early revolutionaries, with almost no exception, acted as though Catholic Christianity was a necessary, if not an ideally desirable, religion for the French nation. Catholic clergymen, including such men as Bishop Talleyrand and Abbé Siéyès, were prominent in the counsels of the National Assembly, and the Assembly made no frontal attacks on Catholicism. At the same time, however, the leaders of the Assembly, including Talleyrand and Siéyès, were nationalists and were resolved on making the church, like all other institutions in France, serve national ends. It was Talleyrand who, joining with Mirabeau, initiated, in October 1789, the confiscation of church property by the state. He argued that such property did not really belong to the church, but to the nation, and that if the rights of the existing clergy were secured, the nation through its representatives was at liberty to apply the property to any purpose of its own. In the following February the Assembly, in the name of liberty, suppressed religious orders and authorized state officials to accept renunciation of vows by monks and nuns. In July 1790 was enacted the so-called "civil constitution of the clergy," in accordance with which the church in France as an organization was to be completely nationalized. Its priests and bishops were to be elected by "the people" (including Protestants, Jews, and freethinkers, as well as Catholics) and were to be salaried by the state; its connection with the pope and with Catholics in other countries was to be reduced to the lowest possible minimum. In November 1790 the National Assembly prescribed that all Catholic clergymen in France should take a special oath "to watch with care over the faithful of the diocese or the parish which is confided to them, to be faithful to the nation, the law, and the king, and to maintain with all their might the constitution decreed by the National Assembly and accepted by the King."

Two forces soon appeared, however, which militated against the successful fruition of the effort to harmonize Catholicism with French nationalism. On the one hand, many Catholics developed hostility to the Revolution: they looked with dismay upon the cancellation of church privileges, the confiscation of church property, and the violation of church law; and in April 1791 the pope formally condemned the "civil constitution of the clergy" and forbade the faithful to obey it. Thenceforth French Catholics were divided into two camps: those who put nationalism ahead of Catholicism and took the oath of allegiance to the state, and those who put Catholicism ahead of nationalism and, following the command of the pope, refused to take the oath of allegiance to the state; the latter became centers of anti-revolutionary agitation. On the other hand, the revolutionaries became more radical; and the Jacobins, already hostile to all "supernatural" religion, now took drastic measures against the Catholic Church on the special grounds that it was anti-revolutionary and that it was under "foreign" control.

Soon the full Jacobin doctrine concerning religion emerged. Christianity, being dangerous to liberty and republicanism and incompatible with national sovereignty, should be proscribed, or at any rate should be reduced to the status of a regulated private cult. The national state—the republic one and indivisible—should supplant the Catholic Church as the object of religious devotion and the dispenser of good works. In other words, religion should be "secularized," that is, it should be strictly subordinated to the national temporal state rather than to an international spiritual church, and it should be utilized for the mission of the nation in this world rather than for the salvation of individual souls in a world to come. Of course, the state might and should tolerate religious vagaries, even superstitions, until such time as the mass of its citizens were duly educated in republican virtue and the right use of reason, provided always that the religious vagaries were not exploited for anti-revolutionary purposes. Likewise, the state might properly establish and favor a religion which would hasten the triumph of reason and republican virtue.

In accordance with this doctrine the Jacobins undertook to de-Christianize France. Priests—at first those who obeyed the pope, and afterwards those too who had disobeyed him—were treated as "suspects." A new calendar substituted a republican week of ten days for the Christian week of seven days. Christian churches were appropriated for nationalist worship or secular purposes. In the one month of November 1793 more than twenty-four hundred churches, including the cathedral of Notre Dame at Paris, were converted into temples of Reason; and on the twenty-fourth of the month the Commune of Paris decreed: "(1) that all churches and temples of whatever religion or sect has existed in Paris shall immediately be closed; (2) that all priests and ministers of any religion whatsoever shall be held personally and individually responsible for all disturbances of which the cause shall proceed from religious opinions; (3) that whoever shall demand that either church or temple shall be opened shall be arrested as a suspect; (4) that the revolutionary committees shall be invited to keep a close watch on all priests; (5) that the Convention shall be petitioned to issue a decree which shall exclude priests from the exercise of public functions of every kind and from all employment in the national factories."

The Jacobins were divided among themselves as to precisely what should be the creed and form of the new national religion. It was the Hébertists who championed the atheistical religion of Reason. Robespierre preferred a deistical religion of the Supreme Being, with a round of special festivals in honor of "the glorious events of the Revolution, the virtues most dear and useful to man, and the greatest benefits of nature."[1] He succeeded in

[1] Here is the quaint list of these festivals: Supreme Being and Nature; Human Species; French People; Benefactors of Humanity; Martyrs of Liberty; Liberty and Equality; the Republic; Liberty of the World; Hatred of Tyrants and Traitors; Truth; Justice; Modesty; Glory and Immortality; Friendship; Frugality; Courage; Good Faith; Heroism; Disinterestedness; Stoicism; Love; Conjugal Love; Paternal Love; Maternal Tenderness; Filial Piety; Infancy; Youth; Manhood; Old Age; Misfortune; Agriculture; Industry; Our Forefathers; Posterity; Happiness.

beheading the Hébertists and supplanting Reason with the Supreme Being. But the religion of the Supreme Being speedily fell with the fall of Robespierre's own head, and thenceforth a number of curious little sects vied with one another, quite harmlessly and ineffectually, to become the orthodox expression of Jacobin religion.

Eventually, in the last days of the Convention and under the Directory—as extreme Jacobin influence waned, —liberty of worship, even of Catholic worship, was permitted and church buildings were restored on the condition that the clergy should submit to national law. The agreement entered into between Napoleon Bonaparte and the pope at the beginning of the nineteenth century admitted that Roman Catholicism was "the religion of the majority of the French people," and again made the Catholic Church a state church in France, but, in good Jacobin style, it stressed the supremacy of the national state and left the way open for the civil government to set up other and rival state churches.

In the long run, some of the basic doctrines of Jacobinism in respect of religion were to triumph. Though in France Christianity was to revive and the Catholic Church was to regain a good deal of moral influence, the profession of Christianity was to be severely personal and voluntary; the church was to be patriotic as well as catholic; and the ecclesiastical organization, shorn of most of its traditional privileges and civil functions, was to be rigidly restricted to purely religious services. The state, rather than the church, was to assume the leadership in education, charity, and social welfare and to enjoy the financial resources which would make such leadership possible and necessary. The individual Frenchman, no matter how faithful a Christian he might be, was to look primarily to the state for immediate succor and was to honor and reverence the state accordingly. This "secularization" of Christianity proved to be an outstanding achievement of the French Revolution. It has contributed enormously to the strength of nationalism in the nineteenth and twentieth centuries, not only in France, but elsewhere throughout the world. It is an abiding legacy of Jacobin nationalism.

With the secularization of religion arose a new need for the national state to serve as the chief agency of social welfare. Previously it was the church which had been expected and able to conduct not only educational establishments but also institutions for the poor and the sick, the halt and the blind, the orphans and the aged, unfortunates of all kinds. Now all these charitable institutions were "secularized," and henceforth their maintenance and development were to be assured less by the church than by the state. Such an outcome was an integral part of the creed of Jacobin nationalism. "Woe and shame to that government which neglects the lot of the poor," wrote Barère[1]; and on his motion the Convention instituted a national fête in honor of misfortune.[2] Because the unfortunate find it difficult to be patriotic, he argued, it is all the more necessary for the republic to give them something to be patriotic about.[3] In his official report to the Convention in May 1794 on social service, Barère

[1] *De la Pensée du Gouvernement Républicain*, p. 114.
[2] *Moniteur*, March 13, 1794, p. 953.
[3] *De la Pensée du Gouvernement Républicain*, p. 107.

proclaimed, amid the plaudits of all the Jacobins, that the nation is debtor to infirmity, old age, and poverty. At that time he definitely proposed that the names of aged and infirm workers and peasants and of poor mothers, wives, or widows of workers and peasants should be inscribed in a "book of national beneficence" and that such persons should receive pensions from the national treasury. He urged further that the national government should provide the sick with medical service, health officers, and hospital care. And he eloquently pleaded that "the distressing word 'poverty' be eradicated from the vocabulary of republicans."[1]

The idea that the national state should be paternalistic in its attitude toward its less fortunate members was a thoroughly Jacobin idea. Indeed, it was one aspect of a much bigger and broader Jacobin idea, the idea that the national state should merit, as well as receive, the supreme loyalty of its citizens by promoting and directing their economic welfare. Before the advent of Jacobinism, French philosophers who interested themselves in economic matters had tended to decry the old mercantilism, the regulation of agriculture, industry, and trade by the state, and to praise a policy of laisser-faire as most conducive to national wealth and prosperity. The early revolutionaries, too, had effected important economic reforms, such as the abolition of guild monopolies and tariff barriers, in the spirit of laisser-faire and in the name of liberty. The Jacobins, however, in their anxiety to assure equality among citizens and to unite the whole nation in enthusiastic loyalty to the republic, thought of economics

[1] *Moniteur*, May 13, 1794, pp. 949-952.

in terms of national policy. It was the Jacobins who, in this respect, were perhaps a bit reactionary. At any rate it was they who revived some of the mercantilist practices of the old Bourbon monarchy and by labelling them "national" laid the foundations for that "economic nationalism" which has been an ubiquitous characteristic of recent times.

In addition to their efforts to regulate the price of foodstuffs for the benefit of consumers, the Jacobins labored, especially after the fall of the Girondists, to confer legislative favors on French agriculture, industry, and commerce. In all these labors and efforts they were actuated by nationalist mercantilist conceptions. They believed that commerce should be especially stimulated, abroad because it would bring gold into the country, and at home because it would unify the nation. They imagined that to secure an advantageous export trade France should protect her industries by high tariffs against foreign competition. "Be on your guard," warned Barère, "against that system of pretended philanthropy which seeks to induce you to abolish tariffs; that system is supported by all the British economists, who wish to induce you to accept it because they know that their own country will have the advantage."[1] Along with tariff protectionism, the Jacobins espoused a vigorous colonial policy, a restrictive navigation act, the subsidizing of a national merchant marine, and a big navy. "The navy," said Barère, "has given the universe to Europe, and Europe to England." The solid foundation for a French navy is the French merchant marine. It destroys the competition of foreign manufac-

[1] *Moniteur*, September 24, 1793, p. 1133.

tures by importing raw materials, by exporting finished products, and by driving away from our ports competing vessels of other nations. A powerful navy is the surest guaranty of colonies, the first incentive of commerce, and the greatest support of industry. "Every vessel built in our ports creates sailors, opens shops, and erects factories."[1]

Barère's economics were those of Jacobin nationalism. "National interest," he said early in his public career, "is a pater familias, foreseeing and industrious."[2] "The vice we ought to cure in this country," he said later at the height of his career, "is the versatility of principles of political economy. . . . What we need is a system of national works, on a grand scale, over the whole territory of the Republic."[3] National unity was to Barère and all the Jacobins the goal of economic policy, and the economic interests of individual citizens were magnified by them into national interests.

[§ 5]

None can seriously question the idealism of the revolutionary Jacobins. Nor should one belittle their very real and very great achievements, which have profoundly influenced our modern world and have made it in many respects a better and more comfortable place for human habitation and development. One should recognize, too, that the "excesses" of the Jacobins—the Terror, the intolerance, the bloodshed—were the outgrowth not ex-

[1] *De la Pensée du Gouvernement Républicain*, p. 34.
[2] *Procès-Verbal de l'Assemblée Nationale*, Vol. XXVI, no. 372.
[3] *Moniteur*, March 13, 1794, pp. 699-700.

clusively of their own fanaticism but of the fanaticism of their opponents at home and abroad. They themselves performed their labors in the midst of a fiery furnace of foreign war and domestic revolt. Their labors would doubtless have been somewhat different, and the nationalism associated with their name would have been of another hue, if no foreign monarchs and no French aristocrats had taken arms against them. It is one of the ironies of history that the most "excessive" Jacobins, both Robespierre and Marat, opposed vigorously the declaration of war by France in 1792 against Austria. They held that war was "the last refuge of scoundrels" and that it would increase the misery of the French people. Robespierre prophesied that it would produce in France a dictator who would destroy liberty.

The tragedy of the Jacobins was that they were idealists, fanatically so, in a wicked world. They instituted or confirmed a host of reforms which they knew to be good, not only for themselves, but for everyone, but which large sections of the world promptly reacted against as being very bad. In the circumstances Jacobin Frenchmen fought and killed, altruistically and enthusiastically. But the more they fought, the more nationalist they grew. Embarking upon the Great War of 1792 in order to make the world safe for liberty, equality, and the right of national self-determination, it was not long before they were waging it primarily for the greater glory of France. Gradually under the influence of war, especially of unprecedented military victories, their attitude toward other peoples underwent a change. Increasingly they tended to dislike and to hate not only tyrannical monarchs and reactionary governments but peoples who failed to rise against their rulers and make common cause with the French Revolution. This led the Jacobins to vindictiveness against foreigners, to pride in and ambition for their own nation, to conquest, and eventually to a new imperialism. It was all gradual and almost imperceptible. Yet by 1797 the French Republic of Jacobin nationalists had incorporated Belgium (with the sanction of a partisan plebiscite) and the German Rhineland (without even the pretense of a plebiscite) and had surrounded itself with a string of vassal states in Holland, Switzerland, and Italy.

The evolution of Jacobin nationalism rendered possible and perhaps inevitable the evolution of the new Jacobin militarism. This militarism became associated with imperialism and afforded the opportunity for the rise of a military dictator. Napoleon Bonaparte fulfilled the prophecy of Maximilien Robespierre. Bonaparte proudly boasted that he was "the son and heir of the Revolution," and, though an Italian by birth and mother-tongue, his heirloom from the Revolution was French nationalism. He was the first Italian (but not the last) to be a nationalist dictator.

Bonaparte based his influence at home and his real strength abroad on Jacobin nationalism. Whether as General, First Consul, or Emperor, he insisted that he was the child of "the people" and he accepted the principle, if not always the practice, of national democratic sovereignty. He emphasized equality and fraternity, and if he abridged liberty he was only doing what his Jacobin predecessors, with loud protestations to the contrary, had done. And all the agencies of nationalist propaganda which the Jacobins had invented, Bonaparte employed to the full. He was strong for nationalist ritual. His legions flew the revolutionary national flag and his bands played the revolutionary national anthem. He built national monuments, celebrated national fêtes, and made the patriotic gesture appropriate to national triumph or national bereavement. No revolutionary Jacobin surpassed Napoleon Bonaparte in effectiveness of patriotic oratory.

Bonaparte took from the Jacobins, also, the idea of "the nations in arms" and made it the cornerstone of his brilliant military career. He took from them, too, the idea of "the nation in public schools" and largely realized it. The importance of the cheap popular press he understood even better than they. He forced it to be unswervingly nationalist and he consciously employed it to stimulate national morale. No French newspaper even mentioned the defeat at Trafalgar so long as Bonaparte was in power, and he hired our old friend Barère to indite journalistic philippics against the English. It was Bonaparte, likewise, who capped the Jacobin patriotic societies with the famous French Legion of Honor.

Utilizing all the means which the Jacobins had put at his disposal for popular propaganda, Napoleon trained a whole generation of Frenchmen in national patriotism. It was Jacobin nationalism in which they were trained, and the most obvious result of their training was their unquestioning willingness to fight and die wherever the Emperor of the French might lead them—into Germany, into Italy, into Austria, into Spain, into Russia. A war which France had begun in 1792 went on almost continuously for twenty-three years and until the battle of

Waterloo in 1815. It was a great war, a general war, a popular war. It wrought far more havoc and destruction and death than any dynastic or commercial war of earlier times. It was the historic, if not the logical, outcome of Jacobin nationalism.

It has been argued by recent apologists, who deem Jacobinism fundamentally pacific rather than bellicose, that nationalism under Napoleon was but a caricature of the original Jacobin nationalism. They may be right. They should bear in mind, however, that every caricature is derived from an original.

CHAPTER IV

TRADITIONAL NATIONALISM

[§ 1]

NOT every thoughtful person in the eighteenth century sympathized with the dominant intellectual tendencies of the "Enlightenment." Here and there in Europe, even before the French Revolution, voices were raised or pens employed in criticism of the "rationalism" of the age and in depreciation of the contemporary faith in natural law, natural rights, and the perfectibility of mankind.

These pens became more caustic, these voices became louder, as the French Revolution developed. It was proclaimed with growing bitterness that the terrors of the Revolution and the ensuing horrors of the Revolutionary and Napoleonic Wars were the inevitable products of the false philosophy of the "Enlightenment" and that the only hope for the true happiness of mankind lay in a return to the thought and institutions of an earlier day. Against the Jacobins, particularly, these "reactionaries" declaimed. It was the Jacobins, they said, who in pursuit of natural law and natural rights had trampled on the higher supernatural law and had violated the fundamental historic rights which were the solid cement of human society. It was the Jacobins who in the name of reason had behaved most unreasonably, who in their attempt to demonstrate the perfectibility of man had amply proved his depravity. Napoleon Bonaparte, his egotism, and his bloodthirstiness were but the fruit which might be expected to consummate the growth of Jacobinism.

The reactionary critics of Jacobinism were humanitarians themselves. With no faith in the inevitably natural "progress" of the human race, they yet believed that man was capable of considerable quiet happiness in his fallen state if only he would learn the lessons of the past and appreciate his own limitations. They ardently believed, moreover, that man in his fallen state had received the gift of tears, and that tears should be shed for human wrong and injustice and suffering. They shed many tears, at least metaphorically, over the sins and frailties of human nature and especially over the cruel slaughter of human beings by Jacobin guillotine in the Place de la Révolution or by Jacobin muskets on the field of battle. It was, above all, in behalf of outraged humanity that they shed most copious tears. The Jacobin "assassins" and "satans" happened to be French, but that was immaterial; they would have been as vehemently denounced if they had been German or English; their adversaries thought of them simply as inhuman. Of course, the reactionaries shed more tears over the aristocratic victims of Jacobin deviltry than over the fate of the masses, but they were sure that the quiet happiness of humanity could be assured less by the masses than by the classes. Aristocrats were the best people. If the best people were guillotined or shot, what hope remained for humanity at large?

Such criticism was expressed by French foes of the Revolution, and likewise by its foes in Germany and

England. In England, perhaps, it received its classical form. Wherever it was expressed, it was accoutered with one very important weapon from the arsenal of Jacobinism; it assumed a kind of nationalism.

England preceded all countries on the Continent in the development of an acute popular consciousness of common nationality. Long before the French Revolution, at a time when Frenchmen had thought of themselves primarily as Burgundians or Gascons or Provençals, Englishmen had been Englishmen and had rallied with real national patriotism to the secularizations of Henry VIII and the exploits of Elizabeth. There had been a nationalist spirit in the political philosophy of Milton and Locke hardly parallelled by their contemporaries on the Continent; and Bolingbroke, the Englishman, was a pioneer in the expounding of a formal doctrine of nationalism. It was natural, therefore, that any Englishman who would enter the lists against Jacobinism should be arrayed in trappings of nationalism.

In the case of Frenchmen, Germans, and other Continentals, it was not quite so natural. Indeed, it might be supposed that a Frenchman who detested the Revolution would detest all its works, including certainly its most characteristic work, which was its nationalism. But nationalism was altogether too profound and too widespread a phenomenon in France during the Revolution to be ignored or overcome by French counter-revolutionaries. These soon recognized that they could not wean their compatriots from Jacobinism if they themselves withheld the milk of French patriotism. They must outdo the

Jacobins in praise of the principle of nationality and in veneration of France.

Besides, as German and other foreign adversaries perceived how effectively the French were inspired by nationalism to defend and spread the Revolution, they began to cherish the idea that nationalism might be invoked among their own peoples in order to stay and turn back the Revolution. A little later, when the Jacobins were no longer on the defensive but were taking the offensive and conquering foreign countries, and when Napoleon, as the evil flower of Jacobinism, was resorting to the most militant despotism and becoming the "scourge of Europe," many of the foreign reactionaries, in the name of humanity, undertook a zealous crusade in behalf of a counter-nationalism. And a considerable number of foreigners who at the outset had been favorably disposed toward the principles of the French Revolution and had been tainted with Jacobin nationalism now joined forces, at least temporarily, with the reactionary nationalists.[1]

In these ways, certain intellectuals who most vigorously opposed the French Revolution and Napoleon proceeded to champion nationalism and to dress it up in distinctive clothes. The clothing was not "reason" or "revolution" but history and tradition. This type of nationalism, like Jacobin nationalism, claimed to be humanitarian, but as the Jacobins departed in one direction from the humanitarian nationalism of Bolingbroke, Rousseau, and Herder, so their opponents departed from it in another direction. The latter made a significant place in their system for aristocracy and an even more significant place for tradi-

[1] For example, Alfieri in Italy and Fichte and Hegel in Germany.

tion. Indeed, their system may most appropriately be termed traditional nationalism.

In order to describe and analyze the tenets of traditional nationalism, it may be convenient to pass in brief review the teachings of three of its most illustrious exponents: Edmund Burke, the Vicomte de Bonald, and Friedrich von Schlegel. Let us begin with Burke.

[§ 2]

Edmund Burke (1729-1797) was seemingly always in opposition to something. Born of a Protestant family of lawyers in Ireland, educated at Trinity College, Dublin, that intellectual bulwark of the "English garrison," and living most of his life in London, he was an opponent of the impairment of any English rights, while he was in Ireland, and an opponent of the impairment of any Irish rights, while he was in England. Trained in the traditional family calling of the law, he forsook it for literature and journalism. Then, after gaining an honorable niche in the literary temple of the "Enlightenment" with his *Philosophical Inquiry into the Origin of the Sublime and the Beautiful* and his *Vindication of Natural Society* and after securing the friendship of such high priests of the "Enlightenment" as Dr. Samuel Johnson and Mr. Edward Gibbon (to say nothing of a fascinating assortment of earls and marquesses), he turned to politics. From 1765 almost continuously until his death he was a Whig member of Parliament and in opposition to the majority whether Tory or Whig. He was against corruption in public office. He was against existing religious disabilities.

He was against the slave trade. He was against any change in the British Constitution—first against any increase of royal authority, and afterwards against any decrease of aristocratic influence. He was against British oppression in India, and his oration against Warren Hastings lasted nine days. He was against British policy in respect of the American colonies and in respect, likewise, of Ireland. From all of which it is manifest that Burke, if temperamentally an "anti," was consistently an humanitarian. He was also a patriot, though a patriot who thought Bolingbroke bombastic and jingoistic. Above all, he was eloquent and matchless in the use of invective, both oral and written.

Burke was about sixty years of age when the French Revolution began. He at once opposed it and prophesied its dangerous magnitude. As it developed, he felt an increasing horror and a mounting fear lest England might be contaminated by Jacobinism. All his powers of opposition, hatred, and invective were brought to bear on the accursed thing; and he dashed off a series of eloquent and immensely effective appeals against the Jacobins: his *Reflections on the Revolution in France* (1790), his three *Memorials on French Affairs* (1791-1793), and his *Thoughts on a Regicide Peace* (1796-1797), interspersed with pamphlets galore. He died while he was collecting funds for French émigrés in England and importuning Pitt not to make peace with the French Republic.

Toward almost everything, Burke's attitude was one of revolt against the characteristic rationalism of eighteenth-century "enlightenment." He detested abstractions and theories and all precise formulas. He denounced Voltaire and Rousseau—and Bolingbroke, too—as mischievous spinners of logic. "I never govern myself, no rational man ever did govern himself, by abstractions and universals. . . . He who does not take circumstances into consideration is not erroneous, but stark mad."[1] Human nature, Burke insisted, must be studied, not as it should be or as it may be presumed to have been once upon a time, but as it has actually functioned in history, in accepted tradition, in tried and tested institutions. History is the best and only certain indication of what man can do. Concrete historical rights are vastly superior to abstract natural rights.

In so far as Burke had an abstract philosophy of his own, it was very rudimentary and was grounded in faith rather than in reason. Behind history, according to him, was Divine Providence, the "Hand of God." God had created man a religious animal. God had willed the state. God had created diverse nationalities. God continued to supervise the whole course of each nation's development. Under Divine guidance, man had passed from a rude and primitive existence into organized society, in which various types of corporate institutions found appropriate places, such as throne, aristocracy, church, judiciary, parliament, electorate, professions, trades, sciences, arts, morals, and manners. All these "just grew," and, on the whole, all grew as they should.

Nationality and the state "just grew." It is idle to discuss how they began; perhaps they began by "contract," but no one knows. In any event, it is the reality of

[1] *Speech on the Petition of the Universalists* (May 11, 1792), Vol. VII (Beaconsfield edition), p. 41.

history and not any fanciful "natural right" which has developed them. The purpose of the state is to promote the welfare of its people, its nationality, but the democratic doctrine of popular sovereignty can hardly serve such a purpose, for it is fallacious in theory and has proved ineffectual in fact. The state was no mere "partnership agreement in a trade of pepper and coffee, calico, or tobacco," to be made suddenly and then to be dissolved at pleasure. Instead, the state was a permanent union whose ends could not be accomplished in any one generation. It was "a partnership, not only between those who are living, but between those who are living, those who are dead, and those who are to be born." The "people"—the nationality—were not distinct from their government, and they had no right to break the social tie which linked them to their forefathers.[1]

There was, then, according to Burke, no general right of revolution, although, it is interesting to note, he approved of five specific revolutions: the English Revolution of 1688; the American Revolution; the Corsican revolt against France; the Polish uprising against Russia; and the insurrections in India against Great Britain. These revolutions, or attempted revolutions, he sanctioned because in his opinion they represented efforts to restore great historic traditions. They were undertaken by whole communities, in concert with their natural leaders, in defense of their due constitutional liberties, and in harmony with their own histories. The French Revolution of 1789 was not a "legitimate" revolution. It broke with tradition; it was undertaken by only a fraction of the French

[1] *Reflections on the Revolution in France*, ed. cit., III, 359.

nation and in defiance of the proper national leaders; and it violated the national constitution. Hence, it was evil, and to Burke all its works were anathema.

Three aspects of Burke's traditional nationalism deserve special attention. In the first place, in line with Bolingbroke and Blackstone, Burke stressed and glorified the aristocratic, political nationalism of the British, and particularly the "British Constitution" as the supreme embodiment of the "genius" of the English nation and its historical experience. Like Bolingbroke, Burke perceived in the crown, the landed nobility, and the national established church the most useful adornments of the venerable Constitution; for any one to presume to lay violent hands on them would be anti-patriotic sacrilege. He was willing to admit the need of some reform in detail, but reform must not be revolution and must be accomplished gradually and as a truly national enterprise. The British, Burke boasted, by adhering to tradition had given the whole world a lesson in perfect government and true liberty which the French Jacobins might well take to heart. "Have these gentlemen [the Jacobins] never heard . . . of anything between the despotism of the monarch and the despotism of the multitude? Have they never heard of a monarchy directed by laws, controlled by a judicious check, from the reason and feeling of the people at large, acting by a suitable and permanent organ?"[1]

Secondly, Burke went much farther than Bolingbroke or Blackstone in developing a philosophy about nationality as such. Indeed, Burke stands with Herder as a pioneer in the exposition of the principle of nationality.

[1] *Ibid.*, III, 395.

The word "nationality" he did not use, but the thing is unmistakable. Nationality, according to Burke, does not signify a mere geographical entity or just an aggregate of individuals who happen at a given moment to live under a common government. Nationality is a concrete expression of "continuity," of an extension of people in time as well as in numbers and space. It is an outgrowth of common political, legal, and religious institutions and traditions, and, most of all, of long continued uniformity of manners and customs. Any aggregation of persons who have lived together in such wise for a long time and have undergone the same historical evolution will constitute a nationality. Each nationality, by means of historical evolution, is likely to develop a distinctive character.

Thirdly, the traditional nationalism of Burke was not quite so exclusive or paramount as the contemporary nationalism of the Jacobins. Not all human loyalties were to be absorbed into a supreme loyalty to the democratic national state. On the contrary, Burke advanced and pressed the idea of a hierarchy of loyalties, each supreme in its own sphere and all perfectly "natural," because all are "traditional." For example, man is and should be loyal to his family, and therefore the state should exalt the family, especially its educational rôle. Again, man is and should be loyal to his locality or "region"; "regionalism" is traditional and hence natural, and the nation should respect and foster it as a necessary preliminary to love of an extensive country or nationality. Of course, man is and should be loyal to the national state, but the state should be the guarantor of other loyalties and certainly should not be exclusive or intolerant in its demands upon its citizens. Then, above the nation, man is and should be loyal to the world and to humanity and should loyally seek to assure peace among the nations of mankind. Here, however, Burke had in mind, not a formal federation of theoretically equal states or any particular agency of international coöperation, but a kind of aristocratic mission for his own countrymen whereby they were to give "knightly succor" to nations in distress, especially to such as were distressed by Jacobinism, and whereby they were to act both as protectors of small nationalities in Europe and as "trustees" of backward peoples in the British Empire.[1] It will be noted that the traditionalism of Burke permitted a happy union, under humanitarian auspices, of nationalism and imperialism. And, finally, topping all other loyalties, man is and should be loyal to God, and it is not the business of the state to dictate to the individual conscience or to interfere with traditional religion.

Burke was a nationalist, but his nationalism was, in its most significant aspects, the very antithesis of Jacobin nationalism. It was traditional, and it was frankly aristocratic. Against the democratic nationalism of the Jacobins Burke was fiery and vehement; he termed it "a spirit," "a new evil," "a vast spectre," and, by that most expressive word in the English language, "a thing"; in one place he called it "a strange, nameless, wild, enthusiastic thing."[2] He hated it and would destroy it utterly. He demanded,

---

[1] "We ought to elevate our minds to the greatness of that trust to which the order of Providence has called us." *Speech on Conciliation*, March 22, 1775, Vol. II (Beaconsfield edition), p. 181.

[2] *Correspondence* (London, 1844), Vol. III, pp. 204, 209; *Thoughts on a Regicide Peace*, Vol. V (Beaconsfield edition), p. 238.

ever more insistently, a counter "enthusiasm" on the part of the English government and the English people. Death overtook him in the midst of his clamors for grand and grander coalitions of European Powers against the France of the Jacobins.

[§ 3]

Louis-Gabriel-Ambroise, Vicomte de Bonald (1754-1840) was of a noble family in southern France which had long served the King and been most faithful to the Catholic Church. He was no exception to the family tradition. While he was at college in Paris, he combatted the prevalent skepticism and took sharp issue with "enlightened" rationalists among his teachers and fellow students. After serving his king as an officer in the royal army, he married and settled down upon his ancestral estate as a country gentleman. The outbreak of the Revolution, four years later, did not immediately disturb him; his peasants did not molest him or his property. It was not until 1791, when the National Assembly put into force the civil constitution of the clergy, that Bonald openly expressed hostility to the Revolution. He then joined the émigrés and settled in Germany, where in 1796 he published his first important book—*Théorie du Pouvoir Politique et Religieux*. Returning secretly to France in 1797, he wrote at his hiding place in Paris two other books—*Législation Primitive* and *Essai Analytique*. In 1802, following the reëstablishment of Catholicism in France, he took the oath of allegiance to Napoleon's government, and thenceforth divided his time between journalism and the management of his family estate. He welcomed the restoration of the Bourbons, and condemned the revolution of 1830.

The broad principles of Bonald's philosophy, as set forth in the books which he wrote in the 1790's,[1] are similar to Burke's though less eloquent and more closely reasoned. Bonald argues against Rousseau's conceptions of the state of nature and the social contract. Civilization, he maintains, represents a gradual evolution from savagery, which is bad, to institutional life, which is good. Society in general has developed naturally and is therefore good, and it is likewise with the three specific types of society which Bonald differentiates: (1) domestic society, or the family; (2) religious society, or the church; and (3) political society, or the state. Each of these societies is, or should be, largely independent of the others, and every individual should be loyal to all three simultaneously.

Traditionally, and therefore properly, a fully constituted state has three marks: (1) a public religion, which, though tolerant of minority dissent, should be Catholic for France, Anglican for England, and Lutheran for Prussia; (2) permanent social distinctions, expressed best in a landed nobility, with special privileges and a good deal of autonomy; and (3) executive authority, vested in a monarch. These "marks," Bonald contends, are essential for the assurance of stability to the state and order among its citizens.

[1] These and other writings of Bonald, including his *Démonstration Philosophique du Principe Constitutif de la Société* (1819), are conveniently assembled in the edition of J. P. Migne (Paris, 1864).

Bonald's doctrine of nationalism is similar to Burke's, though somewhat more explicit and considerably more embellished. Bonald dwells at some length on the principle of nationality. Families united into a body "form a nation [nationality] in the relationship of common origin; they form a people in the relationship of common territory; they form a state in the relationship of common laws."[1] He emphasizes, as Burke does not, the importance of language, not only as a distinguishing badge of nationality, but also as the divinely ordained basis of social solidarity. "It is needful for man to think his speech before speaking his thought. Which means that it is needful for man to know speech before speaking—an evident proposition, and one which excludes any idea of the invention of speech by man." Speech indeed is a gift from God, and with speech man must have received the knowledge of moral truth. Hence there is a "primitive, fundamental, and sovereign law" which man had not made and which he cannot abrogate, for it had come down through the ages by means of the speech, the language, of each nationality.[2] From God, according to Bonald, develops each nationality through the agencies of its divine language and its divine law; it certainly could not develop through the agency of impious revolution. As each nationality develops, it acquires a distinctive national character, a distinctive political constitution, and "natural frontiers." Such has been the historical evolution of Frenchmen, Spaniards, and Englishmen, and such will

---

[1] *Législation Primitive*, Vol. I (Migne edition), p. 1243.
[2] Vol. I (Migne edition), pp. 999, 1068, 1074.

be the outcome of the contemporary evolution of Germans and Italians.

Bonald was as patriotic a Frenchman as any Jacobin, though in a different way. It was not the Revolution which aroused his national enthusiasm, but the contemplation of the old historic France. He praised its traditional institutions, social, political, and ecclesiastical: the French family, the French provinces, the French aristocracy, the French monarchy, the French church. He praised the traditional civilizing mission of his nation, the far flung enterprises of French Jesuits and French empire-builders. He praised such traditional heroes and heroines of the French nation as Saint Louis and Jeanne d'Arc. He praised the French "race," the happy blending of the best blood of "Romans, Gauls, and Germans." He never tired of praising the traditional language of his nation. French, he said, is "the most perfect of modern languages, and perhaps of all languages; . . . it follows most closely the natural order of things and their relationships, the object of our thoughts; and it is the most faithful expression of the truest ideas."[1] The French language is "the language of Fénélon and Racine, of Bossuet and Buffon; a language which is simple without baseness, noble without bombast, harmonious without fatigue, precise without obscurity, elegant without affectation, metaphorical without conscious effort; a language which is the veritable expression of a perfected nature."[2]

The mass of Frenchmen are, and always have been, of excellent character. Only the revolutionary Jacobin leaders

[1] Vol. I, p. 1393.
[2] *Ibid.*, p. 329.

are evil. Frenchmen as a whole are "the most enlightened and reasonable people of Europe." "I observe with attention this people, compounded of Romans, Gauls, and Germans; and I think I perceive in its character the national pride of the Roman, the impetuosity of the Gaul, the candor of the German; as I find, in its manners, the urbanity of the first, the vivacity of the second, the simplicity of the third. It is all soul, all sentiment, all action: it feels when others think; it acts when others deliberate; with it, action precedes thought, and feeling precedes action. Terrible in its errors, extreme in its virtues, it has less vice than passion; frivolous, yet capable of constancy; proud, yet capable of docility; impetuous, yet capable of reflection; confident even to the point of insolence, active so as even to perform prodigies, courageous to the point of foolhardiness, its good qualities are its own, and too often its faults are due to those who govern it." [1]

The patriotic feeling of Bonald was as strong as that of the Jacobins, but his philosophy of nationalism was not as extreme or unrestrained. He vigorously combatted the notion that an absolute sovereignty resides in a national state, or in any kind of a state. He recognized no justification, in "nature" or elsewhere, for the state's assumption of supreme authority in all matters. To his way of thinking, the state was but one of the great institutions which tradition had rendered sacred. Other such institutions were the family, the province or "region," social classes and organized professions, and especially the church. Each of these institutions had likewise been rendered sacred by tradition; each was therefore sovereign

[1] Vol. I, p. 295.

in its own sphere; and hence none could reasonably or advantageously be dictated to by the state. Sovereignty, Bonald insisted, is not singular, but plural; and thereby he was providing in his formulation of traditional nationalism for mitigating factors which were notably lacking from the Jacobin philosophy of nationalism.

A kind of internationalism Bonald also envisaged, not so much under the direction of the national states as under that of the church. Europe, he thought, was more than a geographical expression; it was a society, a family, of nations, and to it man owed loyalty as to the family or society within a particular nation. This "general society" of Europe is "the general society of Christian nations, governed by the *jus gentium;* it is called Christianity, or the Christian Republic." [1] In 1815, the very year in which the Tsar Alexander established the Holy Alliance, Bonald wrote in special praise of Leibnitz and King Henry IV for their projects of setting up a Christian Republic, a confederation of Christian nations, with the pope at its head. "Those two fine spirits," he said, "had well judged that Christianity was one great family, composed of older members and of younger members, a society of the weak and the strong, of the large and the small; and that all Christianity was subject to the common law of families and of states, which are governed by divine authority and not by . . . mere balance of power." [2]

[1] Vol. I, p. 1250.
[2] *Ibid.,* p. 520.

[§ 4]

Friedrich von Schlegel (1772-1829) is far less important than Bonald or Burke as a consistent formulator of traditional nationalism. But he is much more instructive than either as an exemplar of a curious intellectual development which during the Revolutionary and Napoleonic eras transformed a considerable number of "enlightened" humanitarians into traditional nationalists.

Born of a family of intellectual distinction, the youngest son of an eminent Lutheran clergyman in Hanover, Friedrich, in company with his older brother August Wilhelm, received an excellent education at the respectable German universities of Göttingen and Leipzig. Though nominally pursuing the study of law and actually following with interest some courses in legal history and political science, he, like his brother, fell under the influence of Herder's writings and proceeded to soak himself in literature, philology, and philosophy. It was not Herder's nationalism, however, which influenced him so much as Herder's humanitarianism and "enlightenment" and Herder's literary and scholarly interests. Indeed, both Schlegels began their literary careers as devotees of classicism and cosmopolitanism. Friedrich, fresh from the university, planned to produce monumental works on Greek and Latin literature and on comparative philology, and for the time was indifferent to the momentous events of the Revolution in neighboring France and to the first faint stirrings of nationalism in Germany. In so far as he took any interest in the contemporaneous world of politics, he appeared to be influenced by Fichte and to view with sympathetic regard the rise of Jacobinism and the spread of its principles in Germany.

About 1796—when he was twenty-four and very melancholy—Friedrich underwent a spiritual change. He abandoned classicism and became a romanticist, and speedily he was recognized as a leader of the new literary movement in Germany. He would spurn classical forms and conventions and classical reliance on reason; he would give free rein to the emotions and would romantically devote his pen to individual passion and folk-poetry. In his romantic enthusiasm, he gathered about him an interesting group of young like-minded writers.[1] With his brother he established and edited the famous *Athenaeum* as organ of the new movement. He plunged feverishly into the task of translating Shakespeare. As touching personal proof of the depth of his new faith he entered into a romantic liaison with Dorothea Mendelssohn, a Jewess and a divorcee.

Romanticism had been foreshadowed in Germany by Herder, as it had been foreshadowed in France by Rousseau; with the Schlegels it became a beacon-light for European literature, and brought nationalism into bold relief. It was romanticism which kindled the enthusiasm of Friedrich von Schlegel for old German literature, old German history, old German religion. "Nothing is so important," he wrote, "as that the Germans . . . return to the source of their own language and poetry, and liberate from the old documents of their ancestral past that power of old, that noble spirit which, unrecognized

---

[1] Including Tieck, Novalis, Schleiermacher, Bernhardi, etc. Schleiermacher, especially, was to become a nationalist philosopher of importance.

by us, is sleeping in them."[1] One of his most beautifully phrased writings was his plea for a German mythology, which would recreate the past and revive ancestral traditions. He cited other nations which had developed distinctive mythologies to their lasting advantage and called upon the Germans to do likewise. If the Germans would reconstruct a national mythology, they would find "everything which any people had sought in that great phantom of the ages, idealism."[2] Traditionalism was creeping over Schlegel in the guise of romanticism.

Like many a later romantic, Schlegel was made more nationalist by foreign travel. A tour which he and Dorothea made to Paris in 1802 he wrote up in a travel-book, *Reise nach Frankreich*,[3] teeming with expressions of romantic nationalism. For example, in reaching the Rhine he noted that "in no spot is the memory of what the Germans once were, and what they may be, so vivid as on the Rhine. The sight of this majestic stream must fill every German heart with sadness. How it falls and dashes between rocks with giant strength, then . . . dances through fruitful lowlands, and finally is lost in marshy flats—too true a picture of our fatherland, our history, and our character." Whereupon the writer bursts into a song, *Am Rheine*, celebrating the old history and glory of the mighty Rhine with its strong castles and brave knights; Franks, Saxons, and Burgundians had once struggled there for fame—"true German men with German hearts"; and some day in the future it should be so

[1] *Jugendschriften, 1794-1802*, ed. by J. Minor (Vienna, 1882), II, 353.
[2] *Athenaeum*, III, 94-105.
[3] *Deutsche National Litteratur*, Vol. CXLIII, pp. 270-296.

again, when by the mystic spirit of the noble river Germans would perform deeds of heroism as of yore. Later, upon arriving in Lorraine, he was struck by the alien aspect of the very soil and by the strange sound of the French language, "harsh and offensive to the ear." "One sees no more the great rocks and giant trees," he said, "one pines for the fresh forest scent of the soil of the German Fatherland." In another product of his tour, a critique of art galleries which he had visited,[1] he concluded that art "may stray abroad and be enriched with foreign contacts but it must always return home to the place and the nation of which it is the dearest possession, for if it loses the spirit of locality it becomes cold and lifeless. . . . There is much talk of one universal beauty and art, but it is idle; up to the present there has not been a single example of a non-national work of art."

More and more Schlegel turned to German history, particularly of the middle ages; and the more he contemplated the great German traditions of the past, the more religious he—and Dorothea too—became. In 1804 Dorothea was baptized as a Protestant Christian and she and Friedrich were formally married. In 1808 both were received into the Catholic Church. Thenceforth Schlegel, with the encouragement and active assistance of his wife, was an apostle of German nationalism and Catholic Christianity.

In 1809 Schlegel entered the service of the Habsburg Emperor at Vienna and was assigned to the agreeable task of arousing martial patriotic enthusiasm in the Archduke Charles's army which was being prepared to take

[1] *Europa*, Vol. II.

the field against Napoleon. Schlegel was one of the first official promoters of national morale; he edited a patriotic newspaper for the soldiers, and published patriotic poems for the civilians. He felt that a traditional nationalism among the Germans would be more than a match for the Jacobin nationalism of the French, and he was an important factor in the nationalist "regeneration" of Germany which was taking place during the later years of the Napoleonic era.

As a lecturer to polite audiences in Vienna, and also as a journalist, Schlegel increased his fame and propagated his doctrines. His lectures on "Modern History" (1810), on "Old and New Literature" (1812), on "Philosophy of Life" (1827), and on "Philosophy of History" (1828) contained the fruits of his mature reflection. In his last years he was the fervent exponent of mystical reaction.

Schlegel's nationalism, as set forth in his lectures and writings after 1809, was only incidentally political. He accepted without question the traditional political arrangements in Europe, especially the old "Holy Roman Empire of the German Nation," with its feudal and aristocratic features. Germany, he maintained, had been from the most ancient to the present time an example of a natural and highly enlightened theory of the "true state," that is, of government conducted by classes. It had been, moreover, a loose confederacy, in which there was the maximum of local autonomy and in which the prince or duke acted rather as judge than as lawgiver. It had also become, through historic evolution, a feudal state, based on love, friendship, and mutual oaths; a "system of honor and pledges."[1] All this was fine, and it should remain intact. In general, monarchy was the best form of government; it preserved the old patriarchal tradition of close personal relationship between the subjects and the ruler; and it was more stable and less selfish than democracy. Under monarchy, only traditional classes should participate in government—the nobles, the clergy, and the scholars. Representative government of the British type was "a plague," a disease which would reduce monarchy to "the chaos of republicanism."[2]

Tradition in Germany and elsewhere required, according to Schlegel, that the church no less than the state should be recognized as divine. Both state and church were of prime importance, though in different spheres. Together they should form a working union as they had done in the middle ages, the state preserving outward peace and the church promoting inward peace. It would be "monstrous" and "devilish" for the state to take over the government of the church. Just as formerly the papacy had supplied a real need in human society by heading a kind of European Republic, so now anew a European Republic might usefully be built about the papacy, a very loose confederacy with ample room for the free national development of all its members.[3]

It should be, however, a chief purpose of any European confederacy under the pope, and certainly of any inter-

[1] *Über die neuere Geschichte, Sämmtliche Werke,* 10 vols. (Vienna, 1822-1825), Vol. XI, pp. 45-47.
[2] *Concordia,* pp. 62-65, 160-169, 384-389.
[3] *Über die neuere Geschichte, Sämmtliche Werke,* XI, 113. Cf. *Concordia,* pp. 62-65; and *Philosophie des Lebens,* trans. by A. J. W. Morrison (1848), pp. 176, 277, 305-309.

national league under a lay monarch, "to preserve culture," which meant, in Schlegel's mind, "national culture." Rejecting political nationalism of the Jacobin variety and quite willing to accept any form of government which had been hallowed by long tradition, even such an unnational government as that of the Austrian Empire, Schlegel ever insisted that traditional cultural nationalism must be cherished by every people and fostered by every government. So long as states respect and safeguard the national culture of their peoples, it matters little to what state a particular people belongs.

National culture embraces national history, national customs, national art, and, most basically, national language and literature. Schlegel pointed out that the innate richness of the German language was not appreciated until the middle of the eighteenth century, when its "energy and flexibility" began to be recognized; that simultaneously the pride in national language spread throughout Europe; and that in England this pride developed to such a degree that "the Britons fell under the meritorious reproach of too exclusive a nationality."[1] No nation, he declared, unless it has ample stores of poetic tradition and employs them freely in its literature, can hope to attain to a national character. "Every free and independent nation may claim the right to a native literature . . . Without this the national genius will never be self-possessed." It is desirable and proper for cultured persons to know foreign languages, but it should be remembered that "the guardianship of the language of a

[1] *Geschichte der alten und neuen Literatur, Sämmtliche Werke,* I, 2-3 (Bohn trans.)

country is . . . confided to the upper classes of society; let them not abuse that trust . . . The practical application of all acquired tongues should be severely restricted to occasions when they are really indispensable. . . . A nation that tamely looks on whilst it is being despoiled of its idiom forfeits the respect due to independence; it is degraded in the ranks of civilization."[1] And cultured persons must not live aloof from the mass of the people. To produce a full and complete national art, all must participate, else it cannot be truly representative of the nationality.[2]

Indirectly Friedrich von Schlegel contributed much to the popularity of ideas about racial superiority, purity of blood, purity of language, and national soul. In his philological studies[3] he advanced the theory, as immediately influential as it was fundamentally erroneous, that "races" are differentiated by language and that the older and purer a language is, the older and purer is the race, the nationality, which speaks it. Thereby he became not only a formulator of a traditional cultural nationalism but a founder of a new romantic and pseudo-scientific nationalism which was to flourish abundantly in the nineteenth century. Besides, Schlegel contributed much to the popular cult of the ground under one's very feet and to the incorporation of it with the larger cult of nationality. His was the chief influence, for example, in making the Rhine a symbol not only for individuals who lived upon its banks but for the whole German nation, and the Rhine

[1] *Ibid.*, pp. 225-226.
[2] *Ibid.*, p. 3.
[3] Especially, *Über die Sprache und Weisheit der Indier* (1808), *Sämmtliche Werke*, Vol. VIII.

as a subject of nationalist literature was popularized by his poems. In fine, Friedrich von Schlegel brought to the fore the historic past of Germany, with its mythology, its traditions, its old songs, and its old virtues. These had all lived on in the German people from time immemorial and were a part of their life-blood. No other people possessed them, or ever could possess them, and only a German might appreciate their peculiar worth.

[§ 5]

The rise of traditional nationalism was almost if not quite as significant in modern history as the rise of Jacobin nationalism. Edmund Burke had an enormous influence in England and abroad; his nationalist writings went through innumerable editions and were speedily translated into nearly every foreign language. It was he, more than any one else, who in England steeled the courage of the classes and the resolution of the government and buoyed up the military spirit of the nation for the protracted struggle with the French. It was he who on the Continent gave spiritual succor and moral justification to hard-pressed monarchs, aristocrats, churchmen, émigrés, counter-revolutionaries, and leaders of "oppressed peoples." The Vicomte de Bonald was not so widely influential, but he helped materially to clarify the views and to point the objectives of his fellow French émigrés and of many other conservatives and reactionaries throughout Europe, particularly in Catholic Europe. It was Bonald who paved the way for the defense, by Chateaubriand, De Maistre, and Montalembert, of religion and aristocracy on nationalist grounds. Friedrich von Schlegel, ridding himself of any Jacobin taint by a deep bath in romanticism, emerged as the effective preacher of a cultural nationalism, both romantic and traditional, which tolerated the restoration of old boundaries between states and which therefore appealed to the statesmen who redrew the map of Europe after Napoleon's downfall. It was Schlegel who expressed, if he did not invent, the latent nationalism in the Tsar Alexander's grandiose scheme of the Holy Alliance.

The disciples of traditionalism were numerous and socially irreproachable. They included many Tory and Old-Whig Englishmen, many French émigrés, many aristocrats and clergymen, many conservative intellectuals, and many sincerely religious Christians among the various nationalities of Europe. Such eminent gentlemen feared and detested the French Revolution and almost everything that Jacobinism was supposed to stand for: popular sovereignty, individualism, liberty and equality, destruction of privilege, etc. In only one respect did they stoop to imitate the French Jacobins, and that was in their quickening of national consciousness and their exalting of nationality. They learned to combat Jacobinism by representing themselves, in contradistinction to the Jacobins, as the best and most rightful standard-bearers of national patriotism. Their own traditional patriotism, they insisted, was true patriotism, whilst that of the Jacobins was false patriotism.

There were real doctrinal differences between Jacobin and traditional nationalisms. The one based national patriotism on natural rights; the other based it on historic rights. The one was democratic; the other was aristocratic The one was revolutionary; the other was evolutionary, if not reactionary. The one stressed the absolute sovereignty of the national state and strove to develop about it a paramount popular religion of nationalism. The other, while preaching national patriotism, tended to regard sovereignty as plural and sought to reconcile loyalty to the national state with continuing loyalty to class and locality, and, perhaps chiefly, with continuing loyalty to traditional Christianity.

Traditional nationalism, not less than Jacobin nationalism, was heir to the humanitarianism of the eighteenth century, and its legacy from this source it exploited to the full. Traditionalists like Burke, Bonald, and Schlegel, were ever bemoaning the inhumanity of Jacobinism, its intolerance and cruelty, its outrages and atrocities, the savage guillotine which it set in motion and the vast bloody wars which it provoked. It was for the sake of civilization, for the historic rights of small nationalities, for the orderly progress of Europe, for protection against despotism—for the sake of humanity at large—that the traditionalists made their patriotic pleas for popular resistance to French Jacobinism. They were inclined, of course, to look for the millennium in the distant past rather than in the near future and to make light of the Jacobin optimism concerning the speedy triumph of justice and virtue on Earth. Yet they did expect and work for the continuing progress of humanity as it should be unfolded by Providence and expressed in the gradual betterment of civilization. To their way of thinking, such progress could be expedited by means of a traditional nationalism which not only should bring each people to a realization of what was best and noblest in its own past but which also should serve humanity as a whole by strengthening and developing traditional relations among peoples. Christendom should be thought of as a unit. Some sort of international federation should be effected, a coalition or league of states, a confederacy under the pope, or a holy alliance. Imperialism should not be repudiated, but its moral responsibilities rather than its financial profits should be stressed. Imperial nations should regard themselves as trustees of civilization and should seek to foster, not to suppress, native national cultures. Aristocrats should lead the advanced nations; advanced nations should be the patrons of the backward nations; everywhere and in all relationships, the governing principle should be that of *noblesse oblige*.

Such was the theory. But in practice traditional nationalism proved to be as bellicose and violent as the Jacobin variety. It has already been suggested that if Jacobinism had not been opposed by reactionaries in France and in Europe it might not have involved domestic terror and foreign war and might not have produced an excess of nationalism. Similarly, it may here be suggested that if traditionalism had not been confronted with menacing Jacobins in France and with their disciples in other countries it would not have felt the necessity of overcoming them by brute force and in all probability would not have evolved a fierce counter-nationalism. As it was, the Jacobins seemed to be resolved to conquer all Europe for their cause, whilst the traditionalists certainly did their utmost to repulse the Jacobins and to subjugate France. Traditional nationalism was a powerful motive force in back of the revolts within France, particularly in La Vendée, in back of growing popular resistance on the Continent, as exemplified in the nationalist awakenings in Germany, Holland, Portugal, Spain, and even Russia, and in back of the ceaseless military and naval efforts of the British. If Napoleon Bonaparte and his marshals were products of Jacobin nationalism, then traditional nationalism flowered in Pitt and Castlereagh, Nelson and Wellington, the Archduke Charles and the Tsar Alexander. The battle of Waterloo was the climax to a bloody tragedy which for twenty-three years had been enacted on the European stage between the forces of Jacobinism and those of traditionalism. The "son of the Revolution" went down in final defeat before a British nobleman who knew and reverenced his Burke.

The military victory of traditional nationalism in 1815 was not complete, or ultimately decisive. True, Napoleon was gotten rid of and Jacobinism was pushed into a dim, dark background even in France. A Bourbon monarch was restored to the French throne. Nobles and clergymen resumed their traditional rôles. The map of Europe was redrawn, not according to any natural right of national self-determination but in accordance with historic rights and dynastic interests. England greatly extended her trusteeship of backward peoples overseas. The Tsar Alexander fashioned a Holy Alliance with the divine-right monarchs of Austria and Prussia in order to assure to their respective peoples in the future the maintenance of peace and justice in accordance with the maxims of the

Christian religion. All of which was indicative of the triumph of traditionalism.

[§ 6]

But the triumph of traditionalism was more apparent than real. Louis XVIII, upon ascending the throne of his Bourbon ancestors, did several things which his ancestors would not have thought of doing. He was not a great man and perhaps not a good man, but he was enough of a politician, and sufficiently anxious not to be obliged to go again into exile, so as to recognize the need of effecting a compromise within France between Jacobinism and traditionalism. In deference to the latter he banned the revolutionary flag and anthem—the tricolor and the *Marseillaise*—and resuscitated as the national flag of France the traditional standard of the Bourbon family—the white banner with the lilies. On the other hand, in deference to Jacobin sentiment, he promptly issued a Charter, addressing it not, as his ancestors would have done, to "my peoples," but to "the French people," which provided for a constitutional parliamentary government and contained a declaration of the "public rights of the French." After paying lip-service to tradition by explaining that "We have sought the principles of the constitutional charter in the French character and in the venerable monuments of past centuries," His Most Christian Majesty proceeded to insert in the Charter such shocking revolutionary dicta as the following: "All Frenchmen are equal before the law, whatever may be their title or rank. They contribute without distinction to the impositions of the state in proportion to their fortune. They are all equally eligible to civil and military positions. Their personal liberty is likewise guaranteed. No one may be prosecuted or arrested except in the cases and in the manner prescribed by law. All may with equal liberty make profession of their religion and enjoy the same protection for their worship. . . . All investigation of opinions expressed or of votes cast previous to the Restoration is prohibited; oblivion of these is imposed upon the courts and upon the citizens alike."

There were Frenchmen in 1815 who were more consistently and conscientiously traditionalist than Louis XVIII, and they openly objected to his dalliance with Jacobin nationalism. As one of them, a certain Vicomte de Castelbajac, explained to the French Parliament: "In using the word *patrie*, gentlemen, I do not mean the word which has been so much abused, which has served as a pretext for all selfish interests and for all the passions and as an excuse for all crimes; I mean by *patrie* not the soil to which I am attached by shameful laws of usurpation and despotism, but the land of my fathers, with its legitimate government, a government which accords me protection by reason of my obedience to the laws and which I am obliged to serve with fidelity and honor. Thus, for me, gentlemen," the honorable vicomte concluded, "the *patrie* is France with the King; and King and France are inseparable in my eyes for constituting the Fatherland." Between such Frenchmen and those who had been tainted with Jacobinism, a struggle went on for many years after 1815, not so much a sanguinary struggle, though it was punctuated occasionally with bloody riots, as a conflict of ideas and political activities. Eventually, as Jacobinism itself became a French tradition, a mild form of it was incorporated with the rising liberal nationalism, which was thereby enabled to overwhelm the older traditionalism.

Indeed, the rise of liberal nationalism was a noteworthy phenomenon in the nineteenth-century history not only of France but of Great Britain and other European countries. In England, as well as in France, it appealed to a growing number of intellectuals who perceived in its tenets the promise of a happy escape alike from the "excesses" of Jacobinism and from the "reaction" of traditionalism. All over western Europe, nationalism remained a driving force, but its form was to be, for some time after 1815, predominantly liberal.

In eastern Europe, circumstances after 1815, though not nearly so conducive to the rise of liberal nationalism, were distinctly unfavorable to any such development of traditional nationalism as Bonald or Schlegel had envisaged. There Prince Clemens Metternich (1773-1859) was the outstanding statesman; and his early training in old-fashioned diplomacy, the confiscation of his hereditary Rhenish estates by Napoleon, and especially the practical exigencies of his situation as chief governor of the supernational Austrian Empire from 1809 to 1848, rendered him the convinced foe of nationalism in any form. Metternich was certainly a traditionalist in his general political philosophy and in his political policies: he was thoroughly devoted to the old régime, to social inequality, to the maintenance of the traditional privileges of the aristocracy and the church, and he was a most loyal, as well as a very shrewd, servant of the absolute divine-

TRADITIONAL NATIONALISM

right monarchy of the Habsburgs. Like the other staunch traditionalists, he yearned for domestic and international peace which should be based on traditional order and security, and he hated Jacobinism in all its aspects. But he could not believe, with Schlegel, that these ends would be served by nationalism, not even by traditional nationalism. Nationalism in every form he condemned as being too closely associated with Jacobinism, as being essentially subversive of social order and security, as being inherently inimical to the traditional state and specifically to the historic Habsburg Empire, and as being dangerous to the peace of Europe. What would the triumph of nationalism entail? A revolutionary rearrangement of boundaries and therefore a series of great international wars.

So Metternich tried to ignore nationalism. Not even cultural nationalism did he encourage, for he felt that the greater the favors he extended to the language and literature of a particular people, the greater would be its national self-consciousness, and the louder and more dangerous would be its consequent demands for political autonomy and eventually for independence. Accordingly he must suppress any nationalist agitation at home and must quarantine all Austrian lands against nationalist infection from abroad.

The Tsar Alexander, though a trifle tainted with Jacobinism in his early days and always a bit romantic, emerged in 1815 as the great hope of traditional nationalism. He was respected as the traditional autocrat of all the Russias and hailed as the decisive instrument of divine Providence in saving the historic civilization of

Europe. He appeared to be intent upon safeguarding the traditional privileges of social classes and at the same time to be disposed to accord to Poles, Finns, and other peoples within his Empire a wide recognition of their historic national rights. He seemed, moreover, to be championing in his Holy Alliance a European confederacy in the spirit of traditional nationalism.

The Tsar, however, was a colossus with feet of clay, and in his swelling bosom beat a heart timid and very impressionable. It was not long before the practical Metternich gained a complete intellectual ascendancy over the dreaming Alexander. By 1820 the latter formally confessed to the former: "Today I deplore all that I said and did between the years 1815 and 1818. I regret the waste of time, which we must attempt to retrieve. You have correctly judged the state of affairs. Tell me what you desire and what you wish me to do, and I will do it." In this repentant mood Alexander joined Metternich in the movement to stamp out all novelties, nationalism included. To Metternich likewise deferred the weak Emperor of Austria and the fawning King of Prussia, to say nothing of a horde of obliging lesser princes in Germany and Italy. Repression of popular agitation of every kind became the rule of the time in eastern and central Europe, and the Holy Alliance rapidly degenerated into a mere reactionary police-measure for the maintenance of the political and social *status quo*.

Advocates of traditional nationalism were, as a rule, conservative gentlemen, fearful of revolution and accustomed to obey their rulers. Few of them displayed any strong tendency to persevere in nationalist agitation when

Metternich and the monarchs set themselves against it. They were content to rally to the defence of traditions of a personal or social sort and to minimize those which were national. In the circumstances, it was left after 1815 mainly to liberals to champion nationalism in eastern and central Europe, with the result that here, as in western Europe, the succeeding nationalism was predominantly liberal.

Yet it should not be inferred that traditional nationalism utterly perished in the midst of its apparent triumph over Jacobin nationalism. It had been too potent a force to suffer such a fate. It continued to be expressed by aristocrats here and there throughout Europe; it exerted considerable influence on the development of liberal nationalism; and, undergoing something of a revival at the end of the nineteenth century, it was destined to be embodied, in large part, in the integral nationalism of the twentieth century. Before indicating in any detail the later career of traditionalist doctrines, it will be convenient to describe the third type of nationalism which issued from the humanitarianism of the eighteenth century and played a leading rôle in the middle of the nineteenth century—liberal nationalism.

CHAPTER V

LIBERAL NATIONALISM

[§ 1]

MIDWAY between Jacobin and traditional nationalism was liberal nationalism. Like the others, this type originated in the eighteenth century. It originated in England, that country of perpetual compromise and of acute national self-consciousness, and in the mind of Jeremy Bentham, that grave prodigy and professional reformer.

Jeremy Bentham (1748-1832) came of a well-to-do family of London lawyers, respectably Tory in politics, and, as became his station in life, was properly educated at Westminster School, at Queen's College, Oxford, and at Lincoln's Inn, whence he was duly called to the bar in 1772. From a conventional career he was saved by the simple fact that he had a tough mind in a peculiarly weak body. Extraordinarily delicate, almost a dwarf, highly nervous and sensitive, he was a mental prodigy in boyhood, and, much stranger, he continued to be a mental prodigy during his whole life. Temperamentally averse to the practice of law and physically precluded from active politics, yet endowed with alert mind and ample funds, he was the perfect example of the closet philosopher and voluminous encyclopedist. From his singular secluded home and from his own inner consciousness he poured forth a flood of schemes for the reformation of the world. His *Fragment on Government*, published in 1776, the year of the American Declaration of Independence, gave him fame as a political philosopher; and his *Introduction to the Principles of Morals and Legislation*, published in 1789, the year of the French Declaration of the Rights of Man, established his reputation as an acute critic of ethics and jurisprudence.

Thenceforth Bentham's literary output was astounding until 1800 and considerable until his death at the ripe age of eighty-four. During all these years he tackled a great variety of abuses in law, religion, government, and politics; he wrote with equal warmth and diffuseness on logic, language, morals, and economics; he propounded innumerable utopian plans for the care of criminals, for the manufacture of pianos, and for the digging of canals across the isthmuses of Suez and Panama. Utterly devoid of any sense of humor, he was privileged to repose a sublime confidence in himself and his schemes. After his death, his body, according to his express wish, was dissected in the interest of science, and then put together again, dressed in his usual clothes, and placed on exhibition in University College, London. There it may be viewed today by any one who may be morbidly curious to behold the earthly remains of Jeremy Bentham, reformer and philosopher, first of liberal nationalists.

Bentham is best known today as the founder of the philosophy of utilitarianism; and it is certainly true that this philosophy underlay all his systems, including his nationalism. Utilitarianism was a version of hedonism, the idea that the fundamental impulse of man is to seek pleasure and to avoid pain. Pleasure is good; pain is evil. No action or intention is good or bad in itself. The goodness or badness of anything depends purely and simply on its effects, that is, on its tendency to produce happiness for the individual concerned. In this way, motives may sometimes be good and sometimes be bad, according to their consequences. Utility is always to be measured by the good done, that is, by the happiness promoted. This philosophy appears to be selfish and egotistical, and Bentham frankly admitted that it is. But in its application, he argued that each man, in serving his own best interests and therefore in securing his own happiness, will be serving best the interests of his fellows and promoting their greatest happiness. For, whatever acts to make one's fellows unhappy is bound eventually to react upon one's self in the same manner. Hence it is the business of utilitarianism to promote the greatest happiness of individuals, which means "the greatest good of the greatest number." And self-interest, Bentham was at pains to explain in good eighteenth-century style, must be "enlightened" self-interest.

As an utilitarian, Bentham was an apostle of individualism. One does not need to think of society at large, but only of the individual unit in society, for the enlightened self-interest of each individual provides inevitably the enlightened self-interest, that is, the happiness, of all human beings. But as an utilitarian, Bentham was also driven to criticize governments and laws and social behaviors which in his opinion were not promoting the greatest good of the greatest number and to demand their reformation. He immensely admired the American Constitution and other arrangements in the New World and ardently believed that if his own countrymen would imitate the overseas experiments and reduce their complex political and legal practices to a simple written constitution and a logical code of law, they too could immeasurably promote individual, and therefore national, happiness. He spent many years in drafting "reasonable" constitutions and codes for England not only, but, being a good humanitarian and equipped with a most comprehensive mind, for the whole universe likewise.

In his emphasis on individualism and in his enthusiasm for reform, Bentham was one with Rousseau and many other French philosophers of the eighteenth century who were providing building blocks for the subsequent construction of Jacobin nationalism. It might be supposed, therefore, that Bentham would have been sympathetic with Rousseau and the Jacobins. To a certain extent he was sympathetic with them. He surely had none of the fierce emotional hostility to them which characterized Edmund Burke. On the contrary, he said several nice things about the course of events in revolutionary France from 1789 to 1792, and in 1792 he accepted the citizenship which the French Jacobins conferred upon him. Yet he could not be wholly sympathetic with Jacobinism because his basic philosophy differed from Rousseau's in certain significant respects.

In the first place, Bentham was not interested in speculation about the origin of government and law, and he scorned Rousseau's theory of the social contract. To Bentham, there was nothing sacred about any government, as a contract would clearly imply; government, even of democratic character, was a necessary evil. To him the question was not whether government is democratic, whether it is subject to the "popular will," but, rather, whether government is useful, whether it promotes the greatest good of the greatest number. In other words, Bentham was not a democrat on principle or in a mystical sense; he thought that democracy, like any other form of government, should be judged by his utilitarian philosophy.

Secondly, Bentham rejected the doctrine of natural rights, which Rousseau and the Jacobins deeply cherished. Rights, according to Bentham, are established by laws, and laws are established by governments. Nature may have given man a platonic right to anything, but such right has no real significance unless and until a particular government affords protection to the individual who would exercise a particular right. Every "right," moreover, must be judged, not by its naturalness, but solely in accordance with its utility.

Bentham was intent upon limiting, rather than upon extending, the scope and functions of government. He assailed the Leviathan idea of government which Hobbes had propounded; he condemned the Jacobin practice of governmental expansion; his thought was quite antithetical to the later socialist doctrine of the state. According to him, the only proper and justifiable end of government was "the greatest happiness of the greatest number," and this could be assured by just three specific state functions: the assurance of security; the protection of property; and the guaranty of equality of individual opportunity for happiness. Of course, these functions were stated broadly enough to admit of a later interpretation which might justify a vast accession of state power, and contemporary English liberals are prone to drape Bentham's mantle about their own programme of social legislation. But Bentham himself was a strict constructionist in the interpretation of his doctrine of the functions of government. He was a convinced exponent of laisser-faire.

Bentham's laisser-faire had important implications. It meant that the state should enact a minimum of laws and only such as were generally applicable to the defense of public order, private property, and individual equality; the state should be primarily a passive policeman, allowing a wide latitude of freedom to its individual citizens. It meant that the state should respect economic liberty, the freedom of the individual to engage in any profession or industry, to enter into any contract at will with employer or employee, and to trade with whomsoever he would, at home or abroad, without let or hindrance by government. It meant that the state should respect religious liberty, the freedom of the individual to practice any religion or no religion without either favor or persecution on the part of the state; churches should be separated from the state and tolerated as strictly private, voluntary organizations.

Bentham's laisser-faire also meant educational liberty, the freedom of the individual to teach and study, to speak and write, to assemble and form associations, with a minimum of interference by the state, although here Bentham, mindful of his utilitarianism, implied that the state might and should assist actively in enlightening all its citizens about their true interests. Likewise his laisser-faire meant ideally an individual freedom from military conscription and therefore the pursuit of a thoroughly pacifist policy by the state, although here again Bentham, remembering the obligation of government to assure security and protect property, declared that a state might maintain a very small standing army and a large voluntary short-term militia.

The implications of utilitarianism were the planks in the platform of the new political philosophy of liberalism which Bentham championed: an individualism based on enlightened self-interest; an ignoring of the social contract, natural rights, and other metaphysical conceptions, and, instead, a stressing of practical utility; a penchant for systematic, logical, and consistent reforms; and a passive-policeman state, with a government which should allow to the individual very wide liberty, political, economic, religious, educational, and military. It ran counter to the traditionalism of Burke and the British Tories, and to a lesser extent it ran counter also to the Jacobinism of the French Revolutionaries.

The new liberalism gained influential converts. It was put forth by Bentham in England at the very time when the Industrial Revolution was getting under way in that country, when a growing number of middle-class manufacturers and capitalists were substituting large-scale machine-production for the old domestic system of hand-industry and were clamoring against the restrictions which the laws of an old agricultural society had imposed on the new developments. In these circumstances it was not so paradoxical as it sounds that practical English business men allied themselves with a closet philosopher, and that the liberalism of Jeremy Bentham, joining hands with that of economists and capitalists, won the great parliamentary reform of 1832 and shortly afterwards created the British Liberal Party.

Bentham has been so much discussed as utilitarian and liberal that his contributions to nationalism have been grossly underrated or entirely overlooked. Yet liberalism from the outset involved a kind of nationalism, and Bentham was himself a patriot—after a fashion. He could hardly have been an Englishman without being a patriot. Though carping in his criticism of the government and laws of his own country, fulsome in praise of America, and willing to accept citizenship in France, he never forgot that, in the words of Bolingbroke, "he was a Briton still." He, the most logical and pacifist of men, took a somewhat illogical pride in the power of Britain in comparison with other nations.[1] He contended that the English language is superior to all others by reason of its simplicity[2] and proposed to make it the basis of a universal language.[3] He repeatedly referred to "English liberties" in such a manner as to suggest that the English nationality alone possessed a real love of freedom.[4] He made mention of the "English mind"[5] and "the spirit of the British people."[6] He frequently employed such

[1] *Principles of International Law, Works*, 11 vols. (Edinburgh, 1843), II, 556-557.
[2] *Essay on Language, Works*, VIII, 310.
[3] *Chrestomathia, Works*, VIII, 185-187.
[4] For example, *Plan of Parliamentary Reform, Works*, III, 490, 537; *A Plea for the Constitution, Works*, IV, 260, 280.
[5] *A Plea for the Constitution, Works*, IV, 268.
[6] *Ibid.*, IV, 284.

phrases as "every English breast," and "we in England."[1] One is tempted to suspect that his extravagant praise of the United States is attributable to the fact that America was "peopled with men of English race, bred up in English habits, with minds fraught with ideas associated with all English ideas by English language."[2]

Bentham was an English patriot, but he was also, in the best eighteenth-century manner, a good deal of a cosmopolite, and he felt no inner conflict between the two loyalties. He could proclaim that he belonged to no party and to no country,[3] and on occasion could address himself to "My fellow citizens of France! My fellow citizens of England! My fellow citizens of the civilized world! My fellow citizens of future ages!"[4] With the exception of one little fit of temper against the French for having pinned their faith to "natural rights," he displayed in all his voluminous writings not a trace of antagonism or antipathy toward any foreign nation.

National patriotism Bentham accepted as a fact, and as a highly utilitarian fact. He defined it as "sympathy for the feelings of a country's inhabitants, present, future, or both, taken in the aggregate."[5] He insisted that as devotion to the commonweal, and especially to its improvement and reform, national patriotism can be of great service in promoting the greatest good of the greatest number. He clearly recognized, moreover, the existence of nationalities, differentiated from one another by (1)

[1] For example, *Anarchical Fallacies, Works*, II, 502, and *Plan of Parliamentary Reform, Works*, III, 514.
[2] *Radicalism not Dangerous, Works*, III, 612.
[3] *Papers on Codification, Works*, IV, 530.
[4] *To his Fellow Citizens of France, Works*, IV, 499.
[5] *Table of the Springs of Action, Works*, I, 219.

LIBERAL NATIONALISM

race, the "radical frame of mind and body," which operates to make a man of one race feel himself a very different being from a man of another race [1]; (2) climate, particularly heat and cold; and (3) the influence of religion in conditioning popular customs. The very fact that peoples are conscious of differences between them, Bentham went on to explain, is responsible for a deepening of the lines of separation. A people becomes attached to its own laws and customs and suspicious of any that may differ from them. National prejudices and animosities result, which, after all, are nothing more or less than a liking for what is familiar and a dislike for what is strange, but they serve their purpose of accentuating what actually is different between nations and even of fostering a belief in differences which may be only imaginary.[2]

Bentham believed that nationality is the proper basis for state and government. In an address to the French nation, he vehemently urged them to emancipate their colonies on the ground that the colonists were not Frenchmen and should therefore not be subjected to French rule.[3] A like plea he made in behalf of the English colonies. The same principle he invoked to justify his indignation at the partition of Poland.[4] Never would he seek to impose the domination of any particular country upon other peoples; rather, he would help them to find happiness through the establishment of national states

[1] *Introduction to the Principles of Morals and Legislation, Works,* I, 30.
[2] *Cf. On the Influence of Time and Place in Matters of Legislation, Works,* I, 171-184; *Principles of Morals and Legislation, Works,* I, 95; *Anarchical Fallacies, Works,* II, 508.
[3] *Emancipate your Colonies, Works,* IV, 408.
[4] *Papers on Codification, Works,* IV, 529-530.

of their own on liberal principles.[1] Nor did he think that England had a mission to perform toward backward peoples. The purpose in his nationalism, as in all his projects, was to assure the greatest happiness to the greatest number of persons and peoples, and this did not admit of a militant or imperialist spirit or of any aggressive course of action.[2] In his nationalism he was pacifist and anti-imperialist, a "Little Englander," and a stout upholder of the right of national self-determination for all peoples, large and small alike.

Bentham coined the word "international." He used it first in 1789 in his *Introduction to the Principles of Morals and Legislation;* and subsequently in his *Principles of International Law* he made fully apparent the significance which the new word possessed for him. It bespoke a relationship between national states and peoples which should supplant cosmopolitanism and yet mitigate nationalism. The old cosmopolite had attempted to be a "citizen of the world" by spurning nationality and decrying patriotism. The new internationalist should be a good nationalist in order to bring about a better world order. But being a good nationalist meant doing to other nations what you would have them do to you. It meant that while love of country and national zeal were commendable sentiments, national partiality and prejudice were to be eschewed. It

---

[1] *Constitutional Code, Works,* IX, 202; *Radical Reform Bill, Works,* III, 584.

[2] Witness his disgust at the foreign military occupation of France after Waterloo: *Plan of Parliamentary Reform, Works,* III, 436-442. *Cf.* his discussion of nationalist propaganda by newspapers: *Principles of International Law, Works,* II, 555-556; here he appears to rate justice higher than patriotism.

meant also that while the political map of the world should be redrawn on national lines, the emerging national states should compete and coöperate in works good for all humanity.

To Bentham, what was peculiarly bad in existing international relations was war. He was certain that the dynastic and colonial wars which had been waged between European states for two or three centuries had wrought vast evil for a great number of individuals and nations, and he was fearful lest even vaster evil might result from the more intensive and passionate wars of his own day. Consequently he devoted the greater part of his *Principles of International Law* to an exposition of the causes and cure of war. The causes of war, he explained, were: national pride; commercial rivalry; disputes over boundaries; attempts at conquest; disputes over royal succession; quarrels over new discoveries; violations of territory; and religious hatreds. The principal means which he urged of preventing war were: the use of reason; the establishment of free trade; the perfecting of international law; the confederation of nations for mutual defense; international arbitration; and the limitation of armaments. Here was the foundation for a new internationalism, grounded in liberal nationalism.

But Bentham never contented himself with proposing a general principle. He must always present a specific "plan." And so his *Principles of International Law* contained, as its inevitable climax, a "Plan for a Universal and Perpetual Peace." This plan, like a much later pronouncement by a twentieth-century liberal, consisted of fourteen points! Bentham's Fourteen Points were substantially as follows: (1) It is not to the interest of Great Britain to possess any foreign dependencies whatsoever, since they are a cause of war and a source of expense. (2) It is not to her interest to have any treaty of alliance, offensive or defensive, with another Power, since treaties of alliance increase the danger of war. (3) It is not to her interest to have any preferential trade agreement with another Power, for such agreements are useless and mischievous. (4) It is not to her interest to maintain any naval force beyond what is requisite for defense of her commerce against pirates. (5) It is not to her interest to retain her navigation acts or any other measures intended indirectly to contribute to her naval strength. Similarly, it is not to the interest of France (6) to possess foreign dependencies, (7) to have treaties of alliance or (8) preferential trade agreements, (9) to maintain a navy, or (10) to provide indirectly for one. (11) Great Britain and France should embody the foregoing policies in a formal joint agreement and should invite the other nations to accede to it. (12) There should follow a limitation of national armies by general and perpetual treaties. (13) An international court should be established for the peaceful settlement of disputes between nations, consisting of two delegates from each nation, and having power: (a) to render decisions or opinions; (b) to publish its decisions or opinions in all countries; (c) to put a refractory state under the ban of Europe; and, in last resort, (d) to request a contingent of troops from each state in order to enforce the decisions of the court. (14) There should not be secret treaties or secret negotiations between states, *i*nasmuch as secrecy is repugnant both to liberty and to peace.

[§ 2]

Liberal nationalism of the sort championed by Jeremy Bentham originated in England and appealed to a growing number of Englishmen, especially among economists and middle-class "Radicals."[1] These English liberals were pacifist, but they had to face the fact that the French Jacobins and Napoleon were not. In the circumstances, they resigned themselves, particularly during the decade after 1804, to acquiescence in the huge war which their Tory Government of Pitt and Castlereagh was waging against the French Empire. They found solace for their consciences in the fine war-aims which their Government set forth. The huge war, they were told and they grew fond of repeating, was being waged in order to liberate the Continent from Napoleonic militaristic despotism, to free trade and commerce from the shackles of Napoleon's Continental System, and to guarantee the independence of small nations. Such aims were in keeping with liberal philosophy; and the efforts of English arms in Portugal, in Spain, in Italy, in Holland and Belgium, and at the culminating battle of Waterloo, tended to buttress the idea that when Napoleon, the arch-enemy of liberty, was finally removed from the scene, liberalism

[1] John Stuart Mill describes in his *Autobiography* how Bentham gave, as to earlier philosophical radicals, "unity to my conception of things . . . , a creed, a doctrine, a philosophy, . . . the inculcation and diffusion of which could be made the principal outward purpose of a life. And I had a grand conception laid before me of changes to be effected in the condition of mankind through that doctrine."

would emerge triumphant in England and on the Continent. So it transpired that many Englishmen, pacifist at heart, fondly hoped to secure sane lasting peace by means of international war.

Liberal nationalism spread from England to the Continent. In Germany its teachings were appropriated by a goodly number of scholars and poets and statesmen and were utilized in order to arouse national resistance to Napoleon. Wilhelm von Humboldt (1767-1835), who had been in his youth a cosmopolite and had flirted in his young manhood with Jacobinism, now became a liberal nationalist; a Prussian minister of public instruction he played a very influential rôle in the drama of German regeneration, quite patriotic and quite liberal. The great Baron vom Stein (1757-1831) was an ardent admirer of England and especially of such English liberals as Adam Smith and Jeremy Bentham; thence he derived much of the inspiration and many practical suggestions for the reforms which he introduced into Prussian politics and economics and likewise for the plans he evolved for the erection of a national German state along liberal lines.

In Portugal and Spain, also, many of the leaders of the popular uprisings against Napoleon professed devotion to liberal principles which they obtained in considerable part from England and, directly or indirectly, from Jeremy Bentham. The revolutionary Spanish Constitution of 1812 betrayed some Jacobin influence but a larger amount of Benthamite liberal influence. It was the prototype of a series of constitutions which were subsequently framed in southern Europe and in South America and which were characterized by the union of nationalism with liberalism. In the meantime, during the last years of the Napoleonic era, liberal nationalists emerged, not only in Germany and the Iberian Peninsula, but likewise in Italy, Poland, Holland, Belgium, and many another country.

By 1815 liberal nationalism was a fairly definite intellectual movement throughout western and central Europe. It differed from traditional nationalism and also from Jacobin nationalism in several ways. It tended to ignore both historic rights and natural rights. It was chiefly evolutionary, but it was certainly not reactionary, and, whilst tending to be revolutionary in practice, it was not so in theory. It was surely not aristocratic, and, though paying lip-service to democracy, it tended to be middle-class. It stressed the absolute sovereignty of the national state, but sought to limit the implications of this principle by stressing individual liberties—political, economic, and religious—within each national state, and the responsibility of all national states for the establishment and maintenance of international peace.

To define the doctrinal content of liberal nationalism a bit more closely, emphasis should be put upon the fact that it was nationalist. It looked forward to a redrawing of the political map of the world so that each nationality should have an independent state of its own. This would involve the dissolution of each imperial domain into its constituent national elements and at the same time the unification of disjointed parts of a nationality into a new commonwealth.

Likewise, liberal nationalism was emphatically liberal. Just as each national state must be independent of every other, so the citizens of each national state must be free men. They must have personal liberties—liberties of speech, press, worship, and association. They must have economic liberties—freedom of profession, freedom of contract, freedom of trade. Indeed, if all states were national and liberal, free trade, it was argued, would flourish within and among them and would prevent war and insure domestic and international peace.

Liberal nationalism was not only national and liberal. It was also, at least in word and drift, democratic. Its devotees said that they desired democratic as well as national self-determination of peoples. Jeremy Bentham enthusiastically advocated thoroughgoing political democracy as the most promising instrument of national happiness and even expressed the hope that women in time would share with men the right of equal, secret, and virtually universal suffrage.[1] Liberals on the Continent generally endorsed the principle of representative democracy. All held out the promise of a world comprising a peaceful, coöperating group of states which should be free and democratic and liberal and national.

In fact, however, the chief support of liberal nationalism came, as we have seen, from members of the middle class, and these persons were not so immediately intent upon realizing democracy for the masses as upon obtaining control and direction of national government by their own class. They had no burning faith in democracy as a "natural right" or as a dogma, and consequently their

---

[1] Though Bentham was quite ready to give women the vote, he was unwilling to admit them to seats in the democratic legislature. Such admittance, he solemnly declared, would lead to "reciprocal seduction" and result in confusion and ridicule. *Plan of Parliamentary Reform, Works*, III, 463; *Constitutional Code, Works*, IX, 108-109.

devotion to it, unlike that of the Jacobins, lacked fervency. On the other hand, their belief in their own interests and their anxiety to serve them whetted their political ambition and gave rise after 1815 in several countries to agitation for liberal constitutional governments which should rest on electorates of intelligent well-to-do middle-class citizens. At some later but unspecified date, when the masses would learn to seek their true interests and would become literate and thrifty, they too could be enfranchised. In the meanwhile, as Englishmen expressed it, "liberty would slowly broaden out."

Certain agencies of nationalism which the revolutionary Jacobins had invented, the evolutionary Liberals adopted and applied to their own ends. After 1815 leading liberal nationalists were exponents of free popular education in national schools, of universal military training in short-term national militias, of popular journalism, and of patriotic societies, provided always, however, that the new societies, the new journals, the new militias, and the new schools were used to spread the new enlightenment of liberalism, its peculiar doctrines of politics, economics, and religion. Liberty demanded that dissent should be tolerated but not necessarily fostered. Indeed, leading liberals on the Continent were pronouncedly "anti-clerical" as well an anti-aristocratic, and they labored almost as zealously as the Jacobins had done to remove both aristocratic and ecclesiastical influences from the main agencies of nationalist propaganda.

In one important respect, liberal nationalism after 1815 was influenced and partially transformed by traditional nationalism, perhaps not directly, but at any rate indirectly. Jeremy Bentham and other early liberals had been good eighteenth-century gentlemen in that they spurned history, especially medieval history, and, with eyes fixed on the present and future, elaborated by severely logical processes ideal schemes for human betterment. Succeeding liberals, however, came under the spell of that intellectual movement of romanticism which the reaction against eighteenth-century enlightenment had cast and which traditional nationalists were exploiting.

Romanticism, as has already been noted in another connection, stimulated the study and revival of folk-ways and folk-legends, the reading and writing of history, particularly of national history, and the tendency to idealize nationalities and national heroes and to ascribe distinctive characters to the several peoples. Romanticism stimulated traditionalists, and it also stimulated liberals. Byron was not a traditionalist but he was highly romantic. So were Victor Hugo and Mazzini and many another poet or prose lyricist of liberalism. So also were a goodly number of professors and other scholars who delved into history and philology and discovered therein romantic evidence of the long continuing latent liberalism and nationalism of the various European nations. Curiously enough, it was romanticism as much as intelligence, and perhaps more than self-interest, which attracted a growing number of intellectuals to liberal nationalism. It was romanticism, moreover, which supplied a much needed enthusiasm and élan to liberal nationalists. These, in romantic vein, began to talk, with telling effect, of the wrongs and sufferings of "oppressed," even of "enslaved," nationalities. "Liberation" simply had to follow, not only of middle classes but likewise of whole nations.

Nineteenth-century developments of liberal nationalism may be conveniently suggested by brief résumés of the teachings of three of its apostles—a statesman, a scholar, and an agitator; a Frenchman, a German, and an Italian; Guizot, Welcker, and Mazzini. Let us consider, first, the French statesman Guizot.

[§ 3]

It is debatable whether François Guizot (1787-1874) was the scholar in politics or the politician in scholarship, but there can be no question that he was a sincere liberal. Toward love of liberty his very childhood impelled him. He came of the French middle class which on the eve of the great Revolution was in the forefront of the struggle for political liberty. He came of a family of the Protestant minority which particularly needed and demanded religious liberty. He came of a father who died on the guillotine during the Terror, a martyr to personal liberty. François was only seven years of age when his father perished, but he retained throughout his long life a horror of Jacobinism and its intolerances. Educated at Geneva in a sternly Calvinist environment, he was strengthened in his Protestantism and inoculated for life against the antithesis to Jacobinism—reactionary traditionalism. He returned to France in 1805, studied law at Paris, speedily turned to journalism, and in 1812, by an astonishing stroke of luck, was appointed professor of history in the Sorbonne, with Napoleon's approval. But Napoleon's régime was at once too illiberal and too tainted with Jacobinism to satisfy Guizot, and the youthful professor of history welcomed the Bourbon restoration of 1814-1815 with its retention of the rights and privileges won for the middle class by the Revolution. In Louis XVIII's Charter of 1814 Guizot perceived the triumph of political liberalism, the happy compromise between constitutional government and national tradition.

In 1812, the year of his professorial appointment, Guizot married Mlle. Meulan, a lively literary lady of royalist proclivities and romantic bent. With her he collaborated in literary undertakings and by her he undoubtedly was confirmed in his liberal royalism and introduced into the new romantic movement. That he was inherently of romantic nature is suggested by his marriage record. On his first wife's death he married in 1828 her niece, Mlle. Dillon; and then when he was past fifty he wooed and wed the Countess of Lieven, former mistress of Metternich and ex-wife of the Austrian ambassador in London. Each of his three wives testified to the ardor and energy of his affection.

During many years at the Sorbonne, Guizot lectured and wrote extensively on various aspects of history. What are probably his two most famous historical works, his *General History of Civilization in Europe from the Fall of the Roman Empire to the French Revolution* and his *History of Civilization in France from the Fall of the Roman Empire*, were delivered as lectures to large audiences in 1828 and 1829. There was much liberal as well as nationalist propaganda in these works and their historicity has latterly been seriously impugned. The older he grew, the more inclined he seemed to be to dash off historical writings as political tracts. His later *History of the English Revolution* and *Life of Washington* were in essence apologies for liberal monarchy in France. Only in his old age, when he was beyond the pale of practical politics, did he cease to indite political tracts under the guise of "scientific history"; he then went back to his first love, theology, and turned his wordy guns against the higher criticism of the Bible as formerly he had turned them against democracy and illiberalism.

Guizot always had political aspirations. Under the Restoration he was active in the group of politicians, the so-called "Doctrinaires," who upheld Louis XVIII's "liberal" compromise between revolution and reaction and who were equally opposed to republicanism and to any reinstatement of the old régime of absolutism, aristocracy, and church privilege; and when the Doctrinaires were in the ascendant, as from 1815 to 1820 and again after 1828, he held public office. When King Charles X, wobbling too far in the direction of the old régime, was overthrown by the Paris insurrection of July 1830, Guizot played an important part in preventing the establishment of a democratic Jacobin republic and in securing the succession of the liberal middle-class monarchy of Louis Philippe.

Under Louis Philippe, Guizot was in his element. It was to him an ideal government, and he had ample opportunity to satisfy his vanity and his longing for high public office. At the outset he presided over the important ministry of the interior. In 1832 began a second and longer ministry of three and a half years, during which he held a portfolio which he claimed the credit of creating, the ministry of public instruction. No longer did he lecture at the Sorbonne. Why command a company when one can be generalissimo? With remarkable swiftness Guizot made himself supervisor of all education, primary, secondary, and university, within the frontiers of France, superintendent of the various learned societies, director-general of a series of publications founded and maintained by his office, and the father of a gigantic scheme for the preservation of the historical records of his country. Still his ambition was not fulfilled; he had yet to manage the foreign policy of France. And so, from 1840 until the revolution of 1848 he was connected with the foreign office, first, briefly as ambassador to England, and then, for six years as minister of foreign affairs, premier of the cabinet, and in fact if not in name guiding statesman of the nation. From such giddy heights he fell with a resounding thud in the February Revolution and sought consolation in London in the arms of the Countess of Lieven. There we may leave him, without professorship and without public office, though he was to go on wielding a liberal pen for another quarter of a century.

As a statesman Guizot could not be so rigidly theoretical as Bentham had been. He had to qualify Benthamite philosophy according to current exigencies of practical politics. He insisted, of course, that the government of Louis Philippe was the closest approach to ideal liberalism then possible in France. It was constitutional and truly representative of the middle classes, of the brains and wealth of the country. It pursued policies, under his own direction, of international peace abroad and individual freedom at home—freedom of religion, of thought, of industry, of contract. It took a great step beyond that taken by Napoleon in expanding the vast system of state-supported and state-directed schools, to which all French youths were to be free to repair and in which the principles of liberty were to be expounded. It was economical in expenditure and in exercise of authority. It resolutely declined to enact any labor or other legislation which might interfere with the free development of industry or with free relations between employers and employees.

At the same time, in internal policies, Guizot felt the need of combatting the efforts of democrats no less than aristocrats, of Jacobins no less than traditionalists, to subvert the happily existing middle-of-the-road middle-class liberal state. He repeatedly censured democracy, and in a polemic which he wrote against it in 1838 he denounced it as "a war-cry, . . . as a banner raised by the many occupying the lower ranks against the few placed above them"; it had emerged, he said, "only yesterday," and "many generations possibly will pass ere a final verdict of its worth be seen."[1] Besides, he perceived in democracy an adjunct to the new-fangled socialism, to him a most damnable movement, whose triumph must signify that "God and the human race will disappear together" and "only animals in the form of human beings will be left." Democracy, he said, by fomenting disorder and stirring up class hatred, would open the gates to this dread socialism.[2]

[1] *Democracy in Modern Communities*, Eng. trans. (London, 1838), pp. 9, 13-16.
[2] *Democracy in France*, Eng. trans. (London, 1849), pp. 34-37.

Now, it was quite proper that Guizot, as theoretical liberal, should employ the freedom of the press to expose and castigate the anti-liberal character of democracy and socialism. But, as practical statesman, was he to allow like freedom of the press to Jacobins and socialists? Before assuming the responsibility of prime-minister he expressed himself in good Benthamite fashion. "I have ever advocated a free press," he wrote; "I believe it to be, on the whole, more useful than injurious to public morality; and I look upon it as essential to the proper management of public affairs, and to the security of private interests." But, later, at the height of his political power, he noted "its too frequent dangerous aberrations"[1] and proceeded to abridge both the liberty of the press and the liberty of meeting and speech. It was this illiberal policy on the part of a leading liberal which precipitated the revolution of 1848.

Likewise Guizot, though a free trader in theory, retained tariff protectionism as a policy of his government on the ground that France, backward in industry, was not yet ready for the noble experiment. In all his foreign policies, he was pacific at heart, as became a devoted defender of the liberal faith, and many of his Jacobin and traditionalist critics found much fault with him for his "inglorious" conduct of foreign affairs and particularly his subservience to England. Yet, while professing no hostility to the liberal principle of national self-determination, he did not wish to have it applied to the detriment of France and consequently in office he opposed the national unification of Italy, abetted his master's wily

[1] *Memoirs to Illustrate the History of My Time*, Vol. I, pp. 70-71.

LIBERAL NATIONALISM

efforts to draw Spain into closer dynastic alliance with France, and acquiesced in the addition of Algeria to the French colonial empire.

If Guizot was hesitant about encouraging nationalism among neighboring peoples, he seldom neglected an opportunity by vigorous voice or prolific pen to foster it among his own people. His purpose was liberal and his method was romantic. He would evoke those finest things from French history, especially in the realm of culture, which should be the best models for the free French nation of the future. "It is a lamentable mistake and a great indication of weakness in a nation," he declared, "to forget and despise the past." And he proudly acknowledged that while he was lecturing at the Sorbonne it was his "prevailing idea" to infuse in his students "an affectionate respect for the early history of France." [1] Both as regards the past and as regards the future *"la patrie* has a right to our warmest affection." [2]

The report which Guizot presented to the King in October 1830, relative to the appointment of an inspector-general of historic monuments, opened with a romantically patriotic flourish: "Sire, the historic monuments with which the soil of France is covered, are the admiration and envy of educated Europe. As numerous as those of several neighboring countries, and much more diversified, they belong not only to a specific or isolated phase of history, but form a complete series without interval. . . . This marvelous assortment of art should not be left to perish. France could not be indifferent to this remark-

[1] *Ibid.*, I, 322-323.
[2] *General History of Civilization* (New York, 1838), p. 346.

able portion of her glory."[1] In inaugurating his course of lectures on the *General History of Civilization in Europe*, he had already declared "without flattery," though perhaps a bit romantically, that "there is not a single idea, not a single great principle, of civilization which, in order to become universally spread, has not first passed through France."[2]

Guizot's lectures on the *History of Civilization in France* remain as the outstanding romantic expression of his nationalism. At the beginning he explains that he has chosen the subject, not because he and his audience are French ("though patriotism is laudable and justifiable"), but because in following the history of France he will be following the history of that country which most perfectly represents the course of civilization in Europe. He then proceeds to sketch successively the history of England, Prussia, Italy, and Spain, indicating merits and defects in each, as judged by his definition of civilization, which has two aspects, the happy development of society, and the happy development of the individual. Next he discourses at length upon the history of France, showing her superior merits in the development of both aspects of civilization. Whence he concludes: "France has, then, this honor, Gentlemen, that her civilization reproduces, more faithfully than any other, the general type, the fundamental idea, of civilization. It is the most complete, the most true, and so to speak the most civilized. It is this which has placed her at the top rank of disinterested opinion in Europe. France has shown herself at the same time

[1] *Memoirs*, II, 362-363.
[2] *General History of Civilization*, pp. 14-15.

intelligent and powerful, rich in ideas and in the forces at the service of ideas. She has addressed herself at the same time to the mind of peoples and to their desire for social betterment; she has stirred their imagination and ambitions; she has appeared capable of discovering the truth and of making it prevail. . . . We have thus the right, Gentlemen, to regard French civilization as of primary importance, because it is the most significant and the most fruitful." [1]

[§ 4]

Karl Theodor Welcker (1790-1869) was one of those very learned German professors who in their student days at university had witnessed Napoleon's victories and the consequent patriotic awakening in Germany and had been fired with ambition to assume leadership in liberating their country from foreign conquest and domestic despotism. He himself, a native of Hesse, was educated in history and jurisprudence at the universities of Giessen and Heidelberg, and while still a student published in 1813 a noteworthy liberal treatise, *Die letzten Gründe von Recht, Staat, und Strafe*. The next year he issued an address, *Deutschlands Freiheit*, containing a constructive programme for a new liberal Germany. Professor successively at Kiel, Heidelberg, Bonn, and Freiburg, he collaborated with Karl von Rotteck, a like-minded colleague, in the preparation of the famous *Staatslexikon*, an

[1] *Histoire de la Civilisation en France* (Paris, 1840), I, 21-22. Jules Michelet (1798-1874), the contemporary of Guizot, is of course an even better example of the French liberal who wrote patriotic history in romantic vein, but he was a little too much tainted with Jacobinism and he was not a statesman!

encyclopaedia of political science in nineteen volumes (1834-1849), and at the same time entered practical politics, becoming a liberal leader in the parliament of Baden and the editor of a liberal newspaper, *Der Freisinnige*. He participated in the Frankfort National Assembly of 1848 and as a member of its Constitutional Committee helped to formulate the celebrated *Declaration of the Fundamental Rights of the German People*. This was the climax of his personal career and also of the career of liberal nationalism in Germany.

The political philosophy which guided Welcker throughout life he set forth cogently in his youthful work of 1813. Looking back upon the history of mankind he perceived a kind of evolution of political government in three stages from despotism to theocracy to the legal state, corresponding neatly to the three ages of childhood, youth, and manhood in the growth of the individual, and accompanied by a change in the method of social control from force and fear to faith and then on to reason and liberty. Liberty, to him, meant trust in the ability and desire of each individual to develop the greatest possible virtue and happiness; and the legal state, the goal of social evolution, was not to be thought of as an end in itself but simply as the most useful instrument for enabling the individual to realize himself. Welcker contended that it did not matter whether there were natural rights. Everything depended upon historical evolution, and some peoples were ripe for a legal (liberal) state, and some were not.

For thinking men in an advanced stage of development, it was immoral to tolerate either a despotism or a theocracy. Only a legal state was fit for them. And the legal state was defined as a constitutional state in which liberties were itemized and guaranteed against despotism and privilege. Citizens of such a state should not play a merely passive rôle. They should demand and obtain a share in government and legislation, as well as guaranties of their individual liberties. For mature citizens should not accept the doctrine of despots and theocrats that government and legislation are from God. It is indeed not only irrational but blasphemous to assert that everything is from God, evil as well as good. The legal (liberal) state was defined by Welcker, moreover, as a national state, embracing one and only one nationality, on the grounds that nationalities differ very much in degree and stage of evolution and that true liberty is more practicable within a single state based on a single nationality already highly developed. Welcker looked with disfavor upon a world-state and likewise upon any close European confederation as tending to reduce the general level to that of the less developed peoples and consequently as favoring despotism at the expense of liberty. For this reason he was distinctly hostile to the later Holy Alliance. At the same time, however, he looked with distinct disfavor upon revolution or violence as means of overthrowing despotism and establishing the legal state. "Revolution," he said, "seldom brings the highest good."

A new and great liberal Germany Welcker hoped and worked for. It was his idea that the whole German nationality should be brought together in a federal union, with their respective princes under a common emperor and under a written constitution which would provide the most effective guaranties of personal liberty and would assure to the nation and its component parts a truly representative government. Such a government would promote material and cultural well-being at home and, by substituting a short-term popular militia for professional standing armies and by adopting free-trade policies, would repudiate militarism and promote international concord and peace. This idea he broached in his address of 1814. He advanced it vigorously in proposals of 1831 and 1844.[1] And he labored arduously for its realization in the National Assembly which German liberals convened at Frankfort in 1848.

The "Declaration of the Fundamental Rights of the German People," which issued from the Frankfort Assembly in December 1848, is the classic expression of liberal nationalism as championed by Welcker and his kind. Though resembling the revolutionary French "Declaration of the Rights of Man and of the Citizen" (1789) in many respects, particularly in its emphasis on national popular sovereignty, in its definitions of the scope and content of personal liberties, and in its denunciation of titled nobility and class-privileges, the German document betrays distinctively liberal and nationalist features at variance with those of its French prototype. Its very title is less universal and more exclusively nationalist. It makes no reference to natural rights but presupposes, rather, the existence of historical evolution as the basis for the specific and very detailed "rights" which it claims. It is much less

[1] *Die Vervollkommnung der organischen Entwicklung des deutschen Bundes zur bestmöglichen Förderung deutscher Nationaleinheit und deutscher staatsbürgerlichen Freiheit* (Karlsruhe, 1831); *Wichtige Urkunden für den Rechtszustand der deutschen Nation* (Mannheim, 1844).

explicit about political democracy and contains no promise of universal manhood suffrage. And whereas the French declaration dwelt on the "right of revolution," the "right of resistance to oppression," the German declaration includes nothing of the sort. German liberals of 1848, at any rate, were too traditionally and nationally hostile to French Jacobinism to incorporate one of its fundamental doctrines in their formal teaching. Liberalism might seek a new national and world order, but it would do its seeking peacefully and in harmony with the historical evolution which it deemed inevitable but gradual. Which is the main reason, perhaps, why the Frankfort Assembly eventually failed and why German political unity was later achieved under auspices other than those of liberal nationalism.

[§ 5]

Guiseppe Mazzini (1805-1872) was neither statesman nor professor. Yet no advocate of liberal nationalism appeared in the whole nineteenth century who was more vocal or influential than he. He had the advantage over a Welcker or a Guizot of being a fiery gospeller and revivalist.

He was born at Genoa of an eminently respectable middle-class family. His father was a physician in good practice and a professor in the local university. His mother was a woman of great personal beauty as well as of active intellect and strong affections. As a child, he was himself extraordinarily delicate, being unable to walk until he was six years of age, but with a mind as precocious as his body was undeveloped. As a little boy he was an omnivorous reader, and at the university of Genoa he distinguished himself as a youthful prodigy. He was supposed to study law, but while he read much legal literature, he steeped himself in the philosophy and literature of the French Revolution and likewise in the literature of medieval Italy, especially the writings of Dante. From the critical study of the former he derived the basic ideas of his liberalism, and from a somewhat uncritical perusal of the latter he drew the inspiration for his romanticism and his nationalism.

In the dark days which for Italian patriots followed the triumph of Metternich in 1815, Mazzini reflected much, perhaps too much, on the fate that had befallen the once great Italy, now "mutilated, insignificant, and under the heel of foreign oppressors." He was a sad young man and at the age of twenty-two took to wearing black in melancholy mourning for his country. He was sad and romantic and also dreadfully moral and earnest. He readily convinced himself that he had no moral right to follow his profession as a lawyer or his inclination as a literary man, so long as Italy was divided and "enslaved." The duties of man, he averred, were a necessary complement to the rights of man.

In 1830, when he was twenty-five, he joined the secret revolutionary society of the Carbonari, the small but active little group of Italians who during the Napoleonic era had been infected with Jacobinism. He was soon arrested for participating in a riot, imprisoned for six months, and then exiled. While he was languishing in jail, he tells us, he received his "vocation"—a sacred mission—a messiahship—what he termed *"the* modern apostolate." The first fruits of his conversion were his repudiation of the Carbonari as being too underhanded and too Jacobin, and his founding of a new organization which he christened "Young Italy."

"Young Italy," according to Mazzini's plan, was to be a non-secret society with the motto "God and the People." It was to be composed of Italian intellectuals under forty years of age who should dedicate themselves to the task of liberating their country from foreign and domestic tyrants and establishing a unified Italian republic on a popular basis. It was to conduct an incessant agitation among all classes of Italians for the purpose of persuading the whole nation to rise under the leadership of the young intellectuals, to expel the tyrants,[1] and to elect a national convention which would inaugurate the united Italian republic. "Place the youth of the nation at the head of the insurgent masses," urged Mazzini; "you do not appreciate the strength that is latent in young men or what magic influence the voice of youth has on crowds. You will find in youth a host of apostles for the new religion."

"Young Italy" spread rapidly among young men of the middle classes and within a decade counted 60,000 members. Mazzini himself lived in exile, in France and England, but he directed the society from afar with telling effect. He was a poor organizer and a worse administrator,

---

[1] By "tyrants" Mazzini here meant the kings of Sardinia and Naples, the dukes of the minor Italian duchies, and the pope. The pope he would leave in possession of his spiritual office but deprive of temporal power. The others he would depose and expel from Italy. He was as republican as any Jacobin.

yet he did inspire. The flood of pamphlets, epistles, and instructions which he poured out for years may seem pretty bombastic to us, but to the young generation of his day they were supremely eloquent. Thanks to his influence, "Young Italy" and the ideas in back of it became a major factor in the patriotic "resurrection" of the peninsula between 1831 and 1870. Though Mazzini was perpetually plotting as well as inspiring, and though he actually took part in insurrections against the Austrians in 1848 and against the pope in 1849, he was less immediately responsible for the attainment of Italian political unification than was Garibaldi or Cavour. Yet Garibaldi was a disciple of Mazzini, and Cavour, though a royalist rather than a republican, inaugurated policies for the new national state of Italy which were largely in harmony with the liberal nationalism of Mazzini.

The liberal nationalism of Mazzini is evident in all his voluminous writings and especially in his *Autobiography*, in his *Essay on the Duties of Man*, in his *Nationality*, and in his *Faith and the Future*. In none of these writings, however, was it expressed systematically or with cool logic. It glowed with emotion and glistened with rhetoric. It was none the less real because it was sometimes mystical. Altogether, it represented a curious fusion of the liberalism of Bentham and the early French revolutionaries with the romanticism of contemporary poets and novelists and with the philosophic idealism of Fichte and Hegel.

The French Jacobins, according to Mazzini, had failed because they stressed rights and not duties. "A Declaration of Rights furnished no foundation for idealism; it provided no absolutely binding law for man; it set no guide for conduct; it gave no definition to happiness; it neglected the strongest impulses to right action—enthusiasm, love, and a sense of duty." The French Revolution was selfish: "having begun with a Declaration of the Rights of Man, it could end only in a man, who was Napoleon."

But just as a demand for the *rights* of man ushered in the selfish Napoleonic era, so a sense of the *duties* of man will usher in a new era, the "era of collective energies." Life itself is a sacred mission which everyone should take most seriously. This mission involves the moral obligation which we call duty. "We must convince men that they, sons of one God, have here on earth to carry out one law, that each must live not to himself but to others, that the purpose of life is not to possess more or less of happiness but to make ourselves and others better, and that to fight injustice and error everywhere for our brothers' good is not a right only but a duty." Man's central and great duty, Mazzini insists, is to all mankind. And in order to enable man to fulfill his duty to mankind, nationalities and national states exist. "The nation is the God-appointed instrument for the welfare of the human race, and in this alone its moral essence lies. . . . Fatherlands are but workshops of humanity."

Each nation, according to Mazzini, has two important functions to perform. First, it must educate and train its members "in the light of the moral law." Secondly, it must arrange and direct its activities in behalf of humanity at large. "Nationalism," he declared "is what God has prescribed to each people in the work of humanity," and he laid down a "law of nationality" in relation to humanity and duty: "Taking its pace with the march of humanity; having for its starting point the people; for its stepping stones, the consequences of its principle logically deduced and vigorously applied; for its driving force, the strength of all; for its purpose, the amelioration of all and 'the greatest good of the greatest number'; and for its goal, the accomplishment of the task which God has assigned it in the world. There is Nationality."

Mazzini was a zealous humanitarian and a determined internationalist. It was not alone for a liberal nationalist Italy that he labored. His heart throbbed and his pen travelled feverishly in behalf of all "oppressed" nationalities. In 1834 he founded the "Young Europe" association "of men believing in a future of liberty, equality, and fraternity for all mankind, and desirous of consecrating their thoughts and actions to the realization of that future"; and before long there was a "Young Poland," a "Young Hungary," a "Young Ireland," as well as a "Young Italy." All the liberal youth of Europe he sought to fire with nationalist enthusiasm and when he was not conspiring against tyrants in Italy, he was conspiring against tyrants abroad. He looked forward confidently to a human world thoroughly regenerated by a coöperating moral nationalism on the part of the youth in every country.

To Italy, his own country, Mazzini reserved a special rôle in the regeneration of humanity. It was his special duty and the special duty of all Italians, he said, "to love Italy above all earthly things," not in a chauvinist way or to the hurt of any other nation, but always idealistically.

It was their special duty to free Italy, to unify her, to republicanize her, so that she could better perform her duties to humanity. In spite of his country's past and present degradation, Mazzini preached constantly and with firm faith that "a nation which has been enslaved for centuries can regenerate itself through virtue and through self-sacrifice." Italy, he reiterated, has a third life to live. Once she had ruled the world by force through the Roman Empire. Later she had ruled the world by authority through the papacy. Now, the "Third Italy" would arise and would lead the world through the "common consent of the peoples." Then the Italy of the People, "radiant, purified by suffering, will move as an angel of light among the nations that thought her dead."

Personally, Mazzini was gentle and high-minded. His soul instinctively revolted no less against the terrorism and intolerance of the Jacobins than against the tyranny and intolerance of the reactionaries. He was essentially a liberal. To be sure, he resembled the Jacobins rather than Bentham in that he was a convinced republican, and he had a sublime faith in democracy, that is, in *all* the people, which most of the middle-class liberals who succeeded Bentham lacked. Yet he was one with them in seeking "the greatest good of the greatest number," in emphasizing personal liberties, in stressing duties rather than rights, and in laboring for international understanding and peace. Like many of his liberal contemporaries, he drew arguments from the arsenal of German idealism and adorned them with the language and emotion of the romantic movement. He surpassed all the liberals in the emotional intensity of his nationalism.

[§ 6]

The principles and purposes of liberal nationalism were expounded during the first two thirds of the nineteenth century by a host of theorists and agitators. Mazzini was but one among numerous professional propagandists, Welcker but one among innumerable professors, Guizot but one among a multitude of politicians, who espoused and spread the new gospel. To mention a few outstanding names, there were Garibaldi and Cavour in Italy; Gervinus, Gagern, Schmerling, and Lasker in Germany; Michelet, Victor Hugo, Casimir-Perier, and Ledru-Rollin in France; Austin, Grote, Francis Place, and John Mill in England; Korais in Greece; Bluntschli in Switzerland; Kossuth in Hungary; Palacky in Czechoslovakia; Laveleye in Belgium; and Daniel O'Connell in Ireland. The movement attracted the allegiance of the middle classes, particularly of the rising new class of industrial capitalists, including such men as the banker Laffitte in France, the railway-builders Hansemann and Mevissen in Germany, and the manufacturers Cobden and Bright in England; Cavour was not only a liberal doctrinaire and a nationalist statesman but the father of the industrial revolution in Italy and a great capitalist. The movement also enlisted the support of free-trade economists, such as James Mill, M'Culloch, and Nassau Senior in England, Bastiat and Rossi in France, and Prince-Smith and Faucher in Germany. A movement so strongly backed as this could not be kept out of practical politics: new Liberal Parties, appearing in England, Germany, and elsewhere, endorsed it; and it brought sympathetic responses from such statesmen in western and central Europe as Canning, Palmerston, Gladstone, Thiers, Louis Napoleon, and, of course, Cavour.

There were many differences in detail among these sundry apostles as to the scope and implications of liberal nationalism. In general, however, they all assumed that each nationality should be a political unit under an independent constitutional government which would put an end to despotism, aristocracy, and ecclesiastical influence, and assure to every citizen the broadest practicable exercise of personal liberty, political, economic, religious, and educational. They all assumed, moreover, that each liberal national state in serving its true interests and those of its own citizens would be serving the true interests of humanity at large and that "true interests" could best be served by national policies of free-trade, anti-militarism, anti-imperialism, and international cooperation and peace. A few of the apostles of liberal nationalism were devout democrats, but most of them agreed with John Austin's contention that government should be of property-owners inasmuch as the rest of the people do not know their own interests.[1] On the question of intervention in the affairs of a foreign country, they were likewise divided. Some held that such intervention was never permissible, whilst the majority maintained that it might be undertaken to free a people from despotism or alien oppression. All nineteenth-century liberals, however, were sufficiently under the influence of romanticism to feel the liveliest sympathy with the nationalist

[1] John Austin, *A Plea for the Constitution* (London, 1859).

aspirations and struggles of every "oppressed" or "enslaved" people and to shed tears over their plight and subscribe to funds for their relief, if not actually to bear arms in their behalf.

Nineteenth-century liberal nationalism, indeed, drew heavily on romanticism. It was romanticism which not only magnified the sympathy of the general run of liberals, the world over, for the "underdog," for the sufferings of the downtrodden masses and for the misery of enslaved peoples, but also stimulated a vast deal of research by liberal scholars with a view to demonstrating why a particular nationality was great in the past and should be united and free in the future. Liberal professors and literary men under the influence of the romantic movement took a most active part in restoring the purity of national languages, in resuscitating folk-songs and folk-customs, in reviving national traditions, and in arousing popular enthusiasm for national heroes of the past. Incidentally, it should be remarked that they extolled and utilized for their own propaganda certain agencies which the French revolutionaries and Jacobin nationalists had devised, such as national schools, national journals, national societies, and national ceremonies and symbols. It was romantic liberals who composed novel anthems and designed new tricolors for a profusion of would-be nations.

Liberal nationalists were high-minded, optimistic, and devoted to the cause of peace. But optimism and high-mindedness even greater than theirs could not have convinced Metternich and other reactionaries who were in actual control of most of the European states during the first two thirds of the nineteenth century that liberal nationalism was right-headed or essentially pacific. Most of the European states were not national states. The Empires of Russia, Austria, and Turkey comprised numerous nationalities. Neither Germany nor Italy possessed national unity or was much more than a "geographical expression." Belgium was composed of Dutchmen and Frenchmen. Norway was yoked with Sweden, Hungary with Austria, and Ireland with England. Throughout eastern and central Europe, moreover, the existing non-national or super-national states were not liberal states. They lacked written constitutions, representative governments, and guaranties of personal liberties. They supported aristocracies of landed nobility and official clergy. They protected class privileges. They pursued policies of tariff protectionism and dynastic militarism. In the circumstances it gradually became only too obvious that in order to reconstruct Europe on liberal and national foundations it would be necessary for peace-loving liberal nationalists to resort to violence and war. They would have to incite peoples to rise in rebellion against reactionary governments. They would have to arouse peoples to fight for national unity and freedom.

Here, then, was the tragedy of liberal nationalism, not unlike that of the earlier Jacobin nationalism. Its logic and its fine intentions were not sufficient of themselves to insure its triumph. It needs must grasp the sword and slay its adversaries.

The sword, therefore, it repeatedly grasped, and its adversaries it slaughtered in vast numbers. Revolt followed revolt, and war followed war. Under liberal auspices occurred the terrible rebellions of "enslaved" Greeks and Yugoslavs against the Ottoman Empire and of "oppressed" Latin Americans against Spain; the riots of 1820 in Italy and Spain; the widespread insurrections of 1830 in France, Belgium, Germany, and Italy; the even more widespread and deadly insurrections of 1848 in France, Germany, Italy, Austria, Switzerland, and Ireland; the Polish uprisings of 1831 and 1863; the Crimean War of 1854-1856; the wars of Italian unification in 1848-1849, 1859-1860, 1866, and 1870; the wars of German unification in 1848-1849, 1864, 1866, and 1870-1871; and the mighty struggle of 1861-1865 in the United States for the preservation of a national union and the emancipation of an enslaved race.

By 1871 some progress toward the goal of liberal nationalism could be recorded. France and England and a considerable number of other countries were under liberal governments. Germans and Italians possessed national states, and likewise, with full independence or a large degree of autonomy, Greeks and Yugoslavs and Rumanians and Latin Americans. The people of the United States were more completely and irrevocably committed to nationalism, if not to liberalism. And, most portentous event of all, these partial successes of liberal nationalism were so many fertile seeds which were to reach fruition in the later and greatest nationalist war of 1914-1918. Thereafter the whole map of Europe would be radically recast in seeming harmony with the fundamental principles of liberal nationalism. Almost every European nationality would have a national state of its own. Almost all would be confederated in a League of

Nations under a Covenant reminiscent of Jeremy Bentham's "Plan for a Universal and Perpetual Peace."

Yet liberal nationalism in achieving its goal suffered a transformation. Its liberalism waned as its nationalism waxed. Latterly, too, it has had to vie with a newer and more drastic type of nationalism—that which we may term "integral"—and to integral nationalism, liberal nationalism in its evolution has contributed, quite certainly if quite unwittingly. To the doctrine of integral nationalism, we may now attend.

CHAPTER VI

INTEGRAL NATIONALISM

[§ 1]

HUMANITARIAN nationalism, born in the eighteenth century, did not wholly die in the Revolutionary and Napoleonic Wars at the close of that century. Something of its soul lived on in the differentiated nationalisms of Jacobins, traditionalists, and liberals, and still inspires a goodly number of idealists who dream of the promotion of the welfare and progress of all humanity by means of mutual respect of national states or national cultures.

Liberal nationalism, arising in the nineteenth century through the fusion of the teachings of Jeremy Bentham with the democratic dogma of Jacobinism and with the historical tendency of romanticism, has not perished in the World War of 1914-1918. It is still with us, very much with us. It nowadays arouses the "oppressed" nationalities of Asia and Africa, as formerly it aroused the "oppressed" nationalities of Europe. It still looks forward hopefully and optimistically to a world of independent national states, liberal and democratic, co-operating in a universal league of nations. Woodrow Wilson, whom some persons have the temerity to describe as the "last of the liberals," is dead, but his soul goes marching on; and Aristide Briand and Ramsay Mac-

INTEGRAL NATIONALISM

Donald, as well as Hindu and Chinese liberals, still live. In the twentieth century, however, particularly in Europe and America, has come clearly to light yet another and novel brand of nationalism, a brand which rather arbitrarily may be designated as "integral nationalism." The designation is what Charles Maurras employs to describe the nationalist doctrine of his small and hysterical political party in France—the "Action Française" —but it may conveniently be used, without undue imagination or ambiguity, to indicate certain significant elements in Italian Fascism and even Russian Bolshevism and, curiously enough, in the attitude and behavior of millions of nationalists throughout the world who do not indulge in much theorizing and who are certainly unaware that they are integral nationalists.

Integral nationalism may be defined, in the words of Maurras himself, as "the exclusive pursuit of national policies, the absolute maintenance of national integrity, and the steady increase of national power—for a nation declines when it loses military might." It has to do, it will be noted, not with "oppressed" or "subject" nationalities, but rather with nationalities which have already gained their political unity and independence. It is applicable, therefore, to the contemporary nations of Europe and America more than to those of Asia and Africa. Among the latter, liberal nationalism is in the ascendant; among the former, though liberal nationalism is still an active force, integral nationalism has been superimposed upon it and in many minds has actually supplanted it.

Integral nationalism is hostile to the internationalism preached by humanitarians and liberals. It makes the nation, not a means to humanity, not a stepping-stone to a new world order, but an end in itself. It puts national interests alike above those of the individual and above those of humanity. It refuses coöperation with other nations except as such coöperation may serve its own interests real or fancied. It is jingoistic, distrusts other nations, labors to exalt one nation at the expense of others, and relies on physical force. It is militarist and tends to be imperialist. In the face of it, a league of nations or any international sense of peace and security is threatened with sterility and destruction. Besides, in domestic affairs, integral nationalism is highly illiberal and tyrannical. It would oblige all citizens to conform to a common standard of manners and morals and to share the same unreasoning enthusiasm for it. It would subordinate all personal liberties to its own purpose, and if the common people should murmur it would abridge democracy and gag it. All these things it would do "in the national interest."

Such a summary of the teachings of integral nationalism is not derived from the study of a few theorists but, rather, from the observation of hard cold facts in the contemporary world. One has only to note the career of Mussolini and his fellow Fascists in Italy and the enthusiasm, natural or artificial, on the part of the mass of Italians for their régime of integral nationalism. One may also note the development of the Bolshevists in Russia, who, beginning as economic and social reformers, with loud protestations against militarism, imperialism, and nationalism, soon discovered, like the French revolutionaries before them, that the world is not equally prepared for their messianic altruism, and have ended by exalting a peculiarly integral nationalism in the Union of Socialist Soviet Republics—living to themselves alone, serving their own interests, brandishing a sword, destroying democracy and liberty, and worshipping at the shrines of their dictators that are now their national heroes. The extreme nationalism of the Russian Bolshevists is likely to be remembered when the details of their economic experiments shall have been forgotten.

It is obvious, moreover, that the invocation of integral nationalism explains in large part the recent rise of nationalist dictatorships in Hungary, Poland, Turkey, and Yugoslavia, and the remarkable advance of Fascists ("National Socialists") in the 1930 elections in Germany. All over Europe and America, indeed, are unmistakable signs of the depth and power of popular undercurrents of the same phenomenon. In the United States, for example, many of the post-war policies of the national government and the large electoral majorities in support of them are in keeping with widespread tendencies of integral nationalism: refusal to join the League of Nations, reluctance to coöperate with it, refusal to adhere to the World Court except on national American terms, naval rivalry with Great Britain, immigration restrictions, mounting tariff barriers, steady encroachments on the independence of Caribbean peoples, growing intolerance toward minorities at home.

Whence has come this integral nationalism? It seems so different in character and purpose from the nationalisms that were humanitarian or liberal or even traditionalist. Yet it is, in the twentieth century, so widespread.

The answer is that, while we have become acutely conscious of it only recently, it has been in process of fashioning since the middle of the nineteenth century. Its philosophy can be distilled from the writings of a varied and numerous group of theorists in the nineteenth and early twentieth centuries. Among such theorists it may suffice for present illustration to specify certain contributions of Comte, Taine, Barrès, Maurras, and certain Italians. These are discussed in the sections immediately following. But thereafter it will be necessary to indicate the evolution of more general factors in society and politics, particularly the later evolution of liberal nationalism, which have latterly induced statesmen to espouse and large numbers of citizens to accept the practices of integral nationalism.

[§ 2]

Auguste Comte (1798-1857), the founder of positivism and father of sociology, was hardly a nationalist at all, but he summed up and gave currency to ideas which were later exploited by nationalists. He himself was deadly dull and something of an elephant in his moods and loves, but the publication in 1854 of the fourth and last volume of his elephantine *System of Positive Philosophy* was most timely, for, at the right psychological moment, it served solemn notice of a seemingly successful attempt to provide a "scientific" synthesis of hitherto contradictory concepts, and as such it paved the way for the late-nineteenth-century intellectual vogue of positivism and "realism." As good a rationalist as any "enlightened" philosopher of the eighteenth century, Comte could write with unaccustomed fervor and modesty that "Bacon, Descartes, and Galileo will forever be regarded as the founders of the positive philosophy."[1] Yet the philosophy as Comte developed it contained strange ingredients: romanticism as expressed in an evolutionary view of social history; traditionalism as emphasized in laws of human order and progress; liberalism as utilized for verbiage; and, above all, the coördinating application in every detail of the scientific method of the nineteenth century.

From Comte's compound of all these ingredients emerged the new sociology, or, as he styled it, "social physics," embracing the laws of "social statics," governing social order, and the laws of "social dynamics," governing social progress. From it, too, emerged the "law of the three states," the dogma that every human conception and every branch of human knowledge has passed successively through three historical phases: (1) the theological, or fictitious; (2) the metaphysical, or abstract; and (3) the scientific, or positive. In the first phase, Comte explained, man believed that all phenomena are the result of immediate volition either in the object or in some supernatural being. In the second phase—a transitional phase—man mentally replaced capricious divinities by abstract forces and talked much about nature and the causes of phenomena. In the third phase, the dawning positive phase, man no longer seeks for causes but is content with facts. "What is now understood when we speak of an explanation of facts is simply the establish-

[1] *Positive Philosophy*, trans. by Harriet Martineau (1855), p. 731.

ment of a connection between single phenomena and a few general facts, the number of which continually diminishes with the progress of science."[1] In other words, fact-finding was to be the pursuit and the goal of the new positivist era, the assembling and counting of facts, facts, facts—with only contempt for external causes or explanations of facts. It was the intellectual basis of the new "realism." And Comte led the way in directing its application to social phenomena. Social phenomena, he said, are as capable of being grouped under his "laws" as are other phenomena. The true goal of positivism must be social, and the true object of the positivist philosopher must be the reorganization of the moral, religious, and political systems of mankind in accordance with the dictates of fact.

Comte was not a nationalist and he elaborated neither a system nor a critique of nationalism. But implicit in all his writings and incidentally explicit in particular passages were notions which nationalists in the ensuing "realistic" age could and did appropriate for a revised "positive" creed of nationalism. Among such notions was, first, a repudiation of Rousseau and of the Jacobin doctrines derived from the "philosopher of nature." Beyond Bentham and even beyond many of the traditionalists went Comte in condemning the principles of the French Revolution. Rousseau's "state of nature," Comte declared, "is only the metaphysical form of the theological dogma of the degradation of the human race by original sin."[2] The principles of equality, of the right of free inquiry, of personal liberty, and of the sovereignty of the people, he

[1] *Ibid.*, p. 26.   [2] *Ibid.*, p. 413.

described as "revolutionary" principles, having the power to destroy but lacking the needful power to organize. He did admit that they had actually been beneficial in two ways: they had destroyed the worn-out Catholicism of the middle ages, and they had made the welfare of the people the primary aim of the state. But, he insisted, they were largely negative because they were metaphysical. Positivists would subsequently discover better substitutes for them.

Secondly, Comte gave aid and comfort to old aristocratic adversaries of political democracy and likewise to new middle-class proponents of government by men of wealth and brains. Positivism required, said he in his most solemn manner, that society of the future should be directed spiritually by philosopher-priests, who would gather and sort the positive facts, and by women, who would supply the needful emotional uplift, while practically it should be directed by a "patriciate," composed of landowners, manufacturers, merchants, and bankers. The masses of the people, the workers, the "proletariat," should exert moral influence on the direction of society by means of "public opinion," but not otherwise, and certainly they should not attempt themselves to direct society: they are too theological or metaphysical and not sufficiently positive and scientific. Toward the idea of the super-man and the institution of the dictatorship Comte pointed the way. To him one of the greatest heroes in all history had been that "enlightened" Prussian despot, Frederick the Great.

Thirdly, Comte based political organization, that is, the state, not on such metaphysical conceptions as "general will" or "popular consent" but on the positive fact of *force*. Force, he maintained, answers in sociology to tissue in biology. It is the foundation of the social organism. The intellect may modify it in conformity with environment, and the heart may furnish it with suitable springs of action. Nevertheless material force is permanently dominant. Government is "power, essentially material, arising from rank and wealth." While the proletarians are to exert moral force on the direction of society, the patricians are to use physical force. "It is fortunate that the ambition of some families supplies all the rest with that government which they need to control and direct the forces generated by the distribution of functions . . . Force is essential as the basis of every human society. Those who are so indignant with Hobbes's principle would be rather perplexed if they were told that political government must be based on weakness . . . For, through want of a real material force, the basis of power would have to be found in the intellect or the heart, and they are far too feeble for such a purpose. Their sole business is to modify an already existing system of control, and till material force has succeeded in forming this, neither the intellect nor the heart can have much effect on society. Whenever force as a fundamental base for politics is absent, they will seek as far as they can to restore it, without attempting to supply its place. Social science would remain forever in the cloud-land of metaphysics, if we hesitated to adopt the principle of force as the basis of government." [1]

[1] *System of Positive Polity*, trans. by Bridges et al. (1875), Vol. II, pp. 245-246.

Auguste Comte, let us repeat, was not a nationalist. He himself looked forward to a Western European Republic which should eventually expand into a world-confederation, and of which urban states, rather than national states, should be the units; and his positive philosophy conspicuously included provision for an elaborate religion of humanity, with priests and acolytes, flowers and festivals, candles and incense. Yet by removing humanity from the realm of metaphysics and by basing his proposed world order on material force, Auguste Comte was departing radically from the abstract humanitarianism of eighteenth-century philosophers and was forging a powerful weapon for the most forceful statesmen of the twentieth century—and these happened to be nationalists. Comte was an unconscious contributor to the theory of integral nationalism.

[§ 3]

Hippolyte Adolpe Taine (1828-1893) was another unconscious contributor to the theory of integral nationalism. He, too, effected a most curious compounding of diverse ideas and tendencies in the nineteenth century, but he did so from an artistic, rather than a scientific viewpoint, and with a literary charm which Comte lacked and which therefore exerted immediate influence far beyond Comte's.

Taine came of a good middle-class French family which was strongly Catholic and vigorously anti-Jacobin. He himself as a student at the Collège Bourbon and later at the École Normale Supérieure came under the influence of the German idealists, notably Hegel, and developed a veneration both for tradition and for personal liberty and at the same time a skepticism about religion and morals. Though abandoning the practice of Catholicism, he retained a sentimental regard for it as a beautiful expression of popular aspiration in the past and, he hoped, in the future. Prevented from taking a degree in philosophy because of his avowed agnosticism, he became more critical of the existing political régime in France (that of Louis Napoleon Bonaparte) and more devoted to the cause of individual freedom. He finally took his degree in letters in 1853, at the very time when Comte was completing his gigantic *System of Positive Philosophy;* and positivism exerted no little influence on Taine's subsequent brilliant career.

Taine was an unhappy man. His life, at least until 1870, was a constant succession of feverish writing, worry about finances, physical break-downs, and travels for recuperation, followed by more feverish writing, and interspersed with bitter disappointments. His great *Histoire de la Littérature Anglaise,* submitted to the French Academy for the Prix Bordin in 1864, was rejected on grounds of unorthodoxy. Appointed examiner of admissions for the military school of St. Cyr in 1863, he was practically forced to resign in 1866. At the École des Beaux Arts he held the professorship of history of art and æsthetics from 1865 to 1884, but he was subjected to considerable pressure and criticism. He tried to enlist in the National Guard during the Franco-Prussian War, but was refused because of his health; "my heart has been in mourning for six months," he wrote at the end of 1870.[1]

[1] *Sa Vie et sa Correspondance* (1902), Vol. II, p. 278.

But the terrible national crisis of 1870-1871, whilst overwhelming Taine with sadness, transformed him. It filled him with a deep and abiding conviction that now every loyal Frenchman should give himself to his country and that he himself could best serve France by knowing "her history, her thoughts, her customs, and her people." So he turned from literary criticism to French history and devoted the rest of his life to the composition of his *Origines de la France Contemporaine.* Back of this famous work was Taine's belief that the solution of existing problems can be found in study and understanding of the past and that the most durable political edifice is based upon the character of the people and upon old and tried institutions, "many times repaired and always preserved."[1] With heavy heart but with marvellous literary skill he analyzed and reinterpreted for citizens of the Third Republic the Old Régime and the First Republic.

When Taine's spiritual buffetings and physical ailments are taken into account, it is not surprising that he should have looked upon the world with jaundiced eyes. From the easy optimism of the "enlightened" philosophers of the eighteenth century, with their sublime faith in the natural progress and speedy perfectibility of mankind, he was very far removed. He was a pronounced pessimist. He was appalled by man's animal nature, his brutality, his folly, his avarice. Health of body and sanity of mind seemed to Taine to be simply lucky accidents. He agreed with the great English poet whom he greatly admired that life is a "tale told by an idiot, full of sound and fury, signifying nothing." He regretted his pessimism and

[1] *L'Ancien Régime*, Eng. trans. (1876), pp. v-viii.

wished that he might not be cynical; yet, with the inescapable feeling that he was "living in a house of madmen," he could not refrain from cynicism about the past and the future.[1]

Taine reacted particularly against the optimism of the Jacobins and what appeared to him to be its outcome in the tragedy-comedy of the French Revolution. The Revolution he describes as "the insurrection of mules and horses against men, under the conduct of apes who have the throats of parrots."[2] Its immediate causes, he admits, were the vices of the old régime, which he exposes quite mercilessly, and the hunger and hope of the masses of the nation. But the fundamental cause, he insists, was the Jacobin doctrine, born out of the "Social Contract," whose votaries, drunk with power, proceeded to overturn the edifice of ages in the hashish dream of establishing the millennium. The Jacobins, he contends, were not trying to devise a régime for real flesh-and-blood Frenchmen, but for philosophic abstractions and human automatons. In fixing their minds on abstract formulas, they were no longer able to see man as a positive human being. They became possessed of a monomania, which converted them into lunatics and monsters. The first product of their doctrine was anarchy, and the second was despotism. Personal liberties were sacrificed; and the emigration of the nobles was comparable to the earlier expulsion of

---

[1] *Cf. Sa Vie et sa Correspondance,* I, 53, 55, 58-60, 96, IV, 28; *Ancient Regime,* 239-241; *History of English Literature,* Eng. trans. (1873), II, 45-47; *Carnets de Voyage* (1913), 132; *Notes on Paris,* Eng. trans. (1875), 17, 21, 35, 58, 144, 164, 280, 315, 329-331.

[2] *Sa Vie et sa Correspondance,* III, 266, 325.

the Huguenots: in both instances, France lost some of her best blood and her most gifted leaders.

The damnable effects of Jacobinism, according to Taine, have lasted far beyond the French Revolution. If France has had insurrections, revolutions, and coups d'état in never-ending stream since 1789, the cause is to be found in the acceptance of the Jacobin doctrine of popular sovereignty. If France has pursued a policy of excessive centralization inimical to the historic rights of individuals and institutions, the fault lies in the Jacobin dogma. If the government cherishes such false ideas as that it is necessary for France to play a great rôle in Europe, to free oppressed peoples, to help liberals everywhere, to undertake sensational far-away expeditions, to conquer and to colonize, the responsibility must be attributed to the Jacobins. If the government since 1789 has imagined that it must educate and provide for all the people, and (what is much worse) keep them amused and occupied, it is because of Jacobin example. In short, the root of all the evils of modern France lies in Jacobinism, especially in its acceptance of the theories of social contract and popular sovereignty. Taine takes this for his text in preaching his sermon on contemporary France; and, after hearing him through, there can remain no doubt that he likes his Jacobins "better dead than alive."[1]

Over against Jacobinism, Taine extolled (as far as it was possible for a misanthrope to extol) traditionalism. Indeed, his chief significance for our present purposes is in the fact that he revived and reëmphasized in the second half of the nineteenth century the traditional nationalism

[1] *Ibid.*, IV, 69.

of the school of Burke, Bonald, and Schlegel. In harmony with these, Taine taught that national patriotism is generated spontaneously in man and flowers slowly through processes of history rather than suddenly through acts of revolution. It is one of the noblest of human emotions, comparable with love of beauty and longing for truth. It is a living spring which should be permitted to flow naturally without direction or interference by the state. It automatically inspires every individual with a sense of debt and a desire to discharge the debt to the national society and state. The individual, moreover, bears the same relation to the national state that a single cell bears to an organism; the well-being and very existence of the one depend upon the healthy condition of the other, and hence the prosperity of the whole is the chief concern of its parts.

Furthermore, the citizen owes his debt not only to his national state of the present, but to his national state of preceding centuries. The safety and health of the national society, as it has come down through the ages, must be his interest, his need, and his duty. Because the national state does not belong to the citizens of any particular generation, it must not be revolutionized. "Each generation is simply the temporary manager and responsible trustee of a precious and glorious patrimony which it has received from the former generation, and which it has to transmit to the one that comes after it. Should any of the beneficiaries, through presumption or levity, through rashness or one-sidedness, compromise the charge entrusted to them, they wrong all their predecessors whose sacrifices they invalidate and all their successors whose hopes they frustrate."[1] In this conception of duty to the past and obligation to the future, we have the heart and core of traditional nationalism.

Like earlier traditional nationalists, too, Taine ardently defended monarchy, aristocracy, and regionalism. In his opinion the kings of France had been the makers of France. If it had not been for the thousand years of their hereditary rule and preserving policy, there would be no French nation. The revolutionaries, in their murder of the royal family, had repudiated the race to which they owed their nationality and their patrimony, and patriots who would re-link contemporary France with her glorious past should seek to restore the traditional monarchy.

Likewise, the government which fails to avail itself of the nation's traditional aristocracy loses a rich asset. For, in Taine's opinion, an hereditary aristocracy has great cultural and political value. Culturally, it lends a charm and grace to society, while its leisure provides a rich soil for the growth of literature and art. Politically, it provides a hot-bed for informed national leaders and statesmen, inasmuch as it alone among social classes possesses needful position, education, and opportunity for travel and study. If the French nobles had become oppressive before the Revolution, the fault lay in the situation which allowed them rights without exacting services and not in their character and ability.

It was likewise with the old local and provincial loyalties—the regionalism—which the revolutionaries had deemed incompatible with national patriotism. To

[1] *French Revolution*, Eng. trans. (1878), I, 141-143; *Modern Regime*, Eng. trans. (1890), I, 138-139.

Taine's mind, regionalism was as inherent in French history as nationalism; the former adorned and fed the latter; the latter could not be perfected without respect for the former. Indeed, Taine would piously preserve and restore all the ancient institutions, buildings, customs, and traditions of France, because to him they were essential and inalienable parts of France.

In certain respects Taine departed from the letter, if not the spirit, of earlier traditional nationalism. At least, he put the emphasis differently from Burke and Bonald and more in accordance with the tastes of his own age and the inclinations of later integral nationalists. For example, in the domain of religion. As a "realist" and something of a positivist, he could entertain no lively faith in the dogmas of any supernatural or "revealed" religion; he was completely skeptical of the truth of Christianity; he neither professed nor practiced the Catholic Christianity in which he had been born. Yet as a traditionalist, an æsthete, and a nationalist, he wrote eloquently in behalf of Catholic Christianity and its historic rights and privileges. It might not be true, but it was useful; it was a kind of "moral police" which labored by the side of civil governments to maintain order and obedience, especially in those nations whose power was threatened by the dangerous new theories of democracy and socialism. It might not be true, but it was beautiful; it had performed immeasurable services to human civilization and French culture and was still capable of fostering great literature and great art. It might not be true, but it was a basic element in French nationalism; it had helped to fashion France and to make Frenchmen the fine nation that they were; its worship now and in the future would freshen in Frenchmen "the sentiment of the ideal." Thus Taine advanced a new apology for Catholicism, by coupling a personal rejection of its theology with a social acceptance of its good works. A sad man, he shed tears of regret that he could not personally believe in a faith which was very beautiful, very noble, and very French. It was an apology which orthodox Catholics could hardly applaud, but it appealed to a goodly number of skeptical æsthetes as well as to a larger number of nominal Christians who as integral nationalists desired to utilize a traditional popular faith for nationalist ends.[1]

Taine, also, by exploiting nineteenth-century studies in anthropology and comparative philology and literature, developed and crowned the doctrine of national culture which Schlegel had outlined at the beginning of the century. According to Taine, each nationality has a distinctive culture determined by race, environment, and epoch,[2] and expressed not alone by peculiar institutions but also by peculiar literature, art, and modes of thought. "Race," to him, is fundamental. It determines certain social and intellectual aptitudes. It is the seed which germinates every national culture and contains within itself the limits of potential growth. Taine, like Schlegel, confused biological races with linguistic groups, and he surpassed Schlegel in

[1] Taine's peculiarly æsthetic apology for Catholicism had been foreshadowed, in part, by Chateaubriand and was reinforced in his own time by that great agnostic and artist, Ernest Renan.
[2] Race, environment, and epoch were, in Taine's words, "la race, le milieu, et le moment." These, he explained, are, respectively, the internal mainspring, the external pressure, and the acquired momentum of each national culture. Cf. Lectures on Art, Eng. trans. (1889), I, 215-221; Notes on Paris, 29, 43, 317-318; History of English Literature, I, 8, 17, 25.

attributing to the "Aryan race" and its several branches a superiority over Semitic and Chinese "races." He was in fact one of the foremost formulators of the "Aryan myth."

But, according to Taine, race is modified in detail by environment, and here, as frequently throughout his writings, he borrows a figure from the plant-world to illustrate his point. "Sow a number of seeds of the same vegetable species in different soils, under various temperatures, and let them germinate, grow, bear fruit, and reproduce themselves indefinitely, each on its own soil, and each will adapt itself to its soil, producing several varieties of the same species so much the more distinct as the contrast is greater between the diverse climates."[1] This idea Taine was ever applying in his studies of literature and art. For example, in his celebrated critique of the Netherlands he proceeded on the simple assumption "that in this country water makes grass, grass makes cattle, cattle make cheese, butter, and meat, and all these, with beer, make the inhabitant."[2]

Yet, according to Taine, race and environment do not operate upon a tabula rasa; they are conditioned by time, by the "epoch." Each age becomes the heir to the benefits of preceding ages and thereby adds historic traditions to physical environment and affects the racial development. Again borrowing a figure from the plant-world, Taine explains that "the same plant, under the same temperature, and in the same soil, produces at different steps of its progressive development different formations—buds,

[1] *Lectures on Art*, II, 191.
[2] *Ibid.*, I, 68.

flowers, fruits, seed-vessels—in such a manner that the one which follows must always be preceded by the former, and must spring up from its death."[1]

Race, environment, epoch—these three, then, are the forces which determine national character and national culture. When they are in harmony and combine to complement one another, we have the perfect flowering of national genius, as in France under Louis XIV, in Italy during the Renaissance, and in Germany in the nineteenth century. When, however, they act to annul each other, periods of discord result, such as the seventeenth-century civil war in England or the eighteenth-century revolution in France.

From his clear-cut thesis of nationalist determinism, Taine deduced the corollaries that art is essentially national and that the artist must be inspired by nationalist ideals. An artist, to be truly great, must take his materials from his own country and his own time and furthermore must select from them those traits which best express the national genius and combine them in such a way as to depict most perfectly the national character. Nature itself cannot achieve this perfection because it has only raw materials to work with, but the true artist, working with more malleable metals and with canvas and oils, can realize the ideal towards which his nation has been striving for centuries.[2] It is likewise with literature. Unless a writer expresses and interprets the character of his race and the nature of his country and his age, he cannot pro-

---

[1] *History of English Literature*, I, 21-23.
[2] *Derniers Essais de Critique et d'Histoire* (1903), 300-306; *Voyage en Italie*, Eng. trans. (1889), 147; *Lectures on Art*, I, 157-159, 197, 258-260.

duce great literature.[1] This explains why it is that of the two hundred volumes which Defoe wrote, *Robinson Crusoe* alone attained immortality. In it, he not only presented a problem of universal interest but also painted a living portrait of the typical Englishman, "as he has been for hundreds of years and as he will continue to be for centuries to come." The same is true of Cervantes, of whose numerous dramas and romances only *Don Quixote* is immortal. There are two reasons for this: the knight is one of the eternal types of human history, the heroic sublime visionary; more, he embodies the national character of the Spaniard, chivalrous, morbid, proud, such as eight centuries of crusades and over-charged reveries have made him. Again, to mention another of Taine's almost countless illustrations, Beaumarchais achieved permanent renown in his *Figaro*, because one day he unwittingly drew a picture of himself, "the brave, gay, good-natured, vivacious Frenchman." [2]

Taine in his nationalism was a traditionalist, but at the same time he so suffused it with positivism, fatalism, and personal skepticism (which he called liberty) as to render him less the follower of the earlier traditional nationalism of Burke and Bonald than the forerunner of the later integral nationalism of Barrès and Maurras.

[§ 4]

Maurice Barrès (1862-1923), descended from an old Lorraine family, was a precocious youngster of eight when

[1] *History of English Literature*, I, 35-36, 250; *Lectures on Art*, I, 235; *Sa Vie et sa Correspondance*, II, 204.
[2] *Lectures on Art*, I, 226-234.

the Franco-German war occurred, when conquering Uhlans occupied his native village, and when Alsace and part of Lorraine were ceded by France to the newly founded German Empire. By these events he was profoundly impressed; and as a young man of twenty-two he could write: "Certainly they have a terrible anger, those of our fathers who love us most! And we ourselves, who look back to the dark year in the vague mist of our childhood, feel that the honor of *la Patrie* is embodied in the marching ranks of a regiment; all the military fanfares carry us back to the conquered soil; the waving of the flags seems to us a distant signal to the exiles; our fists clench; and we have only to make ourselves provocative agents."[1] In such a mood Barrès's nationalism was conceived and nourished.

In youth Barrès was high-strung and sensitive, given to introspection and emotional ecstasy. He early became a professed æsthete and suffered much bullying at the hands of his more rugged schoolmates at the lycée in Nancy. He read poetry by the hour. He acquired a supreme veneration for Taine and Renan, whose writings he read and re-read. He was attracted by the positive philosophy of Comte and by the speculations of Hegel and the other German idealists. He dipped into the "realistic" philosophy of Schopenhauer and Nietzsche and brought up from it a firm belief in himself as one of the super-men.

When he was twenty, Barrès went to Paris to study law. But law irked him and he soon turned to literature. For a

---

[1] *Les Taches d'Encre*, Nov. 5, 1884. Cited by Victor Giraud, *Maurice Barrès* (1922), p. 33. There is a valuable discussion of Barrès's nationalist doctrines by E. R. Curtius, *Maurice Barrès und die geistigen Grundlage des französischen Nationalismus* (1921).

number of years he served a literary apprenticeship at the capital, writing reviews for the journals and feeding his soul on poetry, Taine, and the companionship of a youthful group who shared his æsthetic temperament. In 1887 appeared his first important work, *Sous l'oeil des Barbares*. It was the beginning of a trilogy which he completed in 1891 under the inclusive title of *Le Culte du Moi* and which brought him to public attention as the leading French champion of the Nietzschean doctrine of the primacy of the Ego and the superiority of emotion and will over reason.

From praise of personal egotism Barrès passed to praise of national egotism. He was predisposed thereto by early experiences; and the advent of General Boulanger as the "man of action" and the personification of the spirit of French revenge against Germany had decisive influence on the young æsthete. He was elected to the Chamber of Deputies in 1889 by the workmen of Nancy as a disciple of Boulanger and a "socialist nationalist." The collapse of the Boulangist movement convinced Barrès that a doctrine as well as a leader of nationalism was required, and to this end he directed the rest of his life-work.

The title of Barrès's second trilogy was significant, *Le Roman de l'Énergie Nationale*. Its parts, *Les Déracinés, L'Appel au Soldat*, and *Leurs Figures*, were published in 1897, 1900, and 1903 respectively, and were concerned with public affairs,—the corruption of the metropolitan press, the Boulanger episode, the Panama scandals. They bewailed the lack of a French national ideal; they warned of the fate of the individual who withdrew himself from the national group and attempted to live in an artificial atmosphere of his own creation.

Barrès lived and wrote for the most part in Paris, but trips taken at various periods in southern Europe and the Levant were followed now and then by travel-books in which he presented nationalist interpretations of foreign art and character.[1] But he tired of foreign travel rather more easily than his first enthusiasms for Spain and Italy would have led one to expect; and for the greater portion of his life he preferred to spend his holidays in the hills and valleys of Alsace-Lorraine. These sojourns in his native countryside were fuel to the fire of his nationalism, which found expression as time went on in his third great trilogy, *Les Bastions de l'Est*,[2] and in such books as *Les Amitiés Françaises* (1903) and *La Colline Inspirée* (1913).

In these later works Barrès elaborated or underlined things he had already put in a compact volume which he published in 1902 under the title *Scènes et Doctrines du Nationalisme*. Of this volume the Dreyfus affair and the Nancy electoral campaign were the focal points, around which were arranged in somewhat fortuitous grouping the major precepts of his nationalist teaching. But even this volume was not an epitome of all his teaching. It was left for *La Grande Pitié des Églises de France* (1914) and *Une Enquête aux Pays du Levant* (1923) to show him in the additional rôle of nationalist champion of the Catholic Church.

---

[1] *Du Sang, de la Volupté, et de la Mort* (1894); *Amori et Dolori Sacrum* (1903); *Le Voyage de Sparta* (1905); *Greco, ou le Secret de Tolède* (1912); and *Une Jardin sur l'Oronte* (1922).

[2] Comprising *Au Service de l'Allemagne* (1906), *Colette Baudoche, Jeune Fille de Metz* (1909), and *Le Génie du Rhin* (1921).

Barrès's books do not by any means represent the whole of his nationalist activity. He was in Parliament from 1889 to 1893 and again from 1906 to 1910. He was an inveterate journalist: he collaborated for a while with the editors of *Le Figaro* and *Le Journal;* during the Boulangist campaign he edited *Le Cocarde;* he wrote a great deal for *L'Action Française.* From 1899 to 1901 he was closely connected with a patriotic society, the "League of the French Fatherland"; and he was elected president of the "League of Patriots" when Paul Déroulède relinquished that post. He became a member of the French Academy in 1906. He did a considerable amount of speaking both to student groups and to groups of older persons. During the World War his pen was specially busy with articles calculated to maintain the national morale. He also wrote prefaces to many books on subjects with which his name was already connected, particularly patriotic books written during the war and books celebrating the builders of the French nation and the French empire overseas.

With Barrès we pass from the foreshadowings of Comte and Taine into the real substance of integral nationalism, from materials for such a philosophy into a fairly systematic and detailed statement of the philosophy itself. Barrès had begun his literary career as an individualist, an exponent of personal egotism, and it seems plausible to suppose that he might have developed into a thoroughgoing anarchist, or if he could have been a nationalist at all, that he would have been an eagerly liberal nationalist. In fact, however, his apostasy from individualism was early and complete. "The Ego," he confessed, "when subjected to an analysis that is really somewhat serious is reduced to nothing and leaves in its stead only society, of which the Ego is an ephemeral product."[1] So from an interest in individual psychology he turned enthusiastically to an absorbing interest in what he termed social psychology, very thankful, in private, that he had found an honorable way of escape from the bogs of nihilism into which he had been enticed by the dazzling paradoxes of the mad Nietzsche. Henceforth he could not be too bitter in his denunciation of the individualism from which he had apostatized or too ardent in correcting his youthful errors and proving himself the complete nationalist without taint of liberalism. His nature and training were such as to afford him no halting place between personal egotism and national egotism, between a forceful anarchism and a forceful nationalism.

Basic to Barrès's doctrine of integral nationalism is his theory of psychological determinism. No individual possesses an independent reason by means of which he may apprehend truth. We are not masters of the thoughts which arise within us. They do not derive from our own intelligence; rather, they are reactions that express very old physiological dispositions. Even the ideas which we consider most singular, even the most abstract judgments and the most involved metaphysical concepts, are in reality general types of experience and appear inevitably in all human beings that are of the same organism and are beset by the same impressions. There is no liberty of thought. One's psychological processes are determined by the very fact that one happens to belong to a certain race,

[1] *Amori et Dolori Sacrum*, 265.

a certain family. Whether or not we like it, and whether or not we acknowledge it, we are automatons. There is something which does operate in our minds, but this something is eternal; we have only a temporary use of it, and the manner in which we employ it is regulated by our dead ancestors. Bound to each other as if with chains, subjected to the same reflexes, we follow each in the steps and thoughts of his forbears.[1]

Associated with the theory of psychological determinism is the cult of ancestors. No matter how strong the desire, one cannot break away from the chains and claims of one's ancestors. "If I were to become a naturalized Chinaman," Barrès once said, "although I were to conform scrupulously to the dictates of Chinese law, I should not cease to think thoughts that were actually French thoughts and to connect them in a way that was French." Wherefore the dead of one's family or nationality are more powerful than the living and more to be honored.[2] "The spirit of man," Barrès said on another occasion, "is never so active as when it is in close communion with the dead."[3] And true to his word, Barrès was ever visiting graves and glorifying tombs.

The chief aid to the cult of ancestors is the cult of the native soil, the veritable *patria*. Because the memories of the child and his parents and the long line of his ancestors have been intertwined with it, the spirit of the landscape, hovering over its undulating lines and its enwrapping horizons, has special power to draw the individual close to

[1] *Ibid.*, 266; *Scènes et Doctrines du Nationalisme*, 12, 16-17. Cf. *Les Amitiés Françaises*, 21.
[2] *Scènes et Doctrines du Nationalisme*, 41.
[3] *L'Appel au Soldat*, 26.

his own past and to the past of his race. The soul of the soil, indeed, is older than the soul of mankind; it constantly broods over its people and inspires them with its unchanging thoughts and emotions as generation follows generation. Barrès is sure that his own destiny is interwoven with that of his native province in France. "Elsewhere I am as a strange bard singing with uncertainty some broken strophe. But in the country of the Moselle I know myself to be a canticle of the soil, a moment in its eternity, a transient blossom from its bosom—and, if my love be but great enough, I may even become its heart."[1] The best patriots, according to Barrès, are the masses of simple folk who live closest to the soil, for it is they who drink steadily from the sparkling fountain-head of national energy just as their fathers did in days long dead. The native soil together with the ancient cemetery determines the soul of man.

One of the most disquieting aspects of contemporary national life, as Barrès saw it, is that many persons, particularly so-called intellectuals, deliberately tear themselves loose from their native districts, pull up their roots from the soil which can best nourish them, efface from their memories the graves of their forbears, and cut themselves off from their family line, that is to say, from the best part of themselves. Such persons—the *déracinés*, or "uprooted," as Barrès termed them—lose the individual and social usefulness they once possessed and become liabilities rather than assets to the nation. Everything possible must therefore be done to keep people in vital touch

[1] *Les Amitiés Françaises*, 267.

with their native districts and to restrict foreign immigration.[1]

What has so far been sketched may be described as the fundamental assumptions upon which the entire Barrèsian philosophy of integral nationalism rests. Each individual has no freedom of thought or action. He is the projection into the present of his dead ancestors. His native soil is the chief means of awakening in him an affection for his family line, his race, and his nationality. Hence it is desirable that everyone should live in close communion with his ancestors and in close touch with his native district.

On these assumptions Barrès based his conceptions of nation and nationalism. He once told a group of students that a nation is the possession in common of an ancient cemetery and the will to keep its heritage undivided and to make it influential.[2] On another occasion he said that France with its many provinces was like a pudding stone formed in a flowing stream, what geologists call a conglomerate. As the mass moves along, other stones become attached to it and unite firmly with it. The eye can easily detect the separate elements of the outer layer, but the mass is solid in its resistance to outside physical force. If one stone does detach itself and roll away, it is quickly pulverized. Or if it attaches itself to some other conglomerate mass, it does so only after it has lost considerable size and weight.[3] From these notions it follows that there is no

---
[1] *Cf. Les Amitiés Françaises*, 255; *Scènes et Doctrines du Nationalisme*, 45, 80, 127, 206; *Amori et Dolori Sacrum*, 187; *L'Appel au Soldat*, 345; and *Les Déracinés*, passim.
[2] *Scènes et Doctrines du Nationalisme*, 108.
[3] *Ibid.*, 20.

place in the nation for the naturalized foreigner, who may acquire the customs of his adopted country and may give intellectual assent to its ideals, but who shares no memories with his foster-brothers and who cannot embrace their ideal as heartily as he would were it a heritage from his own familiar past. In vain the stranger swears when he becomes naturalized to think and act as a Frenchman. In vain he links his interests with those of France. Blood persists in following the course of nature in spite of oaths and human laws. He is a guest but not a member of the household.

Barrès felt keenly that foreign-born citizens and their children were a great menace to France, for, far from attempting to adapt their views to French life, they were trying to adapt French life to their own views, and if they should succeed in alienating the French population from its inherited ideal, the doom of the French nation would be sealed. Hence, obstacles should be placed in the way of naturalization. Naturalized persons should not be permitted to hold public office. Foreign immigration should be discouraged by imposing taxes on employers of foreign labor and by forbidding the sale of land to aliens. At all costs the French national ideal should be protected.[1]

"But why?" the uprooted individual might ask. "Why struggle to preserve national boundaries that are provocative of continual warfare? Why struggle to preserve a distinct national ideal?" "If nations were to be wiped out," Barrès replied, "the highest and most precious material and spiritual relationships in the world would be endangered. We should have to fear a retrogression of

[1] *Ibid.*, 90-91, 96, 433-474.

civilization. Nationalism is not only a matter of sentiment; it is a rational, aye a mathematical, necessity."[1] To supply French nationalism with an ideal and a programme was the central purpose of Barrès.

In analyzing the condition of contemporary France, Barrès was pained to find a marked lack of what he could construe as a national ideal, an ideal, that is to say, which would actually serve as a unifying principle for all districts and groups in France. Without moral unity, without a generally accepted definition of national purpose, France found herself divided into different camps, each with a different watchword and a different flag, each trying to promote its own interests at the expense of the interests of others. How to unite these warring factions, how to subordinate faction to nation, was the problem.

Barrès perceived in other countries several influences which had made for spiritual unity—a dynasty, or traditional institutions, or common suffering. In France the old dynasty had been discredited, and many traditional institutions had been overthrown by revolution and were now despised. But common suffering might be utilized more efficaciously in France than elsewhere; the disasters of 1870-1871 had already stirred painful national emotions among all Frenchmen. Other traditions and passions might similarly be exploited by giving them the moral justification which was their due, by elevating them to a position of dignity as truths of national import, and by making them master-ideas which would command the loyalty of all the people. And if a master-individual could be found to represent in his person all the master-

[1] *Ibid.*, 99.

ideas of the nation, France would then proceed to achieve the destiny marked out for her. She would become a nation in fact as well as in name.[1]

Among the master-ideas which would cement French nationalism, Barrès emphasized regionalism. A truly nationalist government, he insisted, would not hesitate to make local self-consciousness the cornerstone of its whole administrative system. Men must have tangible reasons for loving their country. The act of paying taxes to a central government is scarcely sufficient to inspire patriotic fervor. But give a man a group in which he can actually work, and the fact that he carries responsibility in that group means that his interests and affections are tied to it and that he will have a better understanding of the main problems which have faced France during the centuries. The group may be that of a whole province or only that of a town, or even that of a profession or occupation. Call it regionalism, or call it syndicalism, as you like, but be sure that you give it a real share in national government—legislature, executive, judiciary, and, above all, education. Such a development would involve a repudiation of the senseless parliamentary system and of the benumbing centralization which had been derived from alien sources. It would represent a return to the sensible traditions of historic France. It would result in the strengthening alike of regionalism and of nationalism.[2]

Another of the master-ideas, according to Barrès, would be language, for what a man is depends to considerable extent on the language he speaks. "Metz would become

[1] *Ibid.*, 101, 107; *Les Déracinés*, 268.
[2] *Scènes et Doctrines du Nationalisme*, 91, 496-497, 501; *Assainissement et Fédéralisme* (1895), 6, 10, 12; *Les Déracinés*, I, 36.

German when the language of Metz should become German."[1] The French language would insure that France should remain French. But the French language must be re-vitalized by purging it of foreign words and dosing it with homely local dialects. To Barrès's ear, the patois of the Moselle valley was more delightful than "the insipid humbug of Montmartre," for the former enshrined a real local wisdom while the latter indicated mere superficiality. Words which spring from the soil represent nice distinctions and are employed by deeply rooted people with sharpened imagination and poetic feeling. People who inhabit salons, on the other hand, use a language which is not of their own fashioning, and with such an instrument of conversation it is natural that they should attribute to themselves, in all good faith, tastes and distastes that have never truly been theirs; they are artificial beings (*hommes-mensonges*).

A third master-idea of French nationalism should be Catholicism. Some persons were inclined to be amused at a Barrès who, like Taine, was a skeptic in private thought but a defender of the Catholic Church in public and national life. Barrès could one day twit the monks of Ghazir about their dislike of Renan and the next day be on his knees in a mood of exaltation, listening raptly to the chanting of the Mass by the same monks. His own explanation of the seeming paradox was nationalist. "It is not necessary to possess a perfect faith in order to have the pleasure of venerating the supreme image of that faith."[2] "The Catholic atmosphere is the one which my

[1] *Les Amitiés Françaises*, 12; *L'Appel au Soldat*, 265-266, 368, 392.
[2] *La Grande Pitié des Églises de France*, 7.

ancestors prepared and developed for me. It is therefore the one which is least injurious for me, the one which will be most favorable for my natural activities."[1] Barrès upheld Catholicism not because it was absolutely true but because it was a national tradition and because, being a national tradition, it provided an atmosphere wherein all Frenchman could experience the greatest stimulation of their natural energies, the highest degree of exaltation. "To so monumental a [French] tradition [as that of Catholicism] one can only compare the musical tradition in Germany. But this German musical tradition dates only from the sixteenth century, while we have had cathedrals since the ninth century. These are the voice, the song of our land, a voice rising from the ground, a song of the times when they were built and of the people who wanted them."[2]

A fourth master-idea of French nationalism should be the full recognition of the traditional love of Frenchmen for heroes, particularly for military heroes. Napoleon was the favorite hero of Barrès. He kept a picture of the Corsican near his work-table and advised his fellow countrymen to renew their national faith at the tomb of that "professor of energy."[3] Napoleon and a glorious France seem to have been synonymous in his thinking. Only by means of such another hero could the "frightful accident" of 1870 be avenged. This helps to explain Barrès's support of Boulanger in 1888-1889 and of Déroulède in 1898. In *L'Appel du Soldat*, the story of the

[1] *Scènes et Doctrines du Nationalisme*, 60.
[2] *La Grande Pitié des Églises de France*, 212. Cf. ibid., 171.
[3] *Les Déracinés*, I, 48. Cf. Paul Acker, *Petites Confessions* (1903), I, 207.

Boulanger episode, his thesis is that the current educational system, the bureaucracy, and parliamentarianism had deranged the country; France could be restored to sanity only by giving the people more regional autonomy and at the same time unifying the regions under a powerful leader, a national hero. The French, he held, were unable to do anything unless it were incarnated in a man, preferably a warrior. Contrasting the young and dashing Boulanger with the old bespectacled Thiers, as representatives respectively of national dictatorship and parliamentary republicanism, he wrote: "In the face of a dull Elysée, inhabited by an old lawyer incapable of a movement coming from the heart, which alone will touch the masses, the young minister of war, seated on his black charger, is an image of splendor which always speaks to a warlike nation."[1] Barrès's ideal for the government of France was a Caesarian republic, a national dictatorship, which, while fostering considerable regionalism, should unite the whole country in pursuit of military glory.

The nationalist programme which Barrès deduced from his master-ideas included the condemnation of internationalism and the acceptance of war as an instrument of national policy in foreign and colonial matters. He was particularly hostile to the "subversive" doctrine of internationalism which he found prevalent among French liberals and Jacobins—the internationalism which stood for disarmament, for the cessation of international wars, and, as he imagined, for the eventual suppression of the national system, the internationalism which "invoked the French Revolution and the Roman Empire in support

[1] *L'Appel au Soldat*, 54.

of the cosmopolitan principles it would foist upon the people." To the Roman Empire Barrès was willing to concede the cosmopolitan principle. But the French Revolution, he pointed out with much truth, had definitely accepted the national principle, and since the Revolution all Europe had been reorganizing itself on a nationalist basis. It was quite evident, he said, that not cosmopolitanism but nationalism was the tendency of the day.[1] It was also quite evident, he said, that the talk of internationalism in France had been started by influential Jews, to whose interest it was that people should believe that all men are brothers, that France should disarm, that nationalism is a mistake and military honor a crime.[2] These Jews had their internationally organized credit-establishments to maintain; and they did not care especially for French traditions or French interests. They merely used French politics to further their own international interests, sucking the blood, meanwhile, of good thrifty Frenchmen.

This sort of thing nationalism must vigorously oppose. The nationalist must make France herself as strong as possible. Why? Because when France rids herself of alien influences and attains full nationhood she will see to it that there is less injustice in the world.[3] Human beings might as well recognize once and for all that the surest safeguard of morality in the world as well as in the nation is for Frenchmen to have guns and cannon, well-trained soldiers, and officers with unquestioned authority.[4]

[1] *Scènes et Doctrines du Nationalisme*, 445.
[2] *Ibid.*, 63, 452.
[3] *Ibid.*, 112.
[4] *Ibid.*, 315. Cf. *L'Ame Française et la Guerre*, I, 7.

France must be a military, though of course not a militarist, nation.

No one needed to inquire of Barrès how he would use his cannon, his soldiers, and his officers. For it was perfectly patent that the chief motivation of his whole nationalist philosophy was a hatred of Germany and a desire to see the French flag floating again over Alsace-Lorraine. Nationalism was the theoretical justification of "the noble instinct of revenge!"[1] A good deal of his writing was intended to heighten anti-German feeling in France. *Au Service de l'Allemagne* and *Colette Baudoche*, belonging to the trilogy *Les Bastions de l'Est*, contain, for example, a generous supply of anecdotes charging the Germans with gross barbarity and displaying in sharp relief the delicacy and good breeding of the ordinary Frenchman. Other works are replete with dark allusions to German character. The legends of Germany are "violent, horrible"; they are marked, like the story of Tristan and Isolde, by "an enthusiasm for suicide."[2] They represent an onrushing wave of Asiatic myth, threatening eventually to submerge the more wholesome traditions of France herself.[3] The German is unable to perceive subtleties and nuances in human relationships.[4] It is even a little doubtful, so Barrès confides to his young son, whether Germans possess souls.[5] And so forth. The cumulative effect of it all was to create an overwhelming sentiment in favor of revenge—and war.

[1] *Scènes et Doctrines du Nationalisme*, 298.
[2] *Les Amitiés Françaises*, 263.
[3] *Ibid.*, 262. Cf. *Le Génie du Rhin*, ch. ii.
[4] *Au Service de l'Allemagne*, 120.
[5] *Les Amitiés Françaises*, 86.

INTEGRAL NATIONALISM

Barrès's nationalism was also imperialist. He was insistent that France should consolidate and extend her colonial dominion, if necessary by force. With hearty approbation he quoted the words of Paul Bouche: "The degree to which we turn our colonial empire to account will largely determine the opinion we shall have of ourselves, of our methods, of our intellectual capacity, of our moral depth, and of our vigor. We cannot succeed overseas without increasing French prestige, and we cannot fail there without greatly lessening our prestige."[1] Barrès maintained that overseas imperialism had become one of the French traditions which it was the duty of nationalists to preserve and develop. The French Catholic missions in the Syria of the twentieth century were continuing the tradition of the French Crusaders of the middle ages.[2] The heroic efforts of contemporary Frenchmen to establish new spheres of influence in Africa should be regarded not so much as novel experiments as a revival of French colonial traditions in America. Barrès protested against the French surrender of Fashoda to England in 1898 as "a cruel betrayal of national honor,"[3] and urged France to appropriate Syria "as the bridgehead to Persia and India."[4]

What Barrès claimed for his own nation, he was unwilling to accord to other nations, at least to "backward" nations. He would destroy native traditions of Syrians and Algerians in order to conserve what he imagined were native traditions of Frenchmen. In this and other respects

[1] *Scènes et Doctrines du Nationalisme*, 382.
[2] *Une Enquête aux Pays du Levant*, I, ch. xvi.
[3] *Scènes et Doctrines du Nationalisme*, 326.
[4] *Une Enquête aux Pays du Levant*, II, 193.

there was much that was illogical and contradictory in Barrès's doctrine of nationalism. But his doctrine was deliberately irrational. It was founded on emotional exaltation and was to be realized through spiritual intoxication. Nationalists should frankly recognize, he said, that facts very often contradict principles, so that principles have to be adapted to facts. Nationalists should cast logic aside and all barren intellectualism. They should judge everything in relationship to the nation as it is. Above all, they should be guided by sentiment and should be driven by national feeling as by a tempest.

[§ 5]

Charles Maurras (1868-   ) has been the rigid doctrinaire of integral nationalism, as Maurice Barrès was its literary sentimentalist. Reared under similar circumstances and coming under much the same intellectual influences, Barrès and Maurras have proved complementary to each other. The latter has builded on the former; and if emotional instability of Barrès contributed to his sentimentalism, the physical infirmity of deafness with which Maurras has been afflicted may have served to render him peculiarly doctrinaire and fanatical.

Maurras, born six years later than Barrès in a small town in Provence and educated at Catholic schools, came to Paris as a youth of twenty and joined the group of young intellectuals whom Barrès had assembled about him. He, too, fell under the spell of Taine and Renan, and, even more, under the spell of the writings of Sainte-Beuve and Comte. He applauded the *culte de moi* as developed in Barrès's first trilogy, but as Barrès, the loyal son of Lorraine, soon abandoned personal egotism for national egotism, so Maurras, a loyal son of Provence, did likewise. Maurras became a regionalist, and followed Mistral in championing a local Provençal nationalism. In the meantime he was supporting himself by contributing reviews and articles to Parisian journals; and in 1895 he published his first pretentious book, *Le Chemin de Paradis*, a collection of essays, similar in form to those of Barrès, but marked by a style in imitation of Anatole France and by a content that was distinctly irreligious and pornographic.

During the Dreyfus crisis in French politics, Maurras evolved and began seriously to preach his doctrine of "nationalisme intégrale." In 1900, in the pages of the *Gazette de France*, he set forth the gospel in the fundamental and famous *Enquête sur la Monarchie*. This he has followed with numerous other works, elaborating certain details: *Kiel et Tanger* (1905) and *Quand les Français ne s'aimaient pas* (1907), criticisms of the foreign and domestic policies of the Third French Republic; *La Politique Religieuse* (1912); *L'Étang de Berre* (1915); *Les Conditions de la Victoire* (1916-1917); *Romantisme et Révolution* (1922); etc.

Meanwhile, with funds supplied by the widow of Marshal Macmahon, Maurras was inaugurating and conducting a movement, which he christened the *Action Française*, in behalf of his integral nationalism and its capstone, the restoration of the traditional French monarchy. There was, first, a "committee," organized in 1898 and transformed in 1905 into a "league." There was, next, a bulletin, founded in 1899 and expanded in 1907 into a daily newspaper which later proliferated special sheets for farmers, students, workingmen, and other groups. There were, finally, a comic magazine, *Leurs Figures;* a publishing plant, the "Nouvelle Librairie Nationale"; a school, the "Institut"; and a special organization, the "Camelots du Roi," for youthful militants. Within the orbit of the Action Française Maurras has drawn a group of brilliant journalists and publicists, including Henri Vaugeois, Jacques Bainville, Léon Daudet, Léon Montesquieu, Louis Dimier, Pierre Lassere, the historian Georges de Pascal, and the theologian Dom Besse; and such well known academicians as Barrès, Bourget, Lemaître, and Le Goffic have written for its publications.

Maurras defines an integral nationalist in France as a person who is "above all, French" and that "without condition." [1] "A true nationalist," he says elsewhere, "places his country above everything; he therefore conceives, treats, and resolves all pending questions in their relation to the national interest." [2] In his exposition of what makes a man a Frenchman and how a Frenchman behaves distinctively, he leans heavily upon the psychological determinism of Barrès and its logical corollaries. He is sure that Frenchmen are made by the dead hand of the past. "The future is born of accumulations of the past, and we ourselves are clearly determined by what has begun to be called almost everywhere 'our dead.' Yes, the dead are more active than the most active of the living. I vouch for

[1] *Enquête sur la Monarchie* (1916 ed.), xli.
[2] *Action Française,* June 10, 1908, p. 969.

it: our initiative comes from the ashes of the dead."[1] "Our manner of thinking, determined in first instance by our fathers and mothers, retains hold of all that our ancestors have been; these are dead only in appearance. They maintain in our nature the character which has been marked in them in other days. . . . The living expression of French nationalism is the result of the vigor of the good and pure blood which we have received from our fathers and mothers."[2] With the resulting "cult of the dead," Maurras, like Barrès, associates the "cult of the soil," for the soil has determined the nature of ancestors and has conditioned the activity of descendants. "The cult of the sacred soil . . . has started; from year to year it will grow; it will be a factor in the renaissance of *la Patrie.*"[3] From the soil and from the race comes the nation, which must inevitably develop certain distinctive traditions; any departure from these traditions is the result of alien influences and is therefore unnatural and must prove fatal to real nationalism.

As to what are the basic traditions of French nationalism, Maurras agrees in general with Barrès and refers to regionalism, syndicalism, the French language, the Catholic religion, hero-worship, hereditary hostility to Germany, and hereditary fondness for overseas expansion. But Maurras, as a close disciple of Comte, puts the emphasis differently from Barrès and provides a curiously logical foundation for his violent criticism of the liberalism and

[1] *Enquête sur la Monarchie,* 497.
[2] *La Politique Religieuse,* xxxiii-xxxiv, 18-19. *Cf. Anthinea,* 241; *Quand les Français ne s'aimaient pas,* 362.
[3] *La Politique Religieuse,* 184. *Cf.* "Système Fédératif," *La Quinzaine,* XII, 66, 70; *L'Étang de Berre,* 51, 184.

Jacobinism which, in his opinion, have temporarily endangered the solid traditions of French nationalism. As a disciple of Comte, he is convinced that the individual is but an "abstraction," that the unit of society is not the individual but the group, especially the family, that the life and preservation of society depend upon its obedience to certain scientific laws, and that among such laws the law of "order through force" is preëminent. All the most glorious and enduring French traditions merge in the forceful preservation of social order, in the leadership of the strong against anarchy and disorder.

According to Maurras, the demon that latterly has sought to put down the strong and has thereby imperilled the traditional social order is none other than individualism, an unwelcome foreign intruder, a daughter of "Hebrew Christianity" and German Idealism. "Hebrew Christianity" is neither French nor scientific: it exalts the weak above the strong; it is a religion of slaves. "The Hebrew Christ comes into the world, redeems the slaves, dethrones the strong, and places the first lower than the last in order that His glory may be sung through life eternal. . . . Almost three hundred and seventy-three Olympiads have passed since the Hebrew cried on his cross: 'It is finished.' Yes, it was finished; since that moment the slave has had governments after his own heart."[1] If Christ's teaching of equality and humility is dangerous, Kant's precepts of justice, duty, and individual morality are quite as dangerous. "In examining the history of the social structure . . . one is impressed with the social nature of man, not with his will; with the reality of

[1] *Le Chemin de Paradis*, 135, 147.

things, not with their justice; one merely verifies a collection of facts, without being able to say whether they are moral or immoral." [1] By exalting the individual and by inculcating love and morality, liberalism and Jacobinism have grievously erred. Individualism, thoroughly unnatural and unsound, has been attended, moreover, by excessive emotionalism and insane sympathy. Such errors must be mercilessly eradicated in order to effect a renaissance of French nationalism.

The oldest and therefore the strongest traditions of France, the surest guarantees of its effective nationalism, are, according to Maurras, (1) the classical spirit inherited from antique Greece and Rome, (2) institutional Catholicism, and (3) the monarchy.

"Classicism" particularly appeals to Maurras, perhaps because of the old historic relationship of his native Provence to Greece and Rome, perhaps because of the influence of Taine and Renan upon him, and his personal fondness for the pagan classics, perhaps because of the example which Greece and especially Rome offered of a forceful imperialism in conjunction with fervent patriotism. At any rate in his *Anthinea* he maintains that French culture is deeply rooted in classical Greek culture and that the French are the modern Greeks. France, moreover, is the "boulevard of classicism"; "all Europe is barbarian in comparison."

In the introduction to one of his essays, Maurras presents an apology for his Roman proclivities: "I am Roman because Rome from the time of the consul Marius and the divine Julius up to the time of the dying

[1] *La Politique Religieuse,* 78-79.

Theodosius hewed out the first boundaries of my France. I am Roman because Rome, the Rome of the priests and popes, has given eternal solidity of sentiment, customs, language, and worship to the political achievements of generals, administrators, and judges. I am Roman because, if my fathers had not been Roman as I am, the first barbarian invasion between the fifth and the tenth century would have made a sort of German or Norwegian out of me. I am Roman because, if my Roman-ness had not been safeguarded, the second barbarian invasion, that of Protestantism in the sixteenth century, would have made a kind of Swiss out of me. I am Roman because I am overflowing with consciousness of my historical, intellectual, and moral being. I am Roman because, if I were not, I would possess almost nothing French. . . . I am Roman in so far as I feel myself a man, that is an animal that builds cities and states and not a rodent or a gnawer of roots; a social animal, and not a lonely flesh-eater; excelling in capitalizing the acquisitions of the past and in deducing rational laws, rather than in destroying by errant hordes, nourished on the vestiges of ruins. I am Roman by all the positive realism of my being, by everything within me that enjoys pleasure, work, thought, memory, reason, science, the arts, politics, and the poetry of living men about me. By virtue of this treasure which Rome received from Athens and deposited in the storehouse of our Paris, Rome incontestably signifies civilization and humanity. I am Roman, I am human. Two identical propositions." [1]

[1] From introduction to *Dilemme de Marc Sangnier*, in *La Politique Religieuse*, 395-396.

Maurras, the skeptic, the pagan, the decrier of Christ and "Hebrew Christianity," has been an energetic apologist of the Catholic Church in France. His *Politique Religieuse* is a lengthy statement of his curious position in the matter, and many of his other writings deal at least incidentally with it. Catholicism is to be esteemed, he has contended, because it is essentially Roman in its organization and customs; because it has been the chief instrument and expression of French culture; and because it is a particularly potent weapon of social solidarity and order which are necessary to French nationalism. The Catholic God is a myth, but the Catholic Church, at least in France, is a useful fact. Catholics themselves, no less than non-Catholics, should recognize the utility of reconciling traditional Catholic Christianity with the principles of Comte. "Differing about the truth, we have come to agree on the useful: divergencies of speculation subsist, but we have reached a practical accord on the value of Catholicism to the nation."

Besides, Catholicism is not "Hebrew Christianity." It is Roman and French. It permits a certain amount of love and sympathy and preaches a certain amount of justice and morality, but, unlike "Hebrew Christianity," it does not let these dangerous tendencies get out of hand. It is not too Christian. "It is not of religion, but of history; it is not of dogma, but of observation and science."[1] The dead of France have been Catholic, and they bid their successors to remain so.[2] Consequently, Catholic defense,

[1] *Ibid.*, 260.
[2] *Ibid.*, 19.

social defense, and national defense are for Frenchmen one and the same thing.[1]

Against the novel and alien tradition of individualism and democracy, Maurras invokes the political and social tradition of old pre-revolutionary France, in which true sociological law prevailed "unmolested by Hebrew and German philosophy." It is in the "old régime" that the "empirical organizer" finds his "realistic politics." Democracy is idealistic and far removed from reality. On the other hand, "empiricism, instead of positing equality even before the law, turns its attention instinctively, but also methodically, to the fact of inherent differences which cannot but strike the eye of the social scientist." It is because the "old France" recognized these inherent differences, because it constructed a natural social order based on facts, that he finds in it an ideal for French nationalism of the past and of the future. A restoration of this "old France," the monarchy of Hugh Capet, Jeanne d'Arc, Henry IV, and Louis XIV, can alone bring France back to health, because it alone has the power to drive Jews, Protestants, Freemasons, and foreigners from power. It

[1] *Ibid.*, 369. It should be noted that a large number of sincere French Catholics, including many members of religious orders and several prelates, as well as laymen, rallied to the support of the Action Française and long regarded Maurras as a glorious apostle whose personal doubts, like those of Saint Thomas, could easily be pardoned in view of his manifold services to the Catholic Church in France and to the cause of French nationalism. Some Catholics, however, were openly critical; and eventually in 1926 Pope Pius XI, with the approval of most of the French bishops, condemned the teachings of Maurras, put his books on the Index, and forbade Catholics to read his newspaper. Since then, Maurras has bitterly assailed the Vatican, and some of his Catholic followers in France have preferred, in the name of nationalism, to follow his lead rather than that of the Pope. Maurras's chief contention has been that the Pope is under the influence of "internationalists, Germans, and the traitorous Briand."

alone can restore real freedom to the French people by granting them a large degree of local and class self-government, which in turn can alone give to French nationalism "concrete form and real substance." And since the traditional monarchy alone can accomplish all these things, no French nationalism is complete or "integral" without monarchy.

To Maurras, the Caesarian republic of Barrès hardly suffices, though it is vastly preferable to a democratic republic. Barrès had objected to the restoration of the old Bourbon monarchy on the grounds that bad government of the Bourbons had precipitated the Revolution and produced the existing sorry state of affairs, that no Bourbon claimant to the throne was capable of leadership, that an effective aristocracy was lacking, and that the monarchists overlooked the historical facts of the nineteenth century. Maurras attempts to answer these objections by asserting that royal power is anterior to its general acceptance; that monarchs are popular because they are rulers, rather than rulers because they are popular; that restoration of aristocracy depends on restoration of monarchy, not the reverse; and that no actual good was done by the "Caesarian republic" of Napoleon III, who placed centralized power at the disposal of Jews, Freemasons, and Protestants. A Caesarian republic, like a democratic republic, must rest in last analysis on democratic elections. Now elections can perhaps represent the sum of particular interests, but it is difficult to think of the national interest as being merely a sum of particular interests, and hence the national interest cannot be adequately served by elections. Furthermore, it is difficult to get the right dictator, and if a good one dies, the country is left without a head, whereas under a monarchy, when the king dies, the people shout *Le roi est mort! Vive le roi!*

Throughout the writings of Charles Maurras and throughout the journalism which he has sponsored, his integral nationalism appears as a breeder of hatreds. He tirelessly preaches hatred of "alien" influences within France: Jewish, Protestant, masonic, liberal, republican, communist, and, latterly, papal. He ceaselessly directs tirades against foreigners: Germans, Englishmen, Americans, Bolshevist Russians. Always he upholds a hundred-per-cent French nationalism, which is at once suspicious and forceful. He is ever expecting the worst, and ever preparing against it by counselling heavier armaments and more unyielding foreign and colonial policies. There is scarcely conceivable an excess of nationalism beyond the integral variety of Maurras, the doctrinaire and the demagogue.

[§ 6]

A prophet, it is said, is not without honor save in his own country. Charles Maurras has certainly received high honor in his own country from the "Action Française"; and some parts of his doctrine of integral nationalism have been widely accepted by his fellow countrymen. But the "Action Française," though noisy, is a small organization and, despite its energetic propaganda, has failed to elect a single member of the French Parliament. The masses of the French people still cling to the Revolutionary principles and practices of individualism and democracy, and their political leaders, devoted to republicanism, still profess a nationalism which at least in form is liberal or Jacobin. It is outside of France that the integral nationalism of Maurras and Barrès has been most thoroughly heeded and most completely put into effect.

Especially in Italy has integral nationalism, under the name of Fascism, largely supplanted, in the activities of the government and in the allegiance of the populace, the earlier types of nationalism. There can be no doubt that the philosophy underlying this Italian development is closely akin to that of Barrès and Maurras—and their odd confederate, Georges Sorel[1]; these Frenchmen have been almost religiously studied by the makers of the Fascist state and the fashioners of its policies; and if they have not created the prevailing thought in Italy, they have clearly expressed it and contributed to it. In Italy Maurras deserves national honors almost as great as those accorded to Mussolini.

Various currents of Italian thought had been running as independent and more or less unconscious tributaries to the main stream of integral nationalism since the time of Mazzini. For example, the German idealism of Hegel, which Maurras rejected and proscribed for integral nationalism in France, had been accepted by an influental group of Italian scholars and utilized by some of them for curiously illiberal nationalist ends.

[1] Georges Sorel, a disciple of Comte, Taine, and Durkheim, is best known as the philosopher of revolutionary syndicalism and the proponent of proletarian violence. He was always, however, very much of a classicist, something of a nationalist, and a kind of crypto-Catholic, and in his last years he wrote articles for the *Action Française*. His famous book, *Reflexions sur la Violence*, could be, and actually has been, a bible for forceful nationalists as well as for forceful socialists.

Hegel was given a vogue in Italy by Francesco De Sanctis (1817-1883), who, while a political prisoner at Naples following the revolutionary uprising of 1848, translated the *Logic* and then began to apply Hegelian æsthetics to literary and historical criticism. During the 1860's and 1870's De Sanctis preached Hegelian politics both as member of the Italian Parliament and as professor at the university of Naples. In the name of idealism he inveighed against the cliques of politicians and the machinations of special interests in the new liberal régime and championed an "idealistic patriotism," which should exalt and dignify the "national interest."

The successor of De Sanctis in the Italian current of Hegelianism, Bertrando Spaventa, upheld the ideal of a strong, omnipotent state. The Italian state, he said, should be strengthened as the German state under Bismarck had been strengthened. More than that, it should be "adored."

Benedetto Croce, the greatest exponent of Hegelian idealism in Italy, though not primarily concerned with politics and always inclining toward liberalism, emphasized in his contributions to the history of philosophy the distinctive and continuous nature of Italian tradition and the importance of the Italian "idea."

Giovanni Gentile, the slightly younger colleague of Croce, revived the Hegelian conception of the state as a spiritual entity and distinguished sharply between the "materialistic" individualism and democracy which had been imported into Italy from France in the nineteenth century and the inherently "idealistic" character of native Italian patriotism as displayed in Dante's idea of the nation, in Machiavelli's idea of unity, and in Vico's idea of social life,—ideas of the sacredness of the nation, the wickedness of foreign oppression, and the need of sacrifice and ideal devotion. Gentile reinterpreted the Italian risorgimento and by means of Hegelian dialectic attempted to show that Mazzini was not a democrat or a republican, but an idealist. Gentile was to be one of the official apologists of Fascism.

Another current of Italian thought which ran independent of, but parallel to, that of Barrès and Maurras had been set in motion by the priest Vincenzo Gioberti (1807-1852) in his famous work, *Del Primato Morale e Civile degli Italiani*, published in 1843. According to Gioberti, Italy was great because it was Catholic, and Catholicism was great because it was Roman. "Italy is the priestly nation among the great body of redeemed peoples; it is the head of Christianity, as other peoples should be its arms, as they actually were in the long war waged by civilization against the sword of the Saracens. Nor did the inhabitants of this peninsula give to other peoples merely divine gifts, but also every other civil and human good; and all the great intellects of Europe, who enhanced in any measure the glory of their countries, lit their lamps at the living flame of Italian genius. . . . The center of the civilizing process is where the center of Catholicism is. . . . Now since Italy is the center of the latter, it follows that Italy is the true head of civilization and Rome is the ideal metropolis of the world . . . Italians, therefore, have the special duty . . . of exercising the primacy which they potentially possess and can rightfully claim." Although Gioberti's pleas were largely neutralized in his own day and for many years afterwards by the antinationalist attitude and policies of the papacy, they became in the long run a classic expression of religious traditions of Rome and the nation, which could be invoked by a growing number of Italians in support of an imperialist and messianic nationalism at variance with the liberal nationalism of a Mazzini.

Curiously resembling in many respects the sentimentalist literary career of Maurice Barrès in France was that of Gabriele d'Annunzio (1863-   ) in Italy. D'Annunzio belonged to a family from Dalmatia, Italy's "irredenta," as Barrès sprang from the French "lost province" of Lorraine. Brought up in the freedom of the open fields and sent to school in Tuscany, D'Annunzio attracted to himself a group of like-minded youthful enthusiasts, and, under the influence of Nietzsche, produced much impassioned poetry in praise of the ego and the super-man. Presently, however, again like Barrès, he turned from personal egotism to national egotism. He sought and found the origin of eternal Italian traditions in pagan Rome; he cultivated a heavy Latin style; he assumed an oracular pose and an imperial bearing. He also, more gradually, discovered the artistic and national utility of Catholic Christianity; he revelled in its cathedrals, vestments, and rites; he pronounced it true because it was beautiful; he proclaimed it sacred because it was Italian and Roman. Besides, he developed and propagated a zeal for the conquest of Dalmatia, Istria, the Trentino, and other parts of "Italia irredenta"; he alternated eloquence with bombast in demands for war against Austria; and he became the idol of the nation by his theatrical seizure of Fiume at the close of the World War.[1]

Just as Barrès and Maurras made some provision in their integral nationalism for working-class syndicalism, so voices were raised in Italy declaring that the radical labor movement could and should be reconciled with a forceful nationalism. Such was that of Filippo Corridoni, "who is now hailed as one of the pioneers and martyrs of Fascism. He was a feverish, violent soul in a delicate body, with the romantic tragic bearing of Mazzini. His occasional tears and his customary bitter laugh, his fierce hatred and flaming oratory made him a powerful proletarian leader. An admirer of the heroes of the Italian risorgimento, he was also profoundly influenced by the writings of Sorel, especially by Sorel's pessimism, his emphasis on the inevitability of violence and suffering, his theory of the moral degradation of the bourgeoisie and of the heroic potentialities in the proletariat. After the war of 1911 [Corridoni] began to develop a new national philosophy for Italian syndicalism, a philosophy which was later revived and expanded by the Fascists. According to him it was the moral duty and tragic fate of the Italian proletariat to continue the struggle for liberty which the Italian bourgeoisie had begun in the risorgimento. . . . The [contemporary] bourgeoisie is a remnant of that degenerate powerful Europe, which for centuries had dominated Italy, and from which the risorgimento had only

---

[1] D'Annunzio has now (1931) "retired to the country and relapsed into humility. In his palatial country hermitage, he is now quietly awaiting his end, praising, in the meantime, the simplicity and poverty of his Franciscan brethren!" H. W. Schneider, *Making the Fascist State* (1928), 244-245. Professor Schneider's book is detailed and excellent on the philosophy as well as on the activities of Fascism.

partially freed it. . . . The class struggle must be intensely national, waged by a young Italy, conscious of its rich cultural heritage, against the international oppression of a more wealthy but more degenerate Europe."[1] In other words, Corridoni merged class struggle in national struggle: Italy represented the noble proletariat, and the rest of Europe the depraved bourgeoisie; between them warfare was inevitable and salutary.

Directly from all these native sources and indirectly from the integral nationalism of Barrès, Maurras, and the Action Française and the syndicalism of Sorel, with its theory of violence, many Italian intellectuals in the first two decades of the twentieth century derived the elements for a new synthesis of Italian nationalism. In the words of Croce,[2] "they were far more opposed to liberalism than to socialism, for many of the new nationalists had been drawn from the socialist ranks; and they approved of the ideas of war and dictatorship; only asking that what the socialists taught about the class war should be applied to war between nations. Like the French [integral] nationalists, they were ready to make mock of the Revolution, the Declaration of the Rights of Man, and democracy; like them, too, they were inclined to support the Roman Church and to receive its support in exchange, seeking a basis of agreement in an 'atheistic Christianity'; they sang the praises of the past, of absolute monarchy, and of classicism after the manner of Boileau; they even at times coquetted with Catholicism, at least in so far as to render it artistic appreciation, D'Annunzio, always the leader in

[1] H. W. Schneider, *op. cit.*, 141-142.
[2] *A History of Italy, 1871-1915*, Eng. trans. (1929), 248-249.

these movements, being the first to do so. . . . A few simple minds, unaccustomed to observe and think, applauded and assented, believing that the [new integral] nationalism, whose brave and eager words they heard, was merely a patriotic reawakening from the socialists' repudiation of love of country and from an over-cautious and prosaic policy on the part of the government. Nevertheless, some of the leading champions of nationalism revealed a different attitude when they said plainly that [the earlier liberal] patriotism and the [new integral] nationalism were 'opposites,' the first being 'altruistic,' the second 'egotistic,' the first aiming at 'service of our country to the death,' the second looking upon nations as 'instruments for promoting the interest of the citizens' or as 'the egotism of the citizens regarded from the national standpoint.' The one was, in short, a moral, or in Nietzschean language, a 'base' ideal, the other utilitarian and 'heroic.' . . . There were also among the [new integral] nationalists those who, recalling Prussian ideas of the state, or under the influence of Pan-Germanism, tried to introduce into Italy a 'religion of the state,' a dark and terrible idol, fantastically remote from human life and seeking to challenge and override it, or a 'religion of the race,' such as had for some time past boasted apostles and priests in various parts of Europe and the world."

In 1910 Italian advocates of integral nationalism founded the "Nationalist Association." Three years later it was transformed into a political party, which at the next general election obtained six seats in the Italian Parliament. In the meantime the imperialist war which Italy waged in 1911-1912 against Turkey for the conquest of

Tripoli aroused enthusiasm for the new nationalism and drew many converts to it from the liberal and republican and even socialist parties. The nationalist newspaper *Idea Nazionale* flourished; such an irredentist society as "Pro Trento e Trieste" grew; and the patriotic cultural "Dante Alighieri" society between 1910 and 1914 doubled its membership and became vehemently nationalist. To these tendencies the World War and the post-war fear of Bolshevism gave widespread encouragement and ultimate decisive support. Integral Italian nationalists, who had polled four thousand votes in 1919, polled four million in 1924; and in October of this year a nationalist dictator "marched on Rome." It was the spectacular advent of Benito Mussolini.

Mussolini had been a Socialist of rather extreme type, strictly Marxian in his view of the class struggle and, though emotionally anti-Austrian, highly critical of national imperialism. As editor of *Avanti*, the leading organ of the Socialist Party, he denounced in no uncertain terms the Tripolitan War. When the World War broke out, however, Mussolini urged in equally certain language that Italy should enter the struggle on the side of the Allies and should put forth every effort to complete her national unification. Read out of the Socialist Party and deprived of the editorship of *Avanti* in November 1914, Mussolini at once founded at Milan a new journal, *Il Popolo d'Italia*, and began to preach a forceful nationalism. Every issue of his journal carried the motto, "He who has steel, has bread," and another (taken from Napoleon), "The revolution is an idea that has found bayonets." Gradually his preaching found favor, not only with middle-class D'Annunzian patriots but with a considerable number of socialist workingmen. Little bands ("fasci") took form and grew in the cities, beginning at Milan; and in January 1915 they held their first general convention at Milan and effected a national organization under the designation of "Fasci d'Azione Rivoluzionari" and the presidency of Mussolini; within the next month there were 105 "fasci" ("bands") with 9,000 members. The Fascist movement was born; it reached maturity in the nationalist revolution of 1924 and the ensuing dictatorship of "Il Duce."

Into the detailed history of the Fascist régime in contemporary Italy it is beyond the province of the present study to go. It may here be pointed out, however, and stressed that the very *raison d'être* of the régime, the motive force in back of it and the goal to which it aspires, is nationalism, and yet not the nationalism that is liberal, Jacobin, or even traditionalist in the Bonald-Burke sense. Like Bonald, Burke, and other early traditionalists, Fascists claim to base their nationalism on history and are intensely anti-individualist and anti-democratic. But unlike the early traditionalists, Fascists absorb all other loyalties in loyalty to the national state and tend to make right synonymous with might. The nationalism of the Fascists, like that of the Action Française, represents a novel synthesis. It is what we have termed integral nationalism.

Italy is the outstanding example of a country where integral nationalism is officially believed in and practiced. But in many other countries of Europe a similar philosophy has been set forth and has attracted numerous disciples, and it would be possible, though repetitious and tiresome, to indicate here the particular intellectual roots of Fascism in Germany, Hungary, Poland, Yugoslavia, Spain and elsewhere. Each of these lands, like Italy and France, has had its own succession of theorists and events that have conspired in our own day to produce a more or less well organized movement in behalf of integral nationalism.

It may seem that in describing the tenets of integral nationalism by reference chiefly to the ideas of four Frenchmen—Comte, Taine, Barrès and Maurras—we have at least implied that these Frenchmen have created the doctrine not only in France but in the other countries. Such a thought, such an implication, is very far from our mind and our intention. We have expounded the philosophy of four Frenchmen because it is peculiarly clear and plain and because it admirably draws together and expresses certain intellectual tendencies which have been common to a large number of nationalists of various countries during the closing years of the nineteenth century and the first quarter of the twentieth century. Maurras certainly has had considerable influence on the formulation of the doctrine of integral nationalism in Fascist Italy as well as in the "Action Française," but enough has probably been said to illustrate our conviction that many of the elements of Italian Fascism are either strictly indigenous or have been imported from countries other than France and that integral nationalism would be a theory and doubtless a fact in Italy today if there had been no Barrès or Maurras.

In Germany, Maurras must have had little or no influence; yet in Germany Adolf Hitler is an outstanding integral nationalist and has a following sufficiently large to elect to Parliament in 1930 more than a hundred "National Socialists" ("Fascists"). Back of these German Fascists is a doctrine of integral nationalism,[1] to which, wittingly or unwittingly, have contributed, parallel with, but largely independent of, our French philosophers, German idealists such as Fichte and Hegel, German critics of individualism and democracy such as Ludwig von Gerlach, German statesmen such as Bismarck, German extollers of race and *Kultur* such as Max Müller, Richard Wagner, and Houston Stewart Chamberlain, German glorifiers of force and the super-man such as Schopenhauer and Nietzsche, German historians and political scientists such as Treitschke.

A cardinal principle of the new integral nationalism which most sharply distinguishes it from all earlier philosophies of nationalism is its admitted and boasted reliance on brute force. This marks alike the gospel of Action Française, Italian and German Fascism, and Russian Bolshevism. Mussolini himself has stated it in picturesque language: "Liberty is not an end but a means. As a means it must be controlled and dominated. This involves force . . . the assembling of the greatest force possible, the inexorable use of force whenever necessary—and by force is meant physical, armed force. . . . When a group or a party is in power it is under an obligation to fortify itself and defend itself against all comers. . . . Liberty is today no longer the chaste and austere virgin

---

[1] For the doctrine, and for interesting side-lights on its formulator, see Adolf Hitler, *Mein Kampf* (1930).

for whom the generations of the first half of the last century fought and died. For the gallant, restless and bitter youth who face the dawn of a new history there are other words that exercise a far greater fascination, and these words are: order, hierarchy, discipline. . . . Fascism [that is, integral nationalism] has already stepped over, and if it be necessary it will turn tranquilly and again step over, the more or less putrescent corpse of the Goddess of Liberty."[1]

[§ 7]

The philosophy of integral nationalism, whether in Germany or in Italy, in France or elsewhere, can be traced, as we have seen, to groups of intellectuals within the several countries during the nineteenth and first years of the twentieth century. But integral nationalism could hardly be the living force that it is among the masses in contemporary Europe and even in contemporary America, giving them attitudes and moving them to action, were it not for certain historical factors which, apart from theories, have prepared the way for popular acceptance of a more intensive and forceful nationalism. Of course, the "masses" do not know that they are "integral nationalists," and many of them would probably profess admiration for "liberal" principles and detestation of "integral" principles, if these should be frankly and fully explained to them. Yet the fact remains, as pointed out in the first section of the present chapter, that the "masses" in most national states today acquiesce in, and on occasion applaud, public policies which partake of the nature

[1] "Forza e Consenso," *Gerarchia* (Milan), March, 1923.

of integral nationalism. Even in countries where personal liberties are still guaranteed, where a republican constitution still exists, and where democratic government still functions, the "masses" tend increasingly to evince a chauvinism, an intolerance, and a fanaticism strangely out of keeping with the individualism and internationalism which an older generation of patriots associated with liberal democratic nationalism.

Three factors may be mentioned as specially operating to convert large numbers of Europeans and Americans from the liberal nationalism which was so popular and altruistic at the middle of the nineteenth century into the integral nationalism which is now so widespread and menacing. One has been the militarist spirit engendered by the wars which were undertaken by liberal nationalists in order to free and unify "oppressed" nationalities. Liberal nationalists, it should be recalled, made pacifism an important part of their creed. They desired neither war nor undue preparedness for war. Their pacifist desires, however, they had to reconcile with their paramount desire to redraw the political map along lines of nationality, and they soon discovered that the only way in which they could accomplish this desire, in the existing world of reality, was to incite armed revolts against tyrants and military uprisings against foreign oppressors. Such revolts and uprisings often led to international complications and wars; and liberal nationalists would have been less than human if they had not viewed these struggles as glorious and the military leaders of them as heroic.

Mazzini, for example, was a pacifist at heart, but to realize his dream of a free and united Italy he felt constrained to wage popular insurrections within his country and a series of wars against Austria; and the insurrections, once successful, and the wars, once won, took on a halo in Italian hearts and were naturally glorified by Italian historians and all Italian patriots, liberals included. It was much the same elsewhere. German liberals failed to unify their country without bloodshed in 1848; but when Bismarck succeeded by means of copious bloodletting in three wars from 1864 to 1871, all German nationalists, liberals included, thenceforth looked upon the German army as not only the creator but also the bulwark of German unity and freedom.

In other words, liberal nationalists themselves unwittingly fashioned a martial monster which helped mightily to transform liberal into integral nationalism. For, once "oppressed" nationalities had won their independence by force of arms and accorded enthusiastic praise to their generals and soldiers, they came more and more to feel that only force of arms could maintain their independence and insure their rightful place and prestige in the world. In this way, newly free and erstwhile peace-loving nations armed themselves as they had never been armed when they were unfree, disunited, and less liberal; they now entered into military rivalry with one another on an unprecedented scale; and the World War of 1914-1918 was a result. And the World War itself, in part a consummation of liberal nationalism, has notoriously been, in many places and among many persons, the powerful spark which has ignited the powder-train of integral nationalism.

A second important factor in the transformation has

been the feeling of superiority engendered by success. Many a would-be nation, inspired by liberal nationalism, began its struggles for freedom and unity in the nineteenth century with humility and noble resolves; and for its plight and self-sacrificing efforts it won the sympathy and sometimes the active support of foreign nations. But when it actually secured unity and freedom, its success seemed to turn the heads of its people. They grew proud of themselves and self-satisfied. In numerous instances they came to feel that they had acquitted themselves so admirably as to prove their superiority over all other peoples and to justify them in ruling "backward" nations. Having reached the goal of liberal nationalism and being flushed with victory, they treated that goal as a starting-point for a continuing race toward integral nationalism.

This subversive effect of success has been illustrated in the history of Germany, Italy, the United States, and many other nations, and is neatly summarized by Bertrand Russell: "'I belong,' the oppressed [liberal] nationalist argues, 'by sympathy and tradition to nation A, but I am subject to a government which is in the hands of nation B. This is an injustice, not only because of the general principle of nationalism, but because nation A is generous, progressive, and civilized, while nation B is oppressive, retrograde, and barbarous'. . . . The inhabitants of nation B are naturally deaf to the claims of abstract justice. . . . Presently, however, in the course of war, nation A acquires its freedom. The energy and pride which have achieved freedom generates a momentum which leads on, almost infallibly, to the attempt at foreign conquest, or to the refusal of liberty to some smaller nation. 'What? You say that nation C, which forms part of our state, has the same rights against us as we had against nation B? But that is absurd. Nation C is swinish and turbulent, incapable of good government, needing a strong hand if it is not to be a menace and a disturbance to all its neighbors.' "[1] It is the integral nationalist who here speaks.

A third factor in the transition from liberal to integral nationalism has been the actual operation of certain propagandist instruments which Jacobin and liberal nationalists had devised and employed within unified national states. Those nationalists had established systems of public schools, directed and controlled by the state and compulsorily attended, the original purpose of which was to make the rising generation literate and to train it for liberty and self-government as well as for particular vocations. As such school-systems expanded and developed and required more funds for their support, they naturally became both more highly centralized and more responsive to mass-prejudices. Soon they were being used for the direct inculcation of nationalism. The majority of their pupils learned enough to be gullible but not enough to be critical. Thus as nationalism became less liberal and more integral, the schools tended at once to reflect and to hasten the process. To a thoughtful person who peruses the scheme which Thomas Jefferson drew up in the eighteenth century for public education in America, the policy which has been pursued in respect of the schools by Mayor William Thompson of Chicago in the twentieth century

[1] Bertrand Russell, *Why Men Fight* (1917), 27-28.

INTEGRAL NATIONALISM

presents a contrast at once ludicrous and tragic. Yet the latter has slowly evolved from the former, as integral nationalism has supplanted liberal nationalism. Or, let the critical student of popular education contrast the programme of studies in the contemporary public schools of France with the programme set forth by Condorcet during the Revolution, or the practical programmes of present-day schools in Italy and Russia with the theories advanced in the middle of the last century by Italians and Russians of liberal persuasion.

The freedom of the press and the freedom of association, like free public schools, were advocated by Jacobins and liberals as means of propagating their principles among the masses. But the new freedom was especially utilized by journalists to establish cheap newspapers which, aiming at the widest and greatest possible circulation, catered increasingly to sensationalism and jingoistic nationalism. Thereby these newspapers contributed to the production of integral nationalists. Similarly the new freedom was attended by the founding of many patriotic societies by liberal revolutionaries or veterans of liberal wars, but these very societies in a second or third generation tended to minimize their liberal origins and to emphasize their extreme nationalism. By the end of the nineteenth century all "progressive" national states possessed army leagues or navy leagues, national defense societies, organizations of sons and daughters of veterans, and a multitude of "yellow" journals, all of which helped immeasurably to prepare peoples for the reception of the practices, if not the philosophy, of integral nationalism.

Now, in the twentieth century, integral nationalism is

essentially religious, fanatically religious. Earlier forms of nationalism, notably the Jacobin and the liberal, were religious, too. But if those earlier forms represented a kind of "New Testament" religion of love and service, with the promise of an apocalypse to the faithful, integral nationalism represents a kind of "Old Testament" religion with jealous and angry gods that insist upon an eye for an eye and a tooth for a tooth.

Integral nationalism involves, according to Maurras, Mussolini, and thousands of other Europeans and Americans, a policy of national selfishness and aggrandizement, a "sacred egoism." Within each national state, its effort is to strengthen and tighten the national bond by every means in its power. Outside, its effort is to make the particular nation feared, or "respected" (as the word goes), by a bold and firm conduct of foreign affairs, backed by military force and accompanied by "prestige." It appeals to the cruder and more exclusively emotional forms of patriotism. Its love of country turns readily into hatred of the alien; its desire for prosperity into competition for territory; and the duty of national service is interpreted as a duty to maintain national unity by unquestioning assent to every decision of government. Political and social ideas appropriate to the new nationalism are instilled into the citizens by the machinery of public education and by compulsory military service; and direct inducement not to surrender these ideas in later life is easily supplied if the national state supervises the press, encourages coöperating patriotic societies, controls appointments in some of the main professions, especially the teaching profession, and is generous in its rewards to leaders of public opinion who are favorable to it.

Such a policy, now actually being followed in a large number of countries, is at once the outgrowth and the antithesis of nineteenth-century liberalism. It ruthlessly suppresses dissentient groups within the nation. It sacrifices whatever seems necessary of the principle of free speech and free thought. It develops a national economy with all the machinery of tariffs, subsidies, bounties, and concessions. In every sphere it penalizes the foreigner; in colonies and "spheres of influence," by frank preference for the trade and capital of the home country; at home, by interposing obstacles to immigration and naturalization. In several countries, particularly in Italy and Russia, it makes itself overwhelmingly important to the citizens by adopting, in varying degrees, national syndicalism or national socialism.[1]

This, then, is integral nationalism, its immediate effects and the factors in its creation and formulation. One of the most important factors in transforming liberal nationalism into integral nationalism, or at any rate in superimposing the latter upon the former, has here been only hinted at. It is the rise of nationalist economic theories and practices. This remains to be considered in the following chapter.

[1] This paragraph and the preceding one are taken, with some verbal changes, from J. L. Stocks, *Patriotism and the Super-State* (1920), an interesting and instructive essay on the contrast between liberal nationalism and integral nationalism, though the author does not use these terms.

CHAPTER VII

ECONOMIC FACTORS IN NATIONALISM

[§ 1]

DEFINITE nationalist doctrines, whether humanitarian, Jacobin, liberal, or traditionalist, were put forth rather suddenly, about a hundred and fifty years ago, in England and France. Having been put forth, they spread very rapidly and very widely; and within the past century and a quarter they have been adopted (and adapted) by Germans, Spaniards, Portuguese, Italians, Slavs, Greeks, Dutch and Belgians, Scandinavians and Finns, Magyars, Bulgarians, Albanians, Irish, Americans, Brazilians, Chileans, Argentinians, Mexicans, Japanese, Chinese, Turks, Siamese, Arabs, Egyptians, Hindus, Filipinos, Koreans, Canadians, Icelanders, Maltese.

The putting forth of nationalist doctrines was one of the mental exercises of the eighteenth century. Primarily it was the work of intellectuals and an expression of current intellectual interests and tendencies. But what has chiefly enabled nationalist doctrines, once put forth, to take hold of the masses of mankind since then, has been a marvellous improvement in the mechanical arts, an improvement which is nowadays termed the Industrial Revolution—the invention of labor-saving machinery, the perfecting of the steam-engine and other motive devices, the extensive use of coal and iron, the mass production of commodities, and the speeding up of transportation and communication. This Industrial Revolution began in a large way in England about a hundred and forty years ago—about the time of the Jacobin Revolution in France —and its intensification in England and its extension throughout the world have parallelled the rise and spread of popular devotion to doctrines of nationalism. The doctrines themselves were originally crystallized in an agricultural society, before the advent of the new industrial machinery, but their acceptance has accompanied, and their complete triumph has followed, the introduction of the new machinery and the transition from an agricultural to an industrial society. It seems to have been a perfectly natural development.

Granting that there was a marked growth of national consciousness in western Europe prior to the Industrial Revolution and that there was a fairly concerted effort on the part of the intellectual class to make their compatriots nationalist, large aggregations of people speaking kindred dialects of the same language—entire nationalities—could not become really unified political entities until there was sufficient improvement of the mechanical arts to admit of swift intercommunication of persons and ideas within a wide area. Nor could the masses of mankind have been inspired with supreme devotion to their respective national states until the Industrial Revolution rendered possible the functioning of effective national government. In other words, the modern age of large-scale production and industrial economy has been prerequisite, in one country after another, and eventually in the world at large, to the ascendancy of nationalism.

It is conceivable, of course, that if no nationalist doctrines had been enunciated and propagated on the eve of the Industrial Revolution, if there had been less national consciousness and more cosmopolitan feeling in countries where the Industrial Revolution began or produced early effects, the great improvement in the mechanical arts and the resulting new economy might have militated against nationalism and paved the way for a world order based on internationalism if not cosmopolitanism. We might now, thanks to the Industrial Revolution, be striving most zealously and purposefully to realize the ideals of eighteenth-century humanitarians rather than those of eighteenth-century nationalists.

As it is, many optimists of the present day are convinced that the Industrial Revolution is fundamentally anti-nationalist, that what nationalist effects it has had during the past century have been incidental and temporary, and that in the long run it must generate increasingly such economic and material forces as will bring peoples into vital interdependence and thereby supplant nationalism with internationalism and cosmopolitanism.

In justification of their conviction, these optimists point to certain facts in the contemporary economic life of industrialized nations. The scope of economic production and consumption is beyond as well as within the frontiers of any particular nation. The sources of raw materials are world-wide. The markets for manufactured commodities are world-wide. Trade is growing between nations. Credit and banking are more and more international; high finance hardly recognizes national boundaries. The demand for labor and the supply of labor are alike international; emigration and immigration proceed on a scale unexampled in human history. Likewise, the scope of communication is beyond as well as within the frontiers of any particular nation. Each country, each nationality, is becoming more closely linked to others by railways, steamships, motor cars, automobiles, aircraft, postal service, telegraph, telephone, radio, and television. Travel is becoming more international. Information for newspapers and the press is being gathered and distributed more internationally. Intellectual movements in one country ramify more and more speedily into other countries. Scientific efforts and achievements are not stopped by national boundaries but are fostered by international congresses and contacts. What is true of these efforts and achievements is equally true of those of a religious or humanitarian nature.

The optimists assert, moreover, that industrial civilization promotes an accelerating progress from localism to cosmopolitanism. Just as, before the Industrial Revolution, most localities were practically self-sufficing and nationalism was therefore impossible, and just as with the advent of the Industrial Revolution, local self-sufficiency gave way to national self-sufficiency and nationalism consequently arose, so now, with the onward sweep of the Industrial Revolution, when world-wide commerce is breaking down even national self-sufficiency, nationalism must quickly decline and be submerged in internationalism. As economic factors made the national state the natural object of popular devotion in the past century, so economic factors, the optimists assert, will inevitably render the League of Nations or some other political expression of human solidarity the natural object of popular devotion in the coming century. Nationalists of any sort, in the extreme view of these optimists, are already old-fashioned and are doomed by economic forces to early extinction.

It is idle for an historian to predict what will eventually come to pass in human evolution. The historian knows that his subject, man, is a highly uncertain animal and has behaved in the past in quite unpredictable ways. There may be scientific laws governing human behavior and social evolution, but there is no agreement among historians or any other group of scholars as to precisely what they are. It may be that contemporary economic developments make a new world order inevitable and that nationalism must evaporate, like morning mist, in the full day of economic internationalism. One may have the will to believe this, but no one knows it as an assured fact.

We do know that there has been an astounding improvement in the mechanical arts during the past hundred and forty years, involving a veritable industrial revolution. We do know that as an accompaniment of this revolution there has been a rapid growth of a kind of economic internationalism—a huge expansion of trade in goods, persons, and ideas across national political frontiers. But it is, or should be, apparent also that there have been during the same hundred and forty years and down at least to the present moment a parallel diffusion and intensification of nationalism, so that the more trade has expanded between nations, the more within each nation various sorts of nationalism have been intensified and recently have given rise to the most intolerant sort, integral nationalism. It seems paradoxical that political nationalism should grow stronger and more virulent as economic internationalism increases. Yet the former is as much a fact in contemporary society as is the latter.

For an understanding of the paradox, it is important to bear in mind that the Industrial Revolution is not necessarily an intellectual revolution. Of itself it is neither nationalist nor internationalist. It is essentially mechanical and material. It has merely provided improved means and greater opportunities for the dissemination of any ideas which influential individuals entertain. Now it so happened that when the Industrial Revolution began, nationalism was becoming a significant intellectual movement, even more significant than internationalism. Consequently, while the newer industrial machinery has been utilized for international ends, it has also been utilized, even more, for nationalist purposes. The obvious international fruits of the Industrial Revolution must not blind our eyes to its intensely nationalist contributions and implications.

It is, indeed, a sustainable hypothesis that, to date at any rate, the effects of the Industrial Revolution have been greater and more significant within national states than between them. The Revolution got under way at a time when the tradition of economic mercantilism was strong, when it was deemed expedient and beneficial for the government of each state to regulate manufacturing and trade in the interests of its own citizens. The Revolution started in the national state of England, whose statesmen and legislators at the time were mercantilists anxious to exploit it for increasing "the wealth of the nation." When, a full generation later, it penetrated into France, it entered another national state and one in which the nationalism of the Jacobins and the mercantilism of Napoleon were firmly established modes of thought. Thenceforth the Industrial Revolution spread always within the retaining walls of existing political states, usually national states, which guided and in large part controlled its local development.

If the whole world could have been industrialized simultaneously and uniformly, national differences might not have been emphasized. As it was, however, no two countries were at any given time in exactly the same stage of industrialization, and each sought, in measure as it possessed or obtained a national government, to assure its own industrial development against degrading competition of neighbors that were more or less advanced than itself.

Under the new industrial system, economic production is primarily national, and only secondarily international. The citizens of an industrialized nation talk almost invariably, and with much reason, of their "national resources," their "national factories and workshops," their "national markets." Economic consumption is international, but, far more, it is national. The home country and its colonies are always the chief market for the sale of the manufactured commodities of an industrialized nation, and they promise to become even more so in the future as so-called backward nations in Asia and Africa undergo industrialization and erect barriers against European and American imports. Hence, trade, while international to a marked degree, is relatively much more national; exports and imports of an industrialized nation do not equal in value what it buys and sells at home. Besides, quite naturally, credit and banking are organized almost wholly within nations in accordance with national law, and if they function internationally, they function, far more, nationally. Labor is organized by nations, and if it has international affiliations, it subordinates them to what it considers to be its own national interests. There is far more travel by people within a nation than between nations. There is more news in the public press about one's nation than about others. All international movements, scientific, religious, and humanitarian, actually flourish principally in national sections and under national organizations.

Moreover, it has been the Industrial Revolution which has rendered practical certain novel agencies of popular propaganda. These might ideally have been put to international purposes, but actually they have been impressed into national service, and, as we have remarked elsewhere, they have made no mean contribution to the contemporary strength and ardor of integral nationalism. Reference here is to schools, armies, journals, and societies. Without the Industrial Revolution, it would be impossible to raise funds, to supply textbooks and material equipment, or to exercise centralized supervision and control requisite to the establishment and maintenance of great systems of free universal schooling. Without the Industrial Revolution, it would be impossible to take all able bodied young men away from productive employment and put them in an army for two or three years, feeding and clothing and housing them and providing them with transport, arms, and hospitals. Without the Industrial Revolution, it would be impossible to produce huge quantities of journals, to collect news for them quickly, to print them in bulk, to distribute them widely, to have a numerous public to read them and much advertising to pay for them. Without the Industrial Revolution, it would be impossible for a propagandist society to flood a large country with written and oral appeals.

Many societies throughout the world today conduct propaganda that is international in nature or object, and some are outright anti-nationalist. Most journals carry some foreign news, and a few are critical of nationalism and try to keep it within reasonable bounds. Public schools, at least in the higher grades, teach foreign languages and something about international relations, and a considerable number of teachers in them are imbued with non-national ideals. Even a national army is not exclusively nationalist; it actually coöperates on occasion with armies of other nations. In all these respects it is the technological advance effected by the Industrial Revolution which makes feasible the large-scale employment of schools, armies, journals, and societies for international and broadly humanitarian purposes. But in the same way it has been rendered feasible to employ the same agencies for nationalist purposes. The technological advance itself is no more favorable to one purpose than to the other. It can be used for either or for both. In fact it has been used for a century, and it is still used, preëminently for nationalist ends. Societies, journals, and schools, as well as armies, are today predominantly nationalist, and the nationalism which they inculcate tends to be more exclusive and more vigorous. Indeed, economic development seems to be a handmaid to nationalist development, rather than the reverse.

[§ 2]

On the eve of the Industrial Revolution, while England and France were still chiefly agricultural countries and at the time when Bolingbroke and Rousseau were penning philosophies of humanitarian nationalism, a group of economic theorists in France—the so-called "Physiocrats"[1] —preached the doctrine that the French people and incidentally all peoples would be better off economically if governmental regulations of manufacturing and restrictions on commerce were abolished; if foodstuffs, raw materials and finished products circulated freely both within and among nations; and if the several states limited their functions to a minimum and pursued pacific foreign policies. Much the same ideas were urged, with a wealth of detail, a fine sonorousness of phrase, and superior logic, by Adam Smith (1723-1790) when the Industrial Revolution was just beginning in England. It was a kind of economic liberalism which was thus espoused in the eighteenth century by the Physiocrats and Adam Smith and which, as the Industrial Revolution progressed and wrought great technological changes in Great Britain, was developed in particular respects and crystallized into economic dogmas (with political implications) by a series of "classical" British theorists, Thomas

[1] Including, particularly, Dr. François Quesnay (1694–1774), Dupont de Nemours, and the Abbé Baudeau. *Cf.* G. Weulersse, *Le Mouvement Physiocratique en France de 1756 à 1770*, 2 vols. (1910).

Robert Malthus (1766-1834), David Ricardo (1772-1823), James Mill (1773-1836), Nassau Senior (1790-1864), et al., culminating in the practical politico-economic activities of the "Manchester School," notably Richard Cobden (1804-1865) and John Bright (1811-1889).

Economic liberalism appealed to the growing number of new and influential factory-owners and operators, to the rising class of industrial capitalists, who readily perceived in it a reasoned justification for the removal of governmental aids to agriculture and handicaps to large-scale industrial production. If, in the name of liberty, organizations of wage-earners could be forbidden, collective bargaining would be prevented and the factory-owner would be enabled to make more favorable terms with factory-workers. If, in the name of liberty, the state could be prevailed upon to refrain from enacting social legislation, taxation would be reduced and labor would be housed, clothed, and worked, most economically, in a competitive open market. If, in the name of liberty, customs duties on the importation of foreign foodstuffs could be repealed, the cost of living would decrease, and industrial employers, enabled to pay smaller wages, would obtain larger profits. If, in the name of liberty, all tariffs could be abrogated and general free trade established, foreign as well as domestic markets would be available for surplus production of the new machinery, and increasing consumption would keep pace with increasing production.

So alluring was the prospect and so rapid was the growth of capitalism that British factory owners succeeded by 1860 in committing the government of their country to economic liberalism. Collective bargaining was frowned upon. Little social legislation was enacted. The "corn laws"—the statutes discriminating against foreign grain—were repealed. And, what was most gratifying to economic liberals in industrialized England, was the advocacy of their principles by a growing number of economists and statesmen in countries that were just beginning to undergo industrialization. J. B. Say (1767-1832), Count Rossi (1787-1848), and Frédéric Bastiat (1801-1850) popularized economic liberalism in France; the bourgeois monarchy of Louis Philippe and Guizot was favorable to it; and in its spirit Napoleon III in 1860 negotiated with Cobden a treaty which removed many restrictions on trade between France and Great Britain. In Germany Baron vom Stein (1757-1831) was an early admirer and disciple of the teachings of Adam Smith, and full-fledged economic liberalism was imported into the country by an Englishman, John Prince-Smith, who, with Julius Faucher, missed no opportunity to propagate it; the Zollverein tended toward a policy of free trade; and in 1862 the Progressive Party ("Fortschrittspartei") took shape in Prussia on a platform of economic liberalism. In Italy, Cavour himself was an enthusiastic advocate of economic liberalism as he was a conspicuous exemplar of the new industrial capitalism.

Leading exponents of economic liberalism were aware that it might be imperilled by ill advised and unenlightened action on the part of political governments, especially by international war and the exceptional conditions created thereby. Consequently they were pacifist in teaching and counsel. They condemned trade disputes, colonial conflicts, international wars. They criticized nationalist emotions. At the same time they were very optimistic as to the eventual triumph of economic liberalism and of the pacifism associated with it. They were sure that their doctrine was in harmony with the spirit of the new industrial age; that as it had been born of improvement of the industrial arts, so it would gather strength and reach maturity with the perfecting of those arts. Material economic conditions, they asserted, were far more decisive than mere political action; they were bound, in the new age, to assure the success of economic liberalism, to guarantee peace throughout the world, and to get rid of the excesses of nationalism. In the heydey of economic liberalism the poet Tennyson envisaged not merely internationalism but an humanitarian cosmopolitanism as the final fruit of the new gospel. In the ode which he wrote for the opening of the International Exhibition at London in 1862, he disclosed his vision to scholars and statesmen:

". . . O ye, the wise who think, the wise who reign,
From growing commerce loose her latest chain,
And let the fair white-winged peacemaker fly
To happy havens under all the sky,
And mix the seasons, and the golden hours,
Till each man finds his own in all men's good,
And all men work in noble brotherhood."

Yet economic liberalism, in fact if not in theory, was never anti-nationalist. It arose within the framework of existing or would-be national states and it operated in a material world which could not practically be divorced from the spiritual and intellectual world in which nationalism was already a lively sentiment and a more or less reasoned aspiration. The Physiocrats wrote primaril\

for France and were not unmoved by currents of humanitarian nationalism which flowed about them. Adam Smith did not entitle his great treatise *The Wealth of the World* or *The Wealth of Individuals;* he named it *The Wealth of Nations.* He and succeeding British economists took their nationality as a matter of course and argued that Great Britain would be peculiarly advantaged if their principles were carried into effect by national law and national administration. And British industrialists seized upon the new economic doctrines and the British masses acquiesced in them and for a time even applauded them as being likely to promote not only individual interests but national interests.

Indeed, economic liberalism from the beginning was closely associated with liberal nationalism. Jeremy Bentham, as has been pointed out in another connection, was an apostle of both; and the individualism which was at the basis of his utilitarian philosophy was common to both. His nationalist disciples were liberal in their economics, and his economic disciples were liberal in their nationalism. Equally for the sake of nationalism and for the sake of "sound economics," liberals labored for a reformation of society, whereby the greatest good of the greatest number of nations as of individuals would be secured by friendly but unfettered competition alike between individuals and between nations. Of course, each nation, like every individual, should exercise the right of self-determination; each should eschew imperial ambitions and monopolistic enterprises; each should pursue policies of reform, retrenchment, and peace. British economic liberals, being liberal nationalists, were notoriously critical of the British Empire and of expenditures on British armaments and notoriously sympathetic with the efforts of "oppressed" peoples, especially those oppressed by heavy tariffs, to establish free and independent governments of their own.

With such substantial backing from the "best thinkers" of the most advanced industrial country in the world, it was natural that most leaders of nationalist movements among oppressed peoples should take their economic beliefs from the classical liberal school in England and fuse them with their own liberal nationalism. This was precisely what happened in the case of the liberal revolutionaries in France in 1830, in Germany in 1848, and in Italy during the Risorgimento. Cavour was an outstanding example of the liberal nationalist who was deeply grateful to Britain for the blessings of economic liberalism. And British liberals, including logical economists and hardheaded factory-owners, were heart and soul with Cavour and "the cause" of Italian liberty, though it is not clear exactly why they were. They were pacifists, and "the cause" involved war. Perhaps they were pro-Italian because Cavour and his associates were free traders while Austria maintained tariff-protectionism and they may have reasoned that it would be more advantageous to the interests of an exporting country like England to deal with a free-trade Italian nation than with a protectionist Austrian Empire. Or it may have been that they were just sentimental enough to sympathize with an underdog and to hope, against reason, that he would soon be on top.

Or it may have been that they thought war in behalf of constitutional Italy to be a lesser evil than peace in support of autocracy in state and church. In any event, they displayed a devotion to the practices of liberal nationalism equal to, if not in excess of, their devotion to the principles of economic liberalism.

It was thus that economic liberalism began to slough off its pacifist skin. Economic liberals of Great Britain, and of other countries too, showed an increasing willingness to lend encouragement, financial aid, and even military support to any struggling nation which promised to promote, and against any Power which was hindering, the national economic interests of their own country. From Canning's intervention in behalf of the Greeks and Latin Americans down to Gladstone's philippics against Austria and Turkey, English liberals, consciously or unconsciously, were abetting nationalism for their own economic purposes and were contributing to the warlike, as well as to the economic, aspect of liberal nationalism. It seems as though economic liberalism was losing its soul by becoming embodied in liberal nationalism.

There was another serious difficulty for economic liberalism. Not all peoples were in the same stage of industrial development, and yet all, in the nineteenth century, were infected with nationalism. The British, being considerably in advance of the others, could most nearly reconcile their nationalism with the dictates of economic liberalism. But the French, while permitting economic liberalism to be taught in their universities and to be professed by some of their statesmen, were disinclined by national interests and national sentiment to apply it fully to public policies. Internally France was willing to forbid labor combinations and to neglect the enactment of social legislation, but externally she was unwilling to embark upon a policy of radical free trade. Her national industries were "infant"; they needed "protection" against competition with the cheap products of older British factories.

The Germans were industrially somewhat more backward than the French. As long as they were importing the bulk of their manufactured commodities and were exporting agricultural products, they could afford to admire Great Britain and to adopt economic liberalism. But at the end of the 1870's German industrialists were sufficiently numerous and influential to obtain from Bismarck a national protective tariff. The German tariff of 1879, dictated by economic and nationalist considerations, was a landmark in the history alike of liberal nationalism and of economic liberalism.

Thenceforth, one nation after another on the Continent of Europe and in America went in for tariff protectionism and also for a wide range of social legislation. The speedily resulting neo-mercantilism was diametrically opposed to the basic principles of economic liberalism, and with the collapse of economic liberalism, its ally, liberal nationalism, suffered a most serious reverse. Yet neo-mercantilism was motivated by nationalist sentiment as well as by economic reasoning, and its rise, if sounding the death-knell of liberal nationalism, heralded the advent of a nationalism which was to be more, rather than less, intense.

[§ 3]

The Industrial Revolution dislocated society and created grave social problems in every country which it touched. Economic liberalism was a doctrine and a programme calculated to enable factory-owners—the new capitalists—to solve their special problems in their own way. As we have seen, it was not necessarily nationalist, but it soon became entangled with liberal nationalism and gradually it helped to transform liberal nationalism into a more acute nationalism which ultimately destroyed economic liberalism itself.

Socialism was a parallel doctrine and programme intended primarily for the solution of the problems of factory-workers—the new proletarians. It was not necessarily nationalist. Indeed, in its principal form it was vehemently anti-nationalist. But in time and at least indirectly, as we shall presently see, it became an actual prop to the nationalist structure which it was intended to overthrow.

The first generation of socialist leaders after the beginning of the Industrial Revolution—such men as Robert Owen (1771-1858) in England and Charles Fourier (1772-1837) in France—were hardly distinguishable in fundamental philosophy from their liberal contemporaries. They talked about individual happiness and the greatest good of the greatest number. They were skeptical of state action and sympathetic with the notion that the state should be a merely "passive policeman." They were strenuous in defense of personal liberty in the realms of religion, education, association, and the press. They did recognize grave abuses in the new industrial order, especially the rapacity of factory-owners and the exploitation of factory-workers,—the long hours, the small wages, the working conditions, the slums, the sweating, which accompanied the conduct of industry for private profit,—and they did develop hostility to the institution and "right" of private property and to the teaching of the classical economists that the distress of the working class was an inevitable and irremediable corollary to economic law.

But in seeking remedies for the situation, these "utopian" or "liberal" socialists were content to counsel the legalization of voluntary trade unions, the enactment of a little factory legislation, and the establishment of communistic farms and workshops by individuals who wished to do so. They were largely indifferent to nationalism and they distrusted the political state, whether national or not. One of their number, the Frenchman Pierre Joseph Proudhon (1809-1865), went so far in his denunciation of the state as the guarantor of private property (which he termed "stolen goods") as to urge the supplanting of the compulsory national state with a loose federation of voluntary associations, and thereby he passed from liberal socialism into anarchism.

A far more systematic and influential socialism—the kind that has had continuing vitality to the present day—was expounded by Karl Marx (1818-1883). Marx was born at Trier in Germany. As the son of a Jewish lawyer who was well-read and conservative, a Prussian patriot, and a convert to Lutheran Christianity, he received a respectable education at the gymnasium in his native town and at the universities of Bonn, Berlin, and Jena. At the universities he was drawn away from the study of the law, for which his father had destined him, to the study of history and philosophy, and, under the influence of professorial disciples of Hegel—the so-called Younger Hegelians—he became possessed, in his father's phrase, "of the demon of revolution," though, to tell the truth, the "demon" was as yet only that of middle-class liberalism. Denied appointment by the existing conservative government to a teaching position in a state university because of his liberalism, he turned to journalism, married most properly, and in 1842-1843 conducted in the pages of the *Rhenische Zeitung* a vigorous campaign for the freedom of the press. He was obviously a good, if somewhat aggressive, liberal; and he bade fair to become a typical liberal nationalist.

But the Prussian government stepped in and altered Marx's fate. It suppressed his newspaper and deprived him of the means of earning a livelihood in Germany. Accordingly, he emigrated to Paris, where he supported himself and his wife by publishing a German newspaper for emigrant compatriots, and where he came into close and significant contact with French Socialists, with a large number of factory-workers, and particularly with Friedrich Engels, like himself a young university-trained German Jew, but one who was freshly returned from England and indelibly stamped with horror at the condition of the industrial proletariat which he had observed in that country. During the next few years Marx talked, read, and pondered much; he was undergoing conversion from middle-class liberalism to working-class socialism. In 1848, in conjunction with Engels, he published a little pamphlet which at that time attracted slight attention but which later acquired great fame. It was the *Communist Manifesto,* the "birth-cry of modern socialism."

The *Manifesto* was no nationalist document. Its interpretation of history, its analysis of contemporary society, and its prophecy for the future not only ignored nationalism but bespoke a philosophy diametrically opposed to nationalism. Marx and Engels started with the assumption that the most important factor in man's historical evolution has been the economic, the material, and went on to demonstrate by citation of selected historical data that struggles between social classes have determined the direction of historical evolution. In the new industrial era, they explained, the struggle is between capitalists and proletarians. "The capitalist class . . . has created more varied and more colossal productive forces than all past generations," but "the system has become too narrow to hold the wealth created in it," and hence has occurred "the paradoxical epidemic of over-production." At the same time, however, "the capitalist class has produced . . . men who will deal it its death-blow—the modern workingmen, the proletarians, . . . crowded into factories." These "are increasing in power and are becoming conscious of their power," and are being reënforced by the lower middle class, the artisans, and the peasants, who are falling into the proletariat. "Until now, all historic movements have been produced by minorities to their profit. The proletarian movement is the movement of the immense majority for the benefit of the majority." It begins with a "national struggle" in each country. But it will become international, for "workingmen have no country."

The practical aims of the "Communists" (that is, the Marxian socialists) should be to make the proletarians "class-conscious," to organize them in a class party, to help them to gain political power, and to abolish middle-class private property which has been "created by the labor of wage-earners for the profit of capitalists." Capital is "social power"; by means of revolution, eventual and inevitable, capital will become "common property." The triumph of the proletariat will involve the destruction of "middle-class freedom" of trade, of the "middle-class family," of traditional religion and morality, and of hostility between nations. "The proletarians have nothing to lose but their chains. They have a world to win. Workingmen of all countries, unite!"

Class consciousness was thus exalted above national consciousness. The individual was expected to be loyal to his class rather than to his nationality. National solidarity, the ardent desire of every nationalist heart, was pronounced chimerical and undesirable. Each nation, it was claimed, comprised the two hostile camps of capitalists and proletarians whose conflict was a fundamental fact and whose fight was to a finish. For wars between nations were to be substituted wars within nations. For a league of nations was to be substituted an association of class-conscious groups, international and even cosmopolitan. All these propositions, according to Marx and Engels, are sure because they are self-evident, because they are in the very nature of things; they are not "inventions of world reformers"; rather, they are expressions "of the actual conditions of an existing class contest and of an historical movement." Nationalism might be imaginary, but the new socialism was very real.

Hardly was the *Communist Manifesto* published when the revolutionary wave of 1848 swept over most of Continental Europe. Marx perceived in it a prompt confirmation of his prophecy: the revolution overspread national frontiers; the masses rose everywhere against classes and despots; and workingmen of one country fraternized with workingmen of other countries. Marx himself returned hurriedly to Germany and revived at Cologne his newspaper, under the name of the *Neue Rhenische Zeitung,* this time as a propagandist sheet for his international "scientific" socialism.

But disappointment and some disillusionment awaited Marx. Middle-class liberals soon obtained the upper hand in the revolutionary movement of 1848. The fraternization of workingmen across national boundaries and their common struggle with capitalists speedily gave way to nationalist conflicts and to struggles for national unity. And in 1849 the restored reactionary government of Prussia again suppressed Marx's newspaper and expelled him from the country. Thenceforth, until his death, he resided in London, growing ever surer of the truth of his basic doctrines but more doubtful of the immediacy of the universal revolution which would give effect to them.

Meanwhile, Marx busied himself with hack-writing, in order to support his increasing family; with the preparation of a ponderous critique of political economy, in order to buttress his creed; and with the formation of an "International Workingmen's Association," in order to prepare the way for the revolution and the resulting triumph of the proletariat. Even this Association—termed by socialists the "First International"—was disappointing. Springing out of a meeting of labor leaders and agitators at the London Exposition of 1862, it adopted general statutes in 1864, and during the ensuing years held annual congresses and organized branches in several countries. But its following was never numerous, and what there was of it fell to quarrelling over the relative merits of Marxian socialism and Proudhonian anarchism and over the relative rights of France and Germany in the War of 1870-1871. The Association held its last sizeable congress at Geneva in 1873, and it was formally dissolved at Philadelphia three years later.

Yet, if Marx failed to organize socialist workingmen internationally, others soon succeeded in organizing them nationally. In Germany, Ferdinand Lassalle (1825-1864), a middle-class Jew who, like Marx, had come under the influence of the Younger Hegelians in the university of Berlin and had had his attention drawn to the plight of industrial workers, published a significant socialist treatise in 1861[1] and two years later organized the "German Social Democratic Party" to work for "universal manhood suffrage in order that, by means of political democracy, governmental support might be obtained for coöperative producers' societies and that thereby social democracy might be established." In 1875 Lassalle's Party was fused with the German branch of Karl Marx's International Workingmen's Association which had been formed in 1869 by Wilhelm Liebknecht, a Saxon scholar, and August

[1] *System der erworbenen Rechte.*

Bebel, a Saxon workingman. The resulting German socialist party accepted the philosophy of the *Communist Manifesto* and added to it the immediate practical programme of Lassalle; and the party grew by leaps and bounds. In 1877 it polled 493,000 votes in the general German elections and sent twelve deputies to the Reichstag. In 1890 it polled 1,427,000 votes and elected 35 deputies. In 1903 it polled 3,000,000 votes and elected 81 deputies. In 1912 it polled 4,250,000 votes and elected 110 deputies. Its enrolled, dues-paying members increased from 25,000 in 1875 to 1,085,000 in 1914.

The German socialist party served as a model for the organization of national socialist parties in other countries—in Austria, Hungary, Italy, Sweden, Denmark, Holland, Belgium, France, Poland, Russia, Great Britain, the United States, Japan, *etc.* Wherever industry developed and became mechanized, there socialist parties took root and Marxian doctrines seemed to flourish. In 1889 an international congress of Marxian socialists was held at Paris, and in 1900 representatives of the several national parties established a formal international organization: a permanent international bureau was set up at Brussels, and provision was made for triennial international congresses; it was the "Second International," which throve up to 1914.

The marked advance of socialism prior to 1914 would seem to signify the growth, as the Industrial Revolution progressed, of a decidedly anti-nationalist and cosmopolitan movement. The movement was not altogether what it seemed to be, however; and its growth was perhaps less connected with mere progress in the mechanical arts than with its own increasing tendency to take account of nationalist aspirations and to adopt nationalist policies. At any rate Marxian socialists, despite their materialist professions, were human, and they could and did glow on occasion with sentiment and spiritual ardor; and there was no more universal object of popular sentiment and spiritual ardor in the nineteenth century than altruistic nationalism. Materialists could not be untouched by it. It was too much in the environment. Marxian socialists were materialists, but they were also something else: they were missionaries, zealous gospellers, emotional reformers; they had, as a rule, the very mental qualities which rendered them specially susceptible to any emotional appeal, even that of nationalism. It should not cause too much surprise to learn that socialism made terms with nationalism on conditions more favorable to the latter than to the former.

In certain respects Marx himself could be regarded as a forerunner of socialistic nationalism. He had had no hostility to the principle of nationality. He had recognized it as a fact, and, furthermore, had extolled it. He had shown a peculiar sentimental attachment to his own fatherland. He had been for years on intimate terms with Mazzini, the apostle of Italian nationalism. He had written sympathetically of the struggles of Italians and Poles and other "exploited" peoples against their "alien exploiters." Besides, he had always had a kind of Hegelian veneration for the political state; he had bitterly assailed the anarchism of Proudhon and the passive-policeman notion which liberals entertained of the state. "Every class-struggle means a political struggle," he and Engels had written in the *Communist Manifesto*. While charging that "present government is simply a committee for the administration of the affairs of the capitalist class," he had steadfastly asserted that the government of the future, to be truly socialistic, must be truly democratic.

Democracy, to Marx, had always been a *sine qua non* of the proletarian state. But how could democracy be practically attained or successfully operated except on the basis of nationality and within the national state? Marx without putting the question in so many words had clearly implied that there was no other answer to it. He had declared that there must be "a national struggle" for democracy within each country; he had provided for "national sections" in the First International; and he had instructed the various national groups of socialists as to the particular tactics which they were to pursue in their respective countries. In a word, Marx had, perhaps unconsciously but no less certainly, linked his proletarian socialism with Jacobin (democratic) nationalism.

Socialist leaders who succeeded Marx tended to maintain and strengthen the link. Lassalle stressed the importance of political democracy and at the same time praised the efforts of Bismarck to unify the German nation. And when, after 1875, national political parties of socialists sprang up in most countries, they included in their platforms not only planks taken from the economic lumber yard of Marx and Engels but also planks lugged out of the nationalist storeroom of the Jacobins. Side by side with demands for public ownership of the means of production, distribution, and exchange, demands which in time they expressed as "the nationalization of industry," they demanded universal suffrage, secret ballot, frequent elections, ministerial responsibility, the abolition of monarchy and aristocracy, the establishment of republican government, and all the other political devices of which Jacobin nationalists had dreamed. They condemned imperialism, militarism, oppression of national minorities, and international war, precisely as Jacobin nationalists might have done if they had been pure theorists instead of practical statesmen. Like the revolutionary Jacobins, the Marxian socialists approved of obligatory education of all children in state schools and of compulsory military training of all youths in a "purely defensive" militia.

Toward the close of the nineteenth century and at the commencement of the twentieth appeared within the ranks of the socialists certain "higher critics" of the gospel according to Marx. These critics held that the Founder was, after all, human; and, being human, he had not been infallible; indeed, he had been mistaken about some matters. Particularly had he been mistaken in his prophecies. He had said, *ex cathedra,* that capital would be concentrated more and more rapidly in fewer and fewer hands, that the vast majority of human beings would correspondingly be reduced to the position of proletarians, and that therefore, in the not distant future, the masses in one country after another would be enabled, by sheer weight of numbers, to establish democratic government and expropriate the capitalists. The critics pointed out that Marx had failed to foresee the ameliorative effect of social legislation and other developments, and some of them, by citing statistics, raised serious doubts whether concentration of capital was actually occurring on any large scale and whether proletarians were ever likely to constitute an absolute majority in any country.

The work of the "higher critics" caused protracted and frequently stormy debates within the several national socialist parties and at congresses of the "Second International" and even led, in some instances, to heresy, apostasy, and schism. One faction, the so-called Reformist faction, following the higher criticism of Eduard Bernstein, argued that inasmuch as the proletarians and socialists did not constitute a majority of citizens in any country, and were not likely, at least in the near future, to constitute such a majority, they should push into the background the class-conflict idea of Marx and should openly coöperate with democratic and liberal middle-class parties in popularizing government and promoting social reform within each nation. This faction was not numerous enough, prior to 1914, to capture the management of any of the socialist parties or to write its theories into their platforms, but it did influence the majority of strict Marxians—the Socialist Fundamentalists—so that the socialist parties in most countries became less and less radical and more and more nationalist.

In Germany, the socialist leaders, particularly after 1907, were far too intent upon rolling up votes at elections to offer vigorous opposition to any policy which appeared to be in the "national interest."[1] In France, the socialists proved themselves quite patriotic by collaborating for years with the radical bourgeois parties, the boasted custo-

---

[1] I have given elsewhere an account of the progressively nationalist character of the German Socialist Party: "German Socialism Reconsidered," *American Historical Review*, October, 1917.

dians of Jacobin tradition. In countries where socialism was relatively strong—in Germany, for instance—it was sometimes argued that any policy which favored an "advanced" nation at the expense of a "backward" nation was helpful to the progress of civilization and therefore of socialism and should be supported by socialists as by other patriots. It was this argument which the socialists of the Fabian Society employed to justify their support of the British conquest of the Boer republics in South Africa. It was the same argument which the socialist parties of all the Great Powers used in explaining why they supported their several national governments in the World War of 1914.

Over against the "Reformists" was another faction, the so-called "Syndicalist" or "direct-action" faction, which, following the "higher criticism" of Georges Sorel, proposed that, lacking a numerical majority, the socialists should push into the background the democratic notions of Marx and by intensifying the class-struggle and resorting to violence should precipitate a revolution and set up a dictatorship of the proletariat. This faction, unlike that of the "Reformists," was not even tolerated by the Socialist Fundamentalists, prior to 1914; read out of the regular socialist parties, except in Russia (where it read the others out), it fashioned the new "revolutionary syndicalist" movement.

Revolutionary syndicalism spread quickly among the trade unionists of southern Europe and for a time filled earnest nationalists of France, Italy, and Spain with chilling fear and gloomy foreboding. In the heat of the World War, however, revolutionary syndicalism disappeared like hoarfrost. One thing it left behind, and that was its doctrine of direct action, violence, and dictatorship. That one thing went into the making of postwar integral nationalism. In Russia, where the direct-action group obtained not only control of the socialist party but also dictatorship of the national state, there was a violent overthrow of capitalism but not of nationalism. The nationalism of Bolshevist Russia is neither liberal nor Jacobin, but it is nationalism none the less.

In fine, Marxian socialism has been a factor in the development of modern nationalism, despite its theoretical setting of class before nation, despite its repeated protestations of internationalism, and despite the apprehensions it has aroused among nationalists of other faiths. Beginning with Marx himself, it has associated its economic doctrines with the nationalist doctrines of democratic Jacobinism; and the association was tightened in Reformist circles before the World War and in the regular socialist parties of most countries after the War. One of its off-shoots has contributed to the rise of Fascist and other forms of integral nationalism. In Russia it has evolved a new interpretation of Marxian economics and a type of intense nationalism.

[§ 4]

Economic liberalism and Marxian socialism were alike formulated as strictly economic doctrines and only gradually assumed nationalist significance and became factors in the nineteenth-century development of nationalism. Simultaneously, however, economic doctrines of a patently nationalist sort were set forth and some of these were especially influential in the evolution of nationalism.

ECONOMIC FACTORS IN NATIONALISM

An early and curious example of nationalist economic doctrine was that propounded by Johann Gottlieb Fichte (1762-1814) in his *Die Geschlossene Handelstaat* ("The Closed Commercial State") published in 1800. Fichte was intermediate between Kant and Hegel in the trinity of the great German idealists and he was a pronounced German nationalist. His nationalism was derived in its cultural aspects from Herder and in its political aspects from Rousseau and the French Jacobins. He was an admirer and apologist of the French Revolution [1]; and if later he denounced the French and extravagantly extolled the language and culture of the Germans,[2] it was because he had always been, like Herder, a cultural nationalist and because he believed that Napoleon had perverted the Revolution. In his last days, he returned, good Jacobin that he was, to a bitter attack on German kings and princes.[3]

Fichte's excursion into economics was undoubtedly a result of his sympathetic observation of actual economic developments in France during the Revolution: the relative self-sufficiency and the virtual nationalization of industry during the years of Jacobin ascendancy; the state control of grain and fixing of prices; the national experiments with paper-money; etc.[4] These developments Fichte rationalized into a philosophical economic system, which

[1] *Cf.* his *Beitrag zur Berichtigung der Urteile des Publikums über die französische Revolution* (1793), in *Sämmtliche Werke*, ed. by J. H. Fichte (1846), Vol. VI, a reply to a book by Wilhelm Rehberg, who had passed strictures on the Revolution in imitation of Edmund Burke.
[2] *Cf. Der Patriotismus und sein Gegenteil* (1806-1807), and the very famous *Reden an die deutsche Nation* (1807-1808).
[3] *Cf. Aus dem Entwurfe einer politischen Schrift in Frühling 1813*, in *Sämmtliche Werke*, VII.
[4] On the economic nationalism of the French Jacobins, see above, pp. 76-79.

in his opinion would remedy the ills alike of mercantilism and laisser-faire and which presumably would serve as a model for every national state.

The national state, according to Fichte, should be the unit of economic life and the guarantor of individual "property." Now, "property" is "the right to work," and therefore, in order to guarantee it, the national state should regulate in detail the work and wages of the economic groups of producers (farmers, foresters, gardeners, *etc.*), artisans (mechanics, manufacturers, *etc.*), and merchants (distributors of goods), and through taxation should provide work and equal wages for the non-economic but needful groups of teachers, officials, and soldiers. With the guaranty of work and wages to every citizen, it would not be necessary for anyone to horde money; the medium of exchange should be not gold or silver but paper script representing the value of a bushel of wheat; and on the death of a citizen all his savings should revert to the state.

The national state should be neither mercantilist nor free-trade; mercantilism led to international jealousies and wars, while free trade resulted in ruthless exploitation of the individual. Rather, if the national state should make itself economically independent of every other country and should close its frontiers to foreign commerce, its individual citizens would be benefitted and motives for war and conquest would be removed. At first it might be necessary to import from abroad machines and technicians in order to develop the self-sufficiency of the nation, and always there would have to be some importation of materials which the climate of the nation would not permit it to produce at home, but such foreign trade should be reduced to a minimum and should be conducted solely by the government of the national state. The only vital contacts which one nation should seek to maintain with others would be intellectual. Foreign travel would be allowed to well-educated citizens, but not to others.

From such an arrangement, Fichte was sure that great happiness would result. Each nation would mind its own business and concentrate on the welfare of all its citizens. The nation would not need a large army or suffer the miseries of war. The citizens would strengthen their national character, attain to a high conception of national honor, and evince a noble national patriotism. Altogether, Fichte's plea was for an economic adjunct to Jacobin nationalism, a kind of national socialism.

Fichte adjudged *The Closed Commercial State* to be one of his very best and most thoughtful works; and, though it had no immediate influence, some of its principal points were reëmphasized by an ensuing generation of more influential economic nationalists. The doctrine of "the right to work" was stressed by Louis Blanc in his proposals for French "national workshops." The notion that "the national state is the institution in which the whole virtue of humanity should be realized" was appropriated from Fichte by Lassalle as the cornerstone of the latter's German Social Democratic Party. Rodbertus's national socialism, according to which the national state should direct all the economic activities of its citizens, was obviously Fichtean. And some of the most peculiar economic experiments of the contemporary Bolshevist government in Russia are curiously reminiscent of the counsels of Fichte in the year 1800.

If Fichte was the protagonist of an economic Jacobin nationalism, others were not lacking to advocate economic policies more in keeping with traditional nationalism. The so-called "Christian socialists" in England and "social Catholics" in France, who during the 1830's and 1840's denounced the selfishness of factory-owners and the un-Christian character of economic liberalism and drew dark pictures of the suffering of the masses under the new industrial system, were actuated perhaps by the fact that as a rule they represented conservative classes whose own economic interests seemed to be threatened by the Industrial Revolution, but they certainly couched their criticisms in terms of traditional morality and patriotism.

Charles Kingsley (1819-1875) may be cited as an example. He was not a professional economist but he was prominent among the Christian socialists and wrote extensively in behalf of the workingmen. Sprung on his father's side from an old English family of country squires and on his mother's side from a respectable family of West Indian planters who had been slave-holders for generations, he grew up with an intense admiration for his own nationality, its glorious traditions and its historical institutions, and with an intense scorn for "inferior" breeds. Like his father he became a clergyman of the Church of England, and eventually he rose to the eminently respectable position of chaplain to Queen Victoria. He was, indeed, a patriot of patriots; and because he was such a good and pious English nationalist, he was anxious that the economic as well as the spiritual welfare of all Englishmen should be the constant care of the nation. "If you feel that it is a noble thing to be an Englishman, especially an English soldier or an English sailor, —a noble and honorable privilege to be allowed to do your duty in the noblest nation and the noblest church which the world ever saw,—then live as Englishmen in covenant with God."[1] And the "covenant with God" required, according to Kingsley, that the English nation should enact such social legislation and pursue such economic policies as would redound most advantageously to Englishmen. With Kingsley and a considerable number of like-minded traditionalists patriotism meant national social reform, and social reform meant more nationalism.[2]

There was one outstanding exponent of liberal nationalism who, contrary to the prevailing tendency of his school, repudiated economic liberalism and offered a defense of tariff protectionism. This was Friedrich List (1789-1846). The son of a prosperous German tanner, he received a good university training; and as a youth, during the Napoleonic period and the attendant patriotic "awakening" in Germany, he became an earnest liberal and an ardent nationalist. After 1815 his exhortations to freedom and national unity cost him a professorial post and a promising government position and landed him in jail.

[1] *True Words for Brave Men*, p. 45. Cf. *Yeast* (1849), *Alton Locke* (1849), etc., *passim*.

[2] In England Benjamin Disraeli (1804-1881), the famous Conservative leader, was conspicuous among advocates of traditional nationalism who were interested in its economic implications; cf. his *Coningsby* (1844) and *Sybil* (1845). In France, the Vicomte de Villeneuve-Bargemont (1784-1850) expressed somewhat similar views in his *Christian Political Economy* (1834) and his *Book of the Afflicted* (1841).

On his release in 1825 he emigrated to the United States and became an American citizen. Enriched by the discovery of valuable coal on his farm in Pennsylvania and brought into some prominence by the journal which he edited for his fellow German-Americans, he was enabled to return to Germany in 1832 in the rôle of United States consul at Leipzig.

In accordance with the doctrines and policies of Alexander Hamilton, whom he had learned to admire during his sojourn in America, List now took a leading part in urging Germany to adopt national economic measures which must hasten the country's political unification—on a liberal basis, he hoped. He helped to create sentiment favorable to the Tariff Union (Zollverein) of the several German states. He aided in the construction of the network of German railways. In 1841 he embodied his ideas in a famous book, *The National System of Political Economy*.[1]

List attacked the cosmopolitan principles of economic liberalism and particularly the universal validity of free trade. Likewise he combatted the notion that the pursuit of immediate private interests by the separate members of the community would promote the highest good of the whole. The nation, to him, was far more important than the world or the individual. The nation had an existence of its own, standing midway between the individual and humanity, and constituting a unity by reason of distinctive language, manners, historical development, culture, and institutions. This unity must be the first condition of the security, the well-being, the progress, and the civ-

[1] *Das nationale System der politischen Ökonomie.*

ilization of the individual and of humanity at large. Consequently private economic interests, like all others, must be subordinated to the maintenance and increase of true national wealth; and inasmuch as the nation has a continuous life, its true wealth must consist, not in the quantity of exchange-values which it possesses at any given time, but in the full, many-sided, and long-term development of all its economic resources. Thus it might happen that the nation, in certain circumstances, should restrict the economic activities and impede the economic interests of some of its citizens in order to confer greater benefits upon the nation as a whole and upon its descendants.

List explained that not all nations were in the same economic situation. Those in the torrid regions were relatively static, depending almost wholly at all times on the production of certain raw materials, while those in the temperate zones passed with greater or less rapidity through four stages of economic development: (1) a pastoral stage; (2) a strictly agricultural stage; (3) a stage in which manufactures were combined with agriculture; and (4) a stage in which commerce as well as manufacturing was combined with agriculture. The last was the climax and goal of economic evolution; it was the stage most favorable to national independence and national culture. It could be attained only by nations in the temperate zones and by these only if and when they took legislative and administrative action requisite to advance them out of the preceding stage. Hence each nation or would-be nation should adopt "industrial politics," that is to say, should purposefully build up its commerce and manufacturing and agriculture.

A nation in the second stage of economic development should follow a policy of free trade with a view to stimulating and improving its agriculture by unhampered intercourse with richer and more cultivated nations, importing foreign manufactures and exporting raw products. Then, when a nation was economically so far advanced that it could manufacture for itself and had entered the third stage, it should employ a system of tariff protection in order to allow growth of the home industries and to save them from being overpowered in their earlier efforts by the competition of more matured foreign industries in the home market. Finally, when a nation arrived at the fourth stage—the ultimate stage—and no longer dreaded foreign competition, free trade might again become the rule, though care must be taken to prevent retrogression: special social legislation might be necessary to preserve the balance between agriculture and manufacturing and between employers and employees, and special subsidies might be needful to maintain the national merchant marine in full vigor.

The practical conclusion which List drew for Germany was that she needed for her economic progress an extended and conveniently bounded territory reaching to the sea-coast on both north and south and an energetic expansion of manufactures and commerce, and that the way to this expansion lay through an economic union of all the German states which would protect "infant" industries and foster a national marine. Thereby Germany would advance into the fourth stage of economic development. Her national political unity must follow and her national culture must flourish.

ECONOMIC FACTORS IN NATIONALISM

List was a professed liberal in politics. He admired the political institutions of England and the United States and desired for the united Germany of his dreams a middle-class government which should function constitutionally and with the utmost guaranty of individual liberty in all spheres outside of the economic. It was not, however, his political liberalism which bore fruit in Germany, but his economic nationalism. Most of his fellow liberals of his own generation were economic liberals; they derived their ideas chiefly from the "classical" English economists and they preached them in Germany in the spirit of cosmopolitan doctrinaires, imagining that the Industrial Revolution was a uniform phenomenon which made them equally applicable to all nations. List, on the other hand, was more of a realist; he perceived that the Industrial Revolution affected the nations differently at different times and that an economic policy which favored the industrialization of England did not necessarily favor the industrialization of Germany; and he was more aware of the intensity of the nationalist sentiment throughout the world and particularly in Germany.

The result was that the influence of the national economic doctrines of List waxed as that of the cosmopolitan economic doctrines of the other liberals waned. German nationalists of conservative and traditionalist stamp could and did accept the economic teachings of List, while rejecting his political counsels; and an increasing number of German industrialists, regardless of nationalist or political bias, foresaw delightful solace for the woes of British competition in List's national programme. Even liberal nationalists of an ensuing generation, growing more in the grace of nationalism than in that of liberalism, came gradually to agree with List's contentions. By 1880 the German national state, under Bismarck's nominal guidance, was actually treading the economic path which had been blazed by Friedrich List.

List was not the only influential advocate of economic nationalism in Germany. Another was Karl Rodbertus (1805-1875), at once more conservative and more radical. Rodbertus led a singularly uneventful life. He was the son of a university professor and he was himself essentially the scholar. After studying law at Göttingen and Berlin and engaging in sundry legal occupations, he bought a landed estate in Pomerania in 1836 and thenceforth divided his time between reading, writing, and superintendence of the estate. He took little part in politics, almost never travelled, and detested "agitation" and "propaganda"; but his books and his voluminous correspondence[1] exercised a great influence on such widely different persons as Karl Marx, Ferdinand Lassalle, Adolf Wagner, and Otto von Bismarck.

Rodbertus was a nationalist, but by no means a liberal. He was very conservative, even traditionalist. He wanted a united Germany, but one which should rally around a national monarch and cherish national history and national culture. At the same time he was shockingly radical, at least to middle-class liberals, in his economic views. He was, indeed, a complete socialist.

Rodbertus maintained that the progress of mankind

[1] *Cf.* especially his *Zur Erkenntniss unserer staatswirtschaftlichen Zustände* (1842); *Soziale Briefe an von Kirchmann* (1850); *Creditnot des Grundbesitzes*, 2nd ed. (1876); and *Briefe* to Adolf Wagner (1878-1879) and to Rudolf Meyer (1882).

was through three stages of economic and social development: the first, "ancient," in which property was primarily in human beings; the second, "past and contemporary," in which property was principally in land and capital; and the third, "still remote," in which property would depend entirely on labor. He claimed that in the "contemporary" stage, the non-laboring classes, by the ownership of land and capital, are enabled to levy virtual tribute on the workers, and, through the evil system of economic competition, they are enabled to levy it in such a proportion that the workers only obtain as much as can barely support them in life. The remedy for this situation and the means of ushering in the future perfect stage of human development would be, according to Rodbertus, the nationalization of land and capital; that is, the abolition of private property and the establishment of socialistic national states. Rodbertus confessed that such a radical reform would be difficult. It would require a vast bureaucracy, a high state of public morality and patriotic feeling, and probably five centuries of preparation. A beginning should be made, however, as soon as possible. Laisser-faire should be repudiated, and the production and distribution of goods should be brought more and more under the management of the national state, directed by a "social" emperor and administered by an ethical bureaucracy.

Less radical than Rodbertus in remedies for economic ills, but equally conservative in politics and more intensely nationalist were the group of professorial German economists who are commonly referred to as the "historical school," in contradistinction to the earlier "classical school" of England. A remarkably gifted and learned group, they were as certain that the Industrial Revolution could and should be utilized to promote nationalism as the classical group were sure that it was leading to cosmopolitanism.

Both Rodbertus and List were interested in history and both employed it, or at any rate a philosophy of history, to sharpen their economic arguments, but they did so incidentally and they are not usually reckoned among the "historical school." The acknowledged founder of the school was W. G. F. Roscher (1817-1894), professor at Göttingen and Leipzig, who in his *Grundriss*, a kind of prospectus which he published in 1843, criticized the *a priori* reasoning, the "logic-mania," of the classical economists and insisted that if economics were to become a true science, based on observation, economists must study history and found their systems on it; furthermore, economics must become, he said, "the science of national development."[1] Practicing what he preached, Roscher published in 1874 a monumental *History of National Economy in Germany* and, before and after, he was bringing out volumes of an even more monumental series on German agriculture, industry, commerce, finance, and poor-relief.[2]

One of the most eminent of the "historical school" was

[1] Similar opinions were clearly expressed shortly afterwards by Bruno Hildebrand, *Die Nationalökonomie der Gegenwart und Zukunft* (1848), and by Karl Knies, *Die politische Ökonomie vom Standpunkte der geschichtlicher Methode* (1853).

[2] *Die Grundlagen der Nationalökonomie* (1854); *Die Nationalökonomie des Ackerbaues und der verwandten Urproduktionszweige* (1859); *Der Nationalökonomie des Handels und Gewerbfleisses* (1881); *System der Finanzwissenschaft* (1886); *System der Armenpflege und Armenpolitik* (1894).

Adolf Wagner (1835-1917), professor in his earlier years at Dorpat and Heidelberg and after 1870 at Berlin, a popular lecturer, a prolific writer, and an efficient organizer and administrator. Wagner held that the teachings of the Physiocrats, Adam Smith, and the other liberal economists were vitiated by having been based on the false premises of "natural right" and "individualism." On the contrary he laid down that the economic position of the individual, instead of depending on so-called natural rights or even on his natural powers, is largely conditioned by the national environment in which he is born, the national laws under which he lives, and the national state to which he belongs, and that all these are themselves historical products. Consequently, economic phenomena cannot be isolated and treated *in vacuo*; such conceptions as freedom and property are partially economic, but also are inextricably juristic and national. And consequently it is idle to study economics apart from national law and politics.

Wagner and other members of the "historical school," in accordance with their principles, conducted many researches into the history of various phases of national economic life and produced many tomes which were not only very erudite but also of great practical utility in indicating how the contemporary state might forward national economic interests. In general the "historical school" tended to support political conservatism as being peculiarly harmonious with Germany's national history and genius and to counsel the adoption of a programme of protectionism and social legislation as being most likely to conserve and strengthen the national tradition and the national morale.[1] In 1872 the German leaders of the "historical school," together with a notable number of sympathetic jurists and administrators, held a conference at Eisenach and issued a manifesto, which, in declaring war on economic liberalism, referred to the national German state as "the great moral institution for the education of humanity" and claimed that it should speedily enact such legislation as "would enable an increasing number of people to participate in the highest benefits of German Kultur." The national state, according to the Eisenach conferees, was to be not a "passive policeman," but a benevolent father and a spiritual guide; it was to foster national agriculture, national industry, national commerce, and national labor. The conference ended with the establishment of a "Union for Social Politics," an organization which labored during the next decade, with complete success, to convince the national government that it should substitute a protective tariff for free trade and at the same time should insure all German workmen against accident, illness, and old age.

The "historical school" of political economy was

[1] Among the more important writings of Wagner were *Beiträge zur Lehre von den Banken* (1857), *System der deutschen Zettelbankgesetzgebung* (1870-1873), "Grundlegung" and "Finanzwissenschaft" in *Lehrbuch der politischen Ökonomie* (1876), and *Agrar- und Industrie-Staat* (1902). Another very famous member of the "historical school" in Germany was Gustav Schmoller (1838-1917), professor successively at Halle, at Strasbourg, and, after 1882, at Berlin, who turned disdainfully away from economic theory and devoted his whole enormous energy to practical problems, sociological studies, and historical research. Among other Germans who are ordinarily counted among the "historical school" were Brentano, Held, Bucher, Sombart, and Schäffle. Outside of Germany, the historical national approach to economics was made during the second half of the nineteenth century by several English scholars, including Toynbee, Cunningham, and Ashley, and by significant scholars in many other countries.

strongest in Germany but it gained influential disciples and imitators in other countries. It was actuated by nationalist, as well as historical, motives and interests, and everywhere it served to emphasize the nationalist character of economic development. Its programme, sometimes contemptuously referred to as "socialism of the chair" or "parlor socialism," was essentially nationalist and extraordinarily influential at the close of the nineteenth century and at the beginning of the twentieth. It incorporated the major lessons of such economic nationalists as Wagner and Roscher, Rodbertus and List, Kingsley and Villeneuve-Bargemont, and even a Fichte. It represented the economic phase of that transition which was going on in "progressive" countries from liberal, Jacobin, or traditionalist nationalism into the contemporary nationalism which is integral.

[§ 5]

The rise of economic nationalism was an impressive fact in the history of industrialized nations of Europe and America during the last two decades of the nineteenth century. It was not an "inevitable" result of continuous improvement of the industrial arts, or of overwhelming influence of economic speculation on the part of a succession of scholars from Fichte to Wagner. The activity of the "historical school" and the gradual transformation of economic liberalism and Marxian socialism in a patriotic direction expressed rather than caused the rise of economic nationalism, and the Industrial Revolution merely rendered it possible. The Industrial Revolution was inherently neither nationalist nor anti-nationalist; and in the earlier part of the nineteenth century the expounders of cosmopolitan economics greatly outnumbered the expounders of national economics. What finally gave the practical victory to the latter was that their doctrines fitted in more perfectly with the rising popular nationalism—Jacobin, liberal, or traditionalist—which, quite apart from economic and industrial considerations, scholars were championing, statesmen were practicing, and schools and journals and armies and societies were teaching.

It is a noteworthy fact that the nationalism engendered in Germany during the Napoleonic era and enormously developed during the wars of national unification from 1864 to 1871 was much more sentimental than economic. In so far as German nationalists were concerned with economics, most of them, prior to 1871, were economic liberals who associated cosmopolitan economics with liberal nationalism. Bismarck himself was a vigorous nationalist of the traditionalist sort, but he was not a professional economist or greatly interested in the new industry, and he was inclined to be bored by discussion of economic questions. As minister-president of Prussia during the wars of national unification and as chancellor of the Empire during the first years of its existence, he at first accepted with little question the widely preached doctrines of the classical economists and followed economic and fiscal policies which were distinctly liberal. But the wars of national unification and the glorious success which attended them served to exaggerate the sentiment of nationalism in Germany and to set a large number of Germans to thinking that the nation should be independent of the rest of the world not only politically but also economically. Consequently the German theorists of economic nationalism who hitherto had been in the minority now speedily became the majority, and a rapidly growing number of Germans turned to them for counsel and guidance.

In this number was Bismarck himself. By 1880 his nationalism had carried him from conservative politics into conservative economics. And it is another noteworthy fact that he, with thousands of fellow German nationalists, embarked upon a thoroughgoing policy of economic nationalism after the achievement of national political unity and at the very time when industrial development was going forward in Germany by leaps and bounds and when, if ever, the Industrial Revolution gave fairest promise of promoting a liberal internationalism if not an idealistic cosmopolitanism.

In December 1878 Bismarck avowed publicly his faith in tariff protectionism as a national German policy. It was in conformity with old German traditions of state-benevolence. It would provide revenue for the new national government and relieve it of undignified dependence on special contributions from its constituent parts. It would protect "infant" industries, safeguard agriculture, and raise the standard of living of the masses. Thereby it would promote the well-being of all the principal classes—manufacturers, farmers, and workingmen,—increase the taxable wealth of the nation, heighten the number and morale of the military force of the nation, and, altogether, render the nation more nearly self-sufficient both for war and for peace, and therefore stronger at home and more respected abroad. In 1879

Bismarck's faith was sealed by act of a majority of the democratically elected representatives of the nation in Reichstag assembled, and a German protective tariff became law. Thereafter, the tariff was frequently revised, but the revisions were almost always "upward"—higher in 1885, still higher in 1887, and to unprecedented heights in 1902. Apparently, the faster that industries ceased to be "infant" and grew up, the more insistent became the nationalist demand that their "protection" be increased; the greater the protection accorded to industry, the louder sounded the demand for corresponding "farm relief."

In the meantime, in February 1879, Bismarck had his titular master, the Emperor William I, solemnly declare in the annual "speech from the throne" that "there must be a positive advancement of the welfare of the working classes by means of national legislation." In 1881, "in order to realize this object," Bismarck informed the Reichstag through the mouth of the Emperor, that "a bill for the national insurance of workmen against industrial accidents will first be laid before you, after which a supplementary measure will be submitted providing for a national organization of sickness insurance. But likewise those who are disabled in consequence of old age or invalidity possess a well-founded claim to a more ample relief on the part of the national state than they have hitherto enjoyed. To find the proper ways and means for making such provision," the national statesman added, "is a difficult task, yet it is one of the highest obligations of every community based, like ours, on Christianity and nationalism." "Proper ways and means" were speedily found, and during the 1880's was elaborated a whole system of national workers' insurance, which, in conjunction with the tariff and with factory legislation and bounties to commercial enterprise and the "nationalization" of railways, telegraphs, and telephones, swept Germany from economic laisser-faire into economic nationalism.

Among the industrialized states of Europe and America, Germany was only a pioneer in the pursuit of economic nationalism. Others quickly followed. In the three decades between 1880 and 1910 almost every such national state adopted tariff protectionism and labor legislation and other policies calculated to steer industrial development within national channels. England, alone among the Great Powers, clung to free trade, but she did so less from faith in its universal desirability than from conviction that it was temporarily useful to her peculiar national interests; and in other respects England vied with nations on the Continent in endeavoring to prove to citizens that they owed their material blessings not so much to economic as to national law. Good British patriots like Austen Chamberlain, David Lloyd George, and Ramsay MacDonald might profess different forms of nationalism, labelled respectively traditionalist, liberal, and socialist, and they might differ among themselves on innumerable matters of detail, but they were quite agreed that economic interests of Englishmen were peculiar national interests and must be protected and promoted by the national government. From the liberalism of John Bright to that of David Lloyd George was a far cry. The Industrial Revolution had progressed meanwhile, and so had economic nationalism and so had economic rivalry among industrialized nations.

Then, too, with the progress of the Industrial Revolution and the rise of economic nationalism, the most "progressive" nations received a new impetus to imperialism. Originally, nationalism had been the antithesis of imperialism, and most kinds of nationalists had usually sympathized with efforts of "oppressed" and "backward" peoples to gain independence at the expense of European empires and colonial dominions. Now, particularly after 1880, there was a strong reaction.

By this time, in industrialed countries, there was need of a greatly augmented supply of raw materials and foodstuffs from "backward" areas, and under the developing system of economic nationalism it began to be argued that such a supply could be obtained more cheaply and would be more stable if a given "progressive" nation owned or controlled a large extent of "backward" lands.

Again, there was need of larger markets for surplus manufactures, and as "progressive" nations put up tariff barriers against each other they increasingly sought compensatory markets in "backward" countries, and it was soon argued that sales could be speeded up if the backward countries were "colonies" or "protectorates." Unfavorable tariffs could be gotten rid of, and requisite internal peace and trade-prestige could be afforded by friendly officials of one's own nationality better than by natives.

Furthermore, there was a growing tendency to export surplus capital from "progressive" countries and to invest it in "backward" countries where rates of interest were higher than at home. Considerable risk was involved in such investment, and, to diminish the risk, the investors, true to the principles of economic nationalism, found it convenient to appeal to their respective national governments for protection of their property abroad and sometimes for the outright political annexation of regions in which they had valuable investments.

Besides, "progressive" nations toward the close of the nineteenth century, thanks to the improved means of warfare and communication which the Industrial Revolution placed at their disposal, were in a vastly better position than nations had been in at any earlier period to conquer and administer distant "backward" areas. In other words, the Industrial Revolution made it natural and relatively easy for national states of Europe and America to embark upon a new imperialism, and many of their leading citizens began to urge them thereto.

The advocates of nationalist imperialism did not confine their arguments to the strictly economic domain. They talked about the inevitability, the blind necessity, of the process; some of them labelled it "manifest destiny." They talked, too, about the problem of "surplus population" at home, maintaining that some of the "surplus" could be supported if the industry of the mother-country were enlarged and buttressed by colonial dominion, and that the rest of the "surplus" could then emigrate, not to foreign countries, but to colonies wherein they would retain their national language, national traditions, and national customs. They talked, also, about the "higher civilization," the solemn duty incumbent upon a civilized nation to "clean up" a "backward" country and prepare it eventually though perhaps remotely for full participation in the blessings of nationalism, to Christianize it, to provide it with schools, sanitation, order, and security. The duty was described in prose as "trusteeship" and in poetry as "the white man's burden."

In Great Britain, in Germany, in France, in Italy, in the United States, in Japan, and even in Spain and Belgium, nationalists conducted, especially after 1880, a good deal of colonial and imperialist propaganda by means of societies, books, lectures, and journals. The nature of the propaganda may be illustrated by a passage from a book by Dr. Karl Peters, a German imperialist nationalist, who was presenting a picture of the blessings which would accrue from the Fatherland's exploitation of German East Africa: "How different will the protectorate then appear! Where today are vast expanses of wilderness, there will then be a thriving economic life.... On the healthful heights a German population will dwell as standard-bearers of German institutions and culture in the Dark Continent. In the lower regions, which today are inhabited only in spots, there will then be a dense, black population, safe and happy under the protection of our Flag and under the sign of the Cross, enjoying the fruits of their own labor. Here also [among the blacks] the German tongue will predominate. And through all its ports German East Africa will conduct a lively exchange of commodities with the Fatherland. Before us stand soberly and solidly the great opportunities which German East Africa offers, and they demand the deliberate energy of our whole nation. In East Africa is an opportunity to wrest from niggardly nature an immense new field for human creative enterprise, and this can be achieved only by earnest and honest work on the part of Germany. The reward which offers is great and worthy of a forward-looking, progressive nation. If Germany succeeds, she will enrich herself ideally and materially, and at the same time she will win the finest triumph which the genius of history can bestow on the civilizing nations of Earth: the triumph of having pushed forward a conservative and backward race and drawn it into the living stream of human development. Only by such activity can the German nationality grasp the supreme palm which Providence offers to a nation's ambition—the palm of impressing its own stamp upon large portions of the Earth's surface and of coöperating in the absolute ennoblement of the human race. A nation which thus places itself voluntarily in the service of the highest tasks which world-history records, will experience in its own soul something of the proud satisfaction which the Earth Spirit in Faust expresses in the beautiful lines:

"'Thus toiling at the whirring loom of Time
I weave the living garment of divinity.'"[1]

Among statesmen, Benjamin Disraeli during his ministry from 1874 to 1880 had already done a good deal to foster the interest of British nationalists in the new imperialism and to acquire new additions to the British colonial empire. Jules Ferry did the same for France, and Bismarck for Germany, in the 1880's. Crispi assumed the official leadership of the movement in Italy, and McKinley and Roosevelt in the United States, in the 1890's and early 1900's. These dates are only those of the factual beginnings of the new nationalist imperialism. No endings are as yet

[1] Karl Peters, *Das Deutsch-Ostafrikanische Schutzgebiet* (1895), p. 418.

dated, except of the German colonial empire, in 1918, and in this case the losses of Germany only meant so many gains for other "progressive" nations in dominion over "backward" lands and peoples.

The new imperialism has doubtless had considerable salutary effect on so-called "backward" peoples, but its ultimate effects on the "progressive" nations which have pursued it would appear to be more dubious. From an economic standpoint it is extremely doubtful whether colonies have actually enriched their mother-countries to any such extent as original advocates of the new imperialism predicted, while on the other hand it is certain that mother-countries have spent vast sums of money on the subjugation, administration, and defense of colonies, and it is reasonably certain that whatever profits have been obtained from colonies have gone chiefly into the pockets of particular individuals or classes in the mother-countries.

From a less strictly economic standpoint, it seems obvious that the new imperialism, in conjunction with other aspects of economic nationalism, has tended to promote among imperialist nations a feeling of superiority and scorn in respect of "backward" peoples, a boastful pride in their own forceful expansion and dominion, and a bumptiousness about their own size and strength. It seems equally obvious that this tendency has been accompanied by increasingly bitter rivalries among the Great Powers and by wars or threats of war of ever greater magnitude between them. The World War is the latest, but presumably not the last, of the great debit charges against nationalist imperialism.

ECONOMIC FACTORS IN NATIONALISM

"The steady increase of national power—for a nation declines when it loses military might": such is the prime object of integral nationalism as defined by Charles Maurras. And to just such an object has the new imperialism palpably contributed. Each national state which would possess colonies must employ military might to acquire, rule, and defend them, and the successful employment of military might for any or all of these purposes, as well as for the earlier purpose of national independence and unity, has come to be regarded as marking an increase of a nation's power and therefore as deserving of the highest praise by the nationalist citizenry. The more imperialist a nation becomes or feels, the more it commits itself to integral nationalism.

Indeed, despite the international and cosmopolitan potentialities of the Industrial Revolution, contemporary economic developments, including tariffs, socialistic experiments, and imperialism, are actually being made to serve narrowly national ends and to fortify integral nationalism. This is at least true of nations which are far advanced in industrialization, that is to say, of most nations of Europe and of the United States and Japan. Of nations which are less advanced and therefore "backward," it is less true, but these are tending to adopt a nationalism of their own as defense against "exploitation" by foreigners and are thus preparing themselves for a régime of economic nationalism when they too shall become industrialized. With the nations of Asia and Africa in the future, as with those of Europe and America today, economic nationalism is likely to prove a powerful aid to integral nationalism.

CHAPTER VIII

CONCLUSION: SOME QUESTIONS CONCERNING NATIONALISM

[§ 1]

IT IS unquestionable that nationalism has been a prime characteristic of modern civilization. Since the eighteenth century the idea that each nationality should cherish its distinctive language and culture and should constitute an independent polity has been advanced by intellectual and political leaders in one country after another and has been accepted and acted upon by the masses of mankind.

The merest tyro in history, or the newspaper-reader who is content with headlines, must know that nationalism is not just a theory which at some future day may or may not be put into practice but that it is a driving force in the world today. From elementary textbooks can be gathered the outlines of the swift story of how nationalism within a century and a half has consolidated France, unified Italy and Germany, and restored political independence to Poland, Finland, Norway, Czechoslovakia, Greece, and the Balkan states, whilst breaking up the Ottoman Empire, the Austrian Empire, the Russian Empire. From a sketchy perusal of newspapers can be gleaned the information that nationalism is stirring Hindus and Chinese and Turks and Filipinos and the most outlandish peoples and that it is threatening the security of overseas possessions of the great imperial Powers of Europe and America.

CONCLUSION

From the slightest observation of the behavior of one's fellows can be obtained evidence that nationalism exerts direct influence on their lives.

For a century and a half major improvements in technology, in the industrial arts, and in material comfort, as well as most developments in the realms of intellect and æsthetics, have been yoked to the service of nationalism. The Industrial Revolution, despite its cosmopolitan potentialities, has been largely nationalized in actual fact. Modern scholarship, despite its scientific claims and its ubiquitous nature, has been preponderantly enlisted in support of nationalism. Philosophies which in origin were not expressly nationalist and were sometimes definitely intended to be anti-nationalist, philosophies such as Christianity, Liberalism, Marxism, and the systems of Hegel, Comte, and Nietzsche, have been copiously drawn upon and frequently distorted for nationalist purposes. The plastic arts, music, and belles-lettres, despite their universal appeal, have become increasingly the product or the pride of national patriots. So much is nationalism a commonplace in the modes of thought and action of the civilized populations of the contemporary world that most men take nationalism for granted. Without serious reflection they imagine it to be the most natural thing in the universe and assume that it must always have existed.

What has given such a vogue to nationalism in recent times? That is the first major question to be raised concerning this most vital phenomenon.

It can hardly be possible that the contemporary vogue of nationalism is attributable to any or all of the philosophers whom we have reviewed in this volume: Bolingbroke, Rousseau, or Herder; Barère or Carnot; Burke, Bonald, or Schlegel; Bentham, Guizot, Welcker, or Mazzini; Barrès, Maurras, or Mussolini; Fichte or List. The importance of these nationalist theorizers, like that of any philosopher, resides in the fact that, having been themselves the result of the phenomenon they discuss rather than its cause, they have formulated and clearly expressed what has been vaguely in the minds of many men.

There are philosophers, of course, who do not express what is in the minds of large numbers of their contemporaries, philosophers who are "behind the times" or "ahead of their time," as the phrases go, and whose formulations pass unnoticed and unheeded by their own generation and sometimes by subsequent generations. The very fact that the nationalist writers whom we have noticed in the preceding chapters have been widely read in their day and thereafter is proof that they were dealing with ideas which in modern times have been continuously popular. To be sure, their "systems" have provided convenient slogans and catchwords for nationalist agitators and have served to crystallize nationalist thinking in particular ways, and thus they have doubtless contributed somewhat to the vogue of nationalism.

But the philosophers of nationalism did not make its vogue. The vogue was there when they appeared on the scene. They merely expressed and gave some emphasis and guidance to it. For the historian they are extremely useful in that they afford him vivid illustrations of current tendencies in nationalist thought. Let us recognize fully, however, the outstanding limitation to their use-

CONCLUSION

fulness. They do not furnish us with any answer to the basic question as to why the masses for a century and a half have acted as if they were influenced by nationalist philosophers more than by others.

The answer to the question must be sought, then, not so much in the philosophers themselves or in their "systems," as in underlying tendencies of our modern age which have given rise to nationalism among the masses as well as among a group of theorizers. This is another way of saying that the question cannot be definitively answered. For there is not likely to be any consensus of opinion even among scholars as to what precisely these "underlying tendencies" are or as to what relationship they bear to one another. All that is really worth our while in the dubious circumstances is to discuss briefly and with a large measure of agnosticism some of the explanations which have been put forth to account for the modern and contemporary vogue of nationalism.

It has been contended that the masses of mankind are instinctively nationalist, that they have always had a latent nationalism which in many instances was forced under cover by ambitious empire-builders but which in every instance was strong enough sooner or later to come into the open and to make statesmen and scholars do its bidding. Just such mass-nationalism has been displayed in modern times, it is contended, as was displayed by various peoples in earlier periods of human history.[1]

[1] Something of this contention was voiced by my friend, Mr. Simeon Strunsky, in a penetrating review which he published of my *Essays on Nationalism* in the *New York Times*. In the review he chided me gently and with his customary sweet reasonableness for placing too much emphasis on the propaganda of nationalism by intellectuals; in his opinion, the masses were nationalist before they were propagandized.

This contention, at least in its extreme form, is, I believe, fallacious. Human beings are social animals and do appear to be equipped with traits which render it possible and necessary for them to live loyally in groups, but the groups do not have to be nationalities. During much the longest periods of recorded history the groups to which individuals have been predominantly loyal have been tribes, clans, cities, provinces, manors, guilds, or polyglot empires. Nationalism is certainly but one expression of human instinct and not a bit more natural or more "latent" than tribalism, clannishness, urbanism, or imperialism. Yet it is nationalism, far more than any other expression of human gregariousness, which has come to the fore in modern times.

It is true that historical records are strewn from earliest times with traces of the existence in greater or less degree of a consciousness of nationality, of a feeling on the part of people who speak a common language that they are different from, and usually superior to, peoples who speak other languages. It is also true that we have historical evidence of the teaching and practicing of genuine nationalism among some peoples at a relatively ancient date, for example among Hebrews, Armenians, and Japanese. Yet such evidence and such records come to us from "intellectuals," and we cannot be quite sure that the "national consciousness" or the "nationalism" therein described was shared by the multitude of peasants and slaves. We can be sure that prior to the eighteenth century A. D. it was not the general rule for civilized nationalities to strive zealously and successfully for political unity and independence, whereas it has been the general rule in the last

CONCLUSION

century and a half. Universal mass-nationalism of this kind, at any rate, has no counterpart in earlier eras; it is peculiar to modern times.

Nor is it at all certain that the "masses" in any country have been directly responsible for the rise of modern nationalism. The movement appears to have gotten under way first among the "intellectual" classes and to have received decisive impetus from the support of the middle classes. In England, where physical environment and political and religious circumstances were peculiarly favorable, a strong national consciousness developed considerably before the eighteenth century, and it may be that English nationalism did spring more or less spontaneously out of mass feeling and sentiment. Even here, the matter is debatable, though it is not within the scope of the present work to indicate the pros and cons in any detail.

Outside of England, however, there can be little question that in the first half of the eighteenth century the masses of Europe, as well as of Asia and America, whilst possessing some consciousness of nationality, thought of themselves chiefly as belonging to a province or a town or an empire, rather than to a national state, and made no serious or effective protest against being transferred from one political domain to another, and that their later thought and action as nationalities were taught them by the intellectual and middle classes of their respective countries.

The inhabitants of France, shortly before the Revolution of 1789, were not a closely knit nationality; they were a congeries of Gascons, Provençals, Artesians, Bretons, Normans, Alsatians, *etc.*, whom their common king addressed as "my peoples"; and they learned to be "the French people" ("la nation française") from middle-class instructors who had already outgrown the cramping bonds of provincial loyalty and who utilized the Revolution as a popular and even compulsory training school in French nationalism. The inhabitants of Germany and those of Italy had fairly to be galvanized into nationalist activity by purposeful currents of propaganda which were set in motion by groups of scholars, publicists, poets, orators, and preachers, chiefly of the middle class. Palacky, the great historian and nationalist of Bohemia, tells us that if the ceiling of the room in which he and a handful of his friends were dining one night had collapsed, the Czech nationalist movement would have been destroyed; the movement was still of a small group and had not yet captured the masses. Equally illuminating tales might be told of the beginnings of nationalism in many countries of eastern and central Europe.

Of course, the speed with which nationalist propaganda within the last century has produced popular effects suggests not only that the seed was good but also that it fell on fertile ground, that it could take root because many persons already had a basic consciousness of nationality. But it is generally true that the masses themselves did not actually grow nationalist fruits and flowers until winds of propaganda had blown upon them seeds of nationalism from particular individuals and classes. It may be pertinent to add that in some cases the nationalism now evinced by the masses bears much the same resemblance to the nationalism of original propagandists that the oak bears to the acorn.

CONCLUSION

It is part of our hypothesis, therefore, that neither the "masses" nor a few philosophers have invented or created modern nationalism. Philosophers, by fashioning and expressing it as doctrine, may have contributed indirectly to its vogue; the "masses," by accepting and acting on it, have undoubtedly contributed directly to its vogue. On the other hand, it is part of our hypothesis that the "first modern nationalists," those whose ideas and attitudes and activities have been rationalized by our philosophers and been imitated by the masses, have been, in the main, men of brains and some means, belonging most often to the middle class. These are the authors and the propagandists of modern nationalism. These have provided the inspiration of nationalist theorizers and the patterns for whole nationalities.

But what has given the great vogue to nationalism? We have pushed the question back a bit, but we have not really answered it. We have explained that the masses have accepted nationalism and therefore have given direct, immediate vogue to it, perhaps because a rising consciousness of nationality specially prepared them, and almost certainly because the teaching and example of influential fellow citizens (particularly of the middle class) bade them so to do. But what has given these influential citizens the impulse to start the vogue, to set the fashions in nationalism? "Certain underlying tendencies," we have ignorantly guessed. Is one of them an instinctive nationalism? We have shown ourselves very skeptical about this suggestion. If nationalism is not "instinctive" with the masses, it can hardly be "instinctive" with the classes; "instinct," by definition, is human, *semper et ubique*.

With the advent of the "economic interpretation of history," it has been urged in some quarters that modern economic development is the "underlying tendency" most basic to the vogue of modern nationalism. The economic argument has been advanced in two different ways. On the one hand, it has been argued by extreme Marxians that while economic developments and the accompanying conflict between capitalists and proletarians must eventuate finally in the triumph of the latter and the establishment of a real brotherhood among nations, nationalism in existing bourgeois society has been, like religion, a kind of soothing syrup which capitalists have administered to the masses in order to divert them from the class conflict. On the other hand, it has been maintained by more moderate disciples of economic determinism that as economic developments have transformed industry from a local to a national basis, so political loyalty has inevitably changed from localism to nationalism, with the added implications in most cases that particular classes now find nationalism to be financially profitable but that in time, when they find it less profitable, it will gradually be supplanted by internationalism. With these contentions we have already dealt, at least indirectly, in the chapter on "Economic Factors in Nationalism." Here it may suffice to reiterate our agnosticism in a few sentences.

Economic developments of the last century and a half may be viewed as naturally making either for or against nationalism. Actually, as we have seen, they have made for nationalism, and for more and more intense nation-

CONCLUSION

alism. This, however, does not necessarily mean that they have "caused" nationalism or are chiefly explanatory of its vogue. It may mean, and in our opinion it probably does mean, that other underlying tendencies have been so strongly nationalist that even economic developments have been pressed into the service of nationalism. We do know that such originally non-nationalist doctrines as economic liberalism and Marxian socialism have been altered in practice until they have come to partake of nationalist character. Certain individuals and classes undoubtedly have profited financially from nationalism, and probably they will continue indefinitely to profit from it. But from evidence now available to us in Russia it seems plausible to imagine that, in measure as nations become proletarian, all citizens will expect to profit from nationalism, and that therefore nationalism will be further intensified. If nationalism is a soothing-syrup, then its efficacy depends less on a theory that capitalists administer it than on the fact that the masses now cry for it.

Besides, exponents of the economic interpretation of nationalism would do well to take a long-range view of history and especially to ponder an interesting contrast between "results" of economic development at the beginning of the Christian era and "results" of economic development in our age. At the earlier time a remarkable expansion of commerce, acceleration of industry, and development of capitalism were attended by the swift expansion of tribal states and city-states of diverse nationalities into a multi-lingual cosmopolitan state known as the Roman Empire; localism was transformed into imperialism; nationalism, if existent at all, was weak. In modern times the vastly greater and more revolutionary growth of industry, commerce, and capital has been accompanied by the welding of rural communities and city-states and simultaneously by the splitting of empires for the common purpose of forming national states; nationalism, supplanting imperialism as well as localism, is strong and triumphant. The contrast certainly suggests that economic development of itself does not create nationalism or cosmopolitanism, but that it merely speeds up a political or intellectual tendency which for other reasons is under way.

It may be, as some assert, that the rise of nationalism is closely associated with the underlying modern tendency toward democracy—political and social. As common people become more literate and more ambitious, they increasingly aspire to have some say in their government and in the promotion of what they think are their interests. As they become more democratically inclined, they discover that they can best and most conveniently operate the necessary machinery of democracy within linguistic frontiers, that is, within nationalities. Hence literacy and democratic desire would logically make for nationalism. True, an humanitarian nationalist like Bolingbroke was a Tory aristocrat and monarchist rather than a democrat, and traditional nationalists like Burke, Bonald, and Schlegel were ostensibly actuated by hatred of democracy. Yet none of these was an absolutist in politics, and all of them, in making out cases for the participation of particular classes in government, may have been responding to democratic stimuli about them. At any rate the middle

CONCLUSION

classes which took the lead in nationalist propaganda took the lead also in democratic agitation. Jacobin nationalism was quite democratic, and the progress of liberal nationalism parallelled the rise of middle-class government and its transformation into national political democracy. Latterly, it should be noted, there has been in very nationalist countries, and in harmony with the doctrine of integral nationalism, a marked reaction against political democracy; but types of social democracy are now stressed as never before in Fascist Italy and Bolshevist Russia, and in last analysis the national "dictators" of the present day rest their authority on the popular will and on their ability to cater to popular desires.

It may be, too, that the rise of nationalism is related to an underlying religious tendency of modern times. It may well be that during and since the eighteenth century the rise of skepticism concerning historic supernatural religion, especially among the intellectual and middle classes, has created an unnatural void for religious emotion and worship, a void which it has seemed preferable to supply with near-by nationalist gods and fervent nationalist cults rather than with far-off cosmopolitan deities and vague humanitarianism. At any rate, modern nationalism assumed from the outset a religious complexion. Jacobin nationalism was essentially religious. Liberal nationalism and traditional nationalism were hardly less so. Integral nationalism has surpassed all its predecessors in rites and ceremonies, in mysticism and devotion, and likewise in intolerance.

Still another "underlying tendency" which may (and, in our opinion, does most plausibly) explain the vogue of nationalism in modern times is the growth of a belief that the state, particularly the national state, can and should promote human progress. The eighteenth century, when systematic nationalist doctrines were first formulated, was a century of eager faith in the "progress" and perfectibility of man and of human society. It was a century, too, of sharp reaction against debates and wars over religious dogmas and of deep yearning to substitute for them a friendly rivalry in good works. It was a century, moreover, of criticism—not merely destructive criticism of existing institutions and practices, but constructive criticism to the end that institutions might be reorganized and practices reformed so as to foster good works and so as to perfect humanity. Such was the set of minds among the generality of intellectuals and middle-class persons in the eighteenth century. They looked for fruition of their ideas not in the supernatural realm but in the realm of human reason and human effort, and hence they turned away from the church and toward the state. It was the state—their respective states—which they would reorganize and reform and which thereupon would assure "progress" to them and their fellows. It did not seem necessary to hypothesize a world-state or a world-confederation of states. Let people belong to the state to which they wish to belong; all such states will naturally vie with one another in the performance of good and enlightened deeds; and just as a member of any church may go to the heaven beyond the skies, so every man by membership in an enlightened national state will share in the heaven on Earth.

CONCLUSION

In this altruistic environment, it was probably natural that leading intellectuals and many a middle-class "friend of the people" should evince nationalism. Some propounded it as doctrine; and the highly altruistic, impressively humanitarian notes of early nationalist philosophers, whether Bolingbroke or Herder, Bentham or Bonald, Burke or Carnot, could hardly fail to strike responsive chords in the breasts of a multitude of eighteenth-century men. The first formal nationalism represented divergent political tendencies—the aristocratic, the democratic, and the non-political, merely cultural—but it constituted a "school" in that it was wholly and vociferously humanitarian. One of its offshoots, Jacobin nationalism, inspired the French Revolution in the name of "the rights of man." Another, traditional nationalism, combatted the Revolution for its outrages against humanity. A third offshoot, liberal nationalism, preserved and handed on to the nineteenth century the spirit of altruism in the form of a tender regard for individual liberty and international peace as well as for the emancipation of "enslaved" peoples. To one or another of these types of nationalism the masses were drawn by altruistic propaganda; and once attached, they proved that they could be as good nationalists as any of the classes. For the masses can afford to be more altruistic than the classes, and perhaps they better understand that man does not live by bread alone.

Of late there has been some disillusionment. An intellectual gulf separates the twentieth century from the eighteenth. Our generation has lost faith in the naturalness and assured continuity of "progress" and has become skeptical of the perfectibility of mankind in this world;

it has denied the validity of human reason and at the same time has begun to criticize the altruism of its predecessors. Yet the masses, and the classes too, remain incorrigibly altruistic. If they are less altruistic about other nations and "backward" peoples, they are more anxious about the welfare of their fellows in their own nationality. If they are less certain of their own ability to perform good works, they are more determined that good works shall be performed by the state, even under a dictatorship. If they are less inclined to reason about the welfare of their national state, they are more willing to sacrifice their lives for it. If they are less pacific and more threatening in their relations with other nations, it is not because they have ceased to look upon international peace as the ultimate goal but because they perceive in militarism and war the most realistic means of arriving at the goal. All this is another way of saying that integral nationalism is now on the increase throughout the world and that in back of it, accounting, we suggest for its vogue, is a widespread popular hope that good may come to the world and its inhabitants.

What has given great vogue to nationalism in modern times? We really do not know. It is a pity that we do not know, for if we did, we could probably make some fairly accurate guess as to the future of nationalism. As it is, we have to content ourselves with hypotheses and suggestions. Of these the most plausible would appear to be the underlying tendency in modern times to regard the national state as the medium through which civilization is best assured and advanced.

CONCLUSION
[§ 2]

Obviously there has been an evolution of modern nationalism both doctrinally and practically. It has not proceeded simultaneously and at equal speed in all parts of the world, but we can clearly discern several stages of it in countries which have been nationalist the longest, and we can guess, from observation of the existing early stage of it in more "backward" countries, the other stages through which it is likely to pass there. Obviously, too, the evolution everywhere has been in the direction of a more and more intense nationalism, and of a nationalism which involves bigger wars or at any rate greater preparedness for war.

This is not wholly in conflict with our hypothesis that altruistic longing for human peace and betterment is the explanation of the modern vogue of nationalism. That there has been enormous betterment of humanity within the last century and a half, especially in material respects, in promotion of physical health, and in provision of creature comforts, admits of no doubt. That much of this betterment has been effected by means of national states, having a greater and closer interest in their citizens than any earlier polity possessed, admits of little doubt. Nationalism in one form or another has almost certainly conferred innumerable blessings on many peoples. Greeks and Poles, for example, must be much better off as citizens of autonomous nations than as subjects of emperors and governing classes differing from them in language, religion, and traditions. And "backward" nations, by becoming nationalist, have increased their own self-respect and freed themselves from imperialist exploitation at home and abroad. Civilization has surely been enriched, as Herder foretold, by the bountiful products of variegated national cultures.[1]

International peace, however, is not one of the blessings which nationalism has conferred upon the world. Humanitarian nationalists of the eighteenth century were sure that if each people cherished its own culture and attended to its own affairs, humanity as a whole would benefit and the reign of peace and reason would speedily begin throughout the world. They were optimists. But the French Revolution with its reign of terror and its sanguinary wars followed forthwith.

Jacobin nationalists at the end of the eighteenth century were certain that if every nation became nationalist and democratic like the French, the glorious principles of liberty, equality, and fraternity would be triumphant throughout the world and international peace would be solidly established. They, too, were optimists. But the devastating, protracted, Napoleonic wars ensued.

Liberal nationalists of the first half of the nineteenth century were convinced that if every "oppressed" nationality was free and possessed its own national language, educational system, militia, and press, it would lie down lamb-like with others of the human flock in the broad green pastures of the world. They, also, were optimists. But a frightful series of wars of national unification quickly succeeded; and events soon proved that

[1] It seems hardly necessary further to labor the advantages of nationalism. They are so obvious, and they are so generally admitted. I have discussed "Nationalism, Curse or Blessing," with special reference to the latter, in my *Essays on Nationalism*.

CONCLUSION

when "oppressed" nationalities actually became free, they transformed themselves from lambs into lions and roared at one another and in the twentieth century fought throughout the whole world the most destructive war in human history.

Integral nationalists of our age are also optimists—in their fashion. They boast that they will maintain and enforce peace by national might. But, inasmuch as "peace" in their philosophy must be that condition of affairs in which each Power helps itself to whatever it wants, still more and worse wars are likely to supervene.

It would seem, in brief, that international rivalries and wars have become progressively more frequent, more general, and more destructive, in measure as nationalism has evolved from its humanitarian prototype, through Jacobin, traditionalist, and liberal phases, into its contemporary integral form. This, we admit, is not a cheerful thought, or one that will give much comfort to optimistic pacifists. Of course, persons who insist on being optimistic or those who like to be reassured that things are going well—even providentially—can reflect that the evolution of nationalism and the intensification of war may be merely parallel developments without any relationship of cause and effect and that therefore right-minded men may check or divert war without worrying about the entirely distinct evolution of nationalism. At the risk of disturbing the peace of mind of such persons, however, we feel obliged to point out that if they base their optimism on that reflection, they are doing precisely what all earlier nationalists did, and are but giving added point to a question of the first magnitude which we here propose: Is there something inevitable in the evolution of nationalism which advances its devotees ever faster toward war while they continue to talk about peace?

The question admits of no final answer, but it invites speculation which may be illuminating. In the first place, let us consider the evolution of nationalism in "progressive" countries, that is, in countries which for a relatively long period have had an acute consciousness of nationality and have been largely industrialized, say among the peoples of western and central Europe and the United States. Here the evolution is fairly clear and may be represented, in certain respects, as describing an imperfect circle.

We start with a state not strictly national, ruled despotically and inefficiently, pursuing mercantilist policies, and constantly prepared for war and frequently engaging in it. We start also with an altruistic impulse on the part of influential commoners and intellectuals in that state to reform it and to make the country, culturally and materially, a happier abode for its inhabitants and a richer contributor to the world's peace and civilization. Then humanitarian nationalism arises. Presently, some of its disciples stress the rôle which the mass of the nation can play in bringing about the new world order which humanitarian nationalism has envisaged, and Jacobin nationalism emerges. Others emphasize the part of the classes, and traditional nationalism appears. Still others urge the importance of individuals, and liberal nationalism takes form.

Almost immediately the Jacobins, backed usually by liberals, proceed to revolutionize a particular state, to

CONCLUSION

reverse many of its practices and traditions, to orient it toward national democracy, and to propagate the new principles among the citizens by means of national schools, armies, societies, and journals. At which the traditionalists take fright and, in conjunction with individuals and groups whom the new order threatens to dispossess, seek to combat the Jacobins. Civil war and international war ensue. Jacobins, gaining the upper hand in one country, become crusaders in behalf of a democratic world. Traditionalists, securing the lead in another country, become crusaders in behalf of an aristocratic world. By and by, a compromise is effected: liberal nationalism comes to the fore, combining a romantic regard for national tradition with a practical use of the agencies and many of the tendencies of Jacobin nationalism.

We have now reached the point where liberal nationalism is in the ascendant: some peoples have free national states and others yearn for them. We have also reached the point where all these peoples are becoming industrialized. There is no tarrying at such a point, however. Peoples who yearn for national independence proceed to acquire it at any costs, even at the expense of deadly wars and sacrifice of liberal principles; and peoples already independent are influenced by their respective agencies of nationalist propaganda to take sides with "oppressed" peoples. The resulting struggles, together with attendant economic developments, give rise among successful peoples to pride in their achievements, to reliance upon force to retain what they have gotten, and to faith in their ability to be both examplars of national self-sufficiency and trustees for "backward" peoples. This process is rationalized as integral nationalism, which brings us back close to the point whence we set out.

We end with states, now emphatically national and tending toward more or less veiled but efficient dictatorships, pursuing mercantilist policies and prepared constantly for war and engaging in it, or threatening to engage in it, frequently and on an ever greater scale.

It seems a long way from Rousseau, Herder, and Mazzini to Maurras, Hitler, and Mussolini, and the route appears to be circuitous. The former preached against the very things which the latter are championing. Yet the latter appear to be a lineal projection of the former. Integral nationalism could hardly be what it is without the pioneering work of humanitarian nationalists, and the nationalism that is exclusive and intolerant has been propagated primarily by popular agencies which were created and fostered by nationalists who were liberal.

In France and Germany it has taken a century and a half to make the circuit from Rousseau and Herder to Maurras and Hitler, and the circuit is not complete, for the nationalism publicly professed in those countries still partakes of liberal as well as of integral character. In Italy it has required slightly less than a century to make the circuit from Mazzini to Mussolini, and here the circuit is relatively more complete. Indeed, if we consider the evolution of nationalism in countries outside of western Europe and the United States, we are struck, especially in eastern Europe, by the accelerated speed with which it has passed from an humanitarian and cultural beginning to an integral and political climax. Poland is resurrected

CONCLUSION

as an act of humanitarian justice and almost at once Poland breathes the breath of integral nationalism. Yugoslavia and Rumania become unified sovereign national states in accordance with the best liberal models and forthwith Yugoslavia and Rumania proceed to behave in the most up-to-date Mussolini-like manner.

In wide areas of the Earth—notably in Asia and Africa —are numerous peoples who hitherto have had relatively little nationalist tradition but who now are showing signs of responding to humanitarian nationalist appeals of intellectuals and middle-class leaders in their midst. Their present position is similar to that of European and American peoples in the eighteenth century or in the middle of the nineteenth. They start with states not strictly national, ruled despotically and inefficiently, and suffering peculiarly from economic exploitation by "progressive" nationalist states. What humanitarian or liberal, what person enamored of modern European usage, can withhold sympathy from these Asiatic and African peoples as they start off on the path of nationalism? But what realist can be sure that that path will not eventually lead in Asia whither it has led in Europe?

If it has taken a century and a half—and many great wars—to redraw the political map of Europe (the smallest of the five continents) along lines of nationality, how long—and how many world-wars—will it take similarly to redraw the map of Asia (the largest of the continents)? If in Europe the acquisition of sovereign national independence has been followed ever faster, particularly in the case of the most recently successful peoples, by the rise of a proud intolerant imperialist nationalism, how soon will the same phenomenon occur in Asia?

It is not strictly true that within a century and a half the political map of Europe has been redrawn along lines of nationality. Great efforts have been expended on the task, and it has been approximately, though not exactly, accomplished as an outcome of the latest Great War. Probably the task can never be exactly accomplished. For there are likely to remain a very large number of "irredentas" in Europe, that is, areas and populations which in the name of nationalism are claimed by two or more national states as rightfully theirs, such as the Polish corridor, the district of Vilna, Upper Silesia, Macedonia, Constantinople, and zones in dispute between Italy and Austria, between Italy and Yugoslavia, between Hungary and Rumania, between Hungary and Yugoslavia, between Italy and Greece. These are so many roots which nourish integral nationalism in the countries concerned. Hungarians and Germans and other "aggrieved" nations are not likely, at the behest of alien pacifists, to diminish propaganda in their schools and armies and journals in behalf of what they deem their national rights and interests; and yet so long as such propaganda continues, it will embitter international relations and threaten war.

If disputed "irredentas" are inevitable and abiding by-products of wars of national unification in Europe, how much the more inevitable and abiding will be those which issue from nationalist wars in Asia? If they fan the flames of integral nationalism in Europe, why not eventually in Asia? Is it not conceivable that pacifists and humanitarians, who now sympathize ardently with nationalist

CONCLUSION

endeavors of China and India to cast off the shackles of European imperialism, would be scandalized, if they could live somewhat beyond the allotted span of life, by a subsequent spectacle of a group of triumphant national states in India and China, inspired with integral nationalism, hating and fighting each other over irredentas, and dominating colonial empires in Europe and America as manifest national destiny or as the colored man's burden? If the future really holds such a spectacle in store, we can be reasonably certain that it will be accompanied by much talk about international peace, about the need of employing force in order to establish and maintain peace.

Is there something inevitable in the evolution of nationalism which advances its devotees ever faster toward war while they continue to talk about peace? There would appear to be something of the sort in the case of Europe since the eighteenth century, and there would seem to be at least a similar beginning in the case of Asia in the twentieth century. Yet we cannot be sure. It must suffice to raise the question, to suggest some of its implications, and to leave it unanswered.

[§ 3]

It may be argued that we are taking too gloomy a view of nationalism and are overemphasizing its bumptious vagaries. Abuses and evils have attended and will continue to attend every spiritual aspiration and every virtue of man. They have attended the past of nationalism, and they will attend the future of nationalism. Let the dead bury the dead; and, the argument runs on, let the distant future take care of itself. What really concerns us is the present and the immediate future, and perhaps nationalism is a current mode which should be adopted by everyone but not taken too seriously by anyone.

One can usually find in the contemporary world, as well as in history, anything that one wishes to find. "Facts" and "proofs," whether of the present or of the past, are not all of one kind. There are enough of various kinds to fortify the convictions of both the optimist and the pessimist, both the pacifist and the militarist, both the person who takes nationalism seriously and the person who disregards it.

The will to believe is always strong in human beings. Faith, as much as hope, springs eternal in the human breast. If we will to believe that nationalism is increasingly dangerous to peace and civilization and that it is almost certain, unless checked, to precipitate an indefinite series of great wars in the future, thousands upon thousands of other men will to believe that a new supernational world-order is now being created in response to an obvious and imperative need for it and that under its aegis the dawn of genuine universal peace is at last in sight.

These other men can certainly offer many evidences for the faith which is within them. Despite tariffs and other artificial devices of economic nationalism, the natural economic interdependence of nations is becoming progressively more apparent and more real. A League of Nations has now been functioning for more than a decade, embracing almost all the national governments of the Earth. The League has helped to keep the peace between Poland and her neighbors, between Italy and Greece, between

CONCLUSION

Yugoslavia and Bulgaria, between Paraguay and Bolivia, between China and Russia. It has accustomed statesmen and diplomats of the several national states to sit down together and to make agreements, on a new friendly basis, concerning international interests in colonies, waterways, labor, and other important matters. It has erected and encouraged the development of an effective World Court for the arbitration and conciliation of international disputes. It has served both as a clearing-house and as a sounding-board for worldwide internationalism.

Alongside of the League of Nations, and supplementing its activities, have been negotiated numerous international agreements of markedly pacific nature and tenor, including the treaties of the Washington conference concerning the Far East and for the limitation of naval armaments, the pact of Locarno for guaranteeing peace between France and Germany, the Kellogg Pact for the general "renunciation of war as an instrument of national policy," the treaties of the London naval conference, *etc.* Statesmen of traditionally hostile nations have even ventured to discuss frankly, without too much heat, such inflammable questions as national security and general disarmament. Notable progress has been made, moreover, toward the liquidation of the World War, such as the rehabilitation, under international auspices, of the finances of Austria, Hungary, Poland, Germany, *etc.;* the Dawes Plan, the Young Plan, and other steps in the solution of the grave problem of reparations; peaceful evacuation of the German Rhineland by the Allies; the establishment of the International Bank. Nor has evidence been lacking of some positive improvement in one of the sorest spots in

Europe—in the relations between France and Germany. Not only may the pact of Locarno and the reparation-agreements be cited, but the mutually respectful collaboration for several years of M. Briand and Herr Stresemann, the foreign ministers of the two countries, and the pooling of certain economic interests by industrialists of the two countries.

Whatever may be thought of these external gestures and actions of national governments in behalf of international peace, whether they be sincere or only superficial, and whether they offset or not the manifestations of integral nationalism within states, it hardly admits of doubt, even on the part of those most fearful of nationalism, that there has been during the past decade, and is now, a widespread popular will-to-peace, a feeling on the part of large numbers of influential citizens that they should not and must not violate an awakening *internationalist* conscience. Never before in human history have so many persons of one nation sought to understand and sympathize with other nations. Never before have peace-societies been so well organized or so active.

The contemporary popular will-to-peace is an extremely interesting phenomenon, but in the minds of some of us lurks a doubt as to its continuously paramount significance. There has long been—at least since the beginning of formal nationalism—a considerable popular will-to-peace, but while statesmen have generally paid lip-service to it on solemn occasions, it has not been stalwart and assertive enough in past crises actually to prevent nationalist wars. Undoubtedly there has been in recent times a much greater degree of popular will-to-peace, but this greater degree is mainly attributable, we submit, to two contemporary developments. One is an increase of international education, a widening comprehension of international affairs and a reasoned recognition of the need for international coöperation in the solution of basic economic problems. The other is a wave of disillusionment about war and what it does, disillusionment which is natural in any generation that has waged a war but which is peculiarly deep in the generation which has suffered from the World War.

As soon as we consider these hopeful developments with some care, we find ourselves faced with major questions. Taking up the matter of disillusionment, the question is, Will popular disillusionment about war prove permanent? In other words, Is it a peg on which we can safely hang our hopes for the future peace of the world, with or without nationalism?

Popular disillusionment about war has never proved permanent in the past, and, though much stronger now than ever before, it may not prove permanent in the future. There is a psychological difficulty which must not be overlooked. A generation that fights a war has personal experience of the ugliness, the brutality, and the sheer boredom of war; it can write and appreciate candid and realistic accounts of what went on at the front and behind the lines; it can detect the buncombe in wartime propaganda; and only with the utmost effort, and quite reluctantly, can it be induced to repeat its military experience. But time goes on. The human mind possesses the faculty, probably merciful, of gradually forgetting unpleasant things in the past and of dwelling only on pleasurable memories. War veterans grow older. They have children and grandchildren. They not only forget many unpleasant things but they tend to reconstruct, even to invent, many romantic war-scenes in order to impress upon their offspring their own youthful prowess and accomplishments. Thus, in time, they proceed to idealize for others the very war which long ago they themselves shuddered at; and another generation, brought up on idealized notions of war and on heroic lessons learned at the knees of fathers and grandfathers, is at last psychologically prepared to repeat the military experience.

At the present moment, the realities of the World War of 1914-1918 are too vivid in the recollections of too many persons to render another World War probable now or within the next decade or two. The disillusionment is too widespread and too thorough. Yet present disillusionment, if more extreme than ever before, is likely to be temporary. The pacifism which it encourages is of emotional exhaustion rather than of reasoned conviction. From its very nature it is not apt to induce a consistent and sustained effort to grapple intellectually with causes of war. In the meantime integral nationalism flourishes in vindictive words which provide excuses for bellicose action. Another vital decision will eventually have to be made between coöperative internationalism and integral nationalism, between peace and war. And it will most likely be the sons or the grandsons of the veterans of the last World War who will have to make the fateful decision.

The high degree of the contemporary popular will-to-peace is mainly attributable, we have suggested, to a widespread disillusionment about the recent World War—a

CONCLUSION

disillusionment, however, which, there is reason to think, may wear off in another generation—and to an increase of international education. International education has surely grown, and is growing. The number of international "institutes" is becoming legion. Crowds of teachers and students are beginning to be exchanged between nations. There are a prodigious number of agencies for acquainting peoples everywhere with international happenings. Yet here, too, is a major question. Is not international education confined in every country, by the very nature of things, to a comparatively small minority, which may or may not exert decisive influence on the masses?

International education seems to be growing among a fairly definite minority. The minority is select and intelligent and of considerable influence. It includes professors, "high-brows," "serious thinkers," and some ladies of leisure, together with liberal sprinklings of clergymen and publicists and exceptional bankers, business men, and labor leaders. On the other hand, the masses in all national states—the bulk of farmers, the general run of business men and shopkeepers, most mechanics and day-laborers, the vast majority of housewives and domestic servants—appear to be almost completely oblivious of international affairs and quite suspicious of the very word "internationalism." Their education is almost wholly nationalist. Outside of asserting what they deem to be particular personal and family interests, and perhaps some business and church interests, they seem content to repeat, parrot-like, such nationalist shibboleths as "my country, right or wrong," "national rights," "national interests," "national honor." It is probably utopian to imagine that in any grave crisis of the future these nationalistically indoctrinated citizens will be swayed by internationalist "high-brows" and "ladies of leisure." It is more plausible to guess that they will be swayed by persons who expect to derive some advantages and preferments from the exploitation of the ignorance and prejudice and emotionalism of the masses.

Hence arises the chief question of all. It is the question whether the masses in a national state can be educated in internationalism and for peace as well as in nationalism and for war. It is a most perplexing question. For education of any sort must be carried on at the present time within the framework of national states and among people who generally are much more interested in nationalism than in internationalism. Education, moreover, is notoriously conservative. Its primary function is usually conceived of as the conserving of the traditions of the past and the handing on of civilization from one generation to the next; and nationalism, rather than internationalism, is now a well established tradition and a distinctive mark of contemporary civilization.

Some persons contend that the significance of the attitude of the masses can easily be exaggerated: that all great reforms have been effected by minorities of determined intellectuals; that, in the present juncture, the masses may be suffered to go on thinking nationally and even to be taught to think nationally; that as leaders of the community become internationalists in thought, word, and deed, they will actually perfect a world order which will operate automatically and which eventually and unconsciously will affect the thought of the whole world;

CONCLUSION

and that then the masses will think, and be taught to think, internationally, quite as naturally and as painlessly as they now think nationally. In other words, it is contended that the solution of the problem of education should be left to an enlightened minority and to fate.

Much doubtless will depend on an intelligent minority. But the rôle of "fate" is not so certain. A minority which relies on the mere succession of events to achieve its ends is likely to experience disappointment and disillusionment. The minority cannot afford to be fatalistic; it must be purposeful and resourceful; it must be frankly and fearlessly propagandist. Nationalism, in all its various forms, has always been more or less purposefully propagated. Internationalism, likewise, must be propagated more or less purposefully.

The question of education is basically not international but national. It cannot be finally resolved by groups of internationally minded persons meeting at Geneva and adopting resolutions for the whole world. Even less can it be resolved by seeking and finding in some foreign country some awful example of extreme rampant nationalism. Wholesale denunciation of Fascism or Bolshevism by foreigners will only serve to strengthen nationalism and weaken internationalism in an Italy or a Russia. The only way to resolve the problem and to make education serve international as well as national ends, to render it preparatory to peace even more than to war, is for enlightened, well-informed citizens to take a hand diligently and farsightedly in shaping the education of their own fellow citizens within their respective national states. Education, like charity, should begin at home—with one's local school-teachers and school-board, with one's local newspaper, with one's own clubs and societies and associations.

Nationalism in many of its doctrines and much of its practice has undoubtedly been a beneficent influence in modern history. Unfortunately, it has tended to evolve a highly intolerant and warlike type which we have arbitrarily termed "integral." Clearly, the outstanding task before national education is to train among the coming generation a large number of men and women of character and reason who will perceive the dangers of integral nationalism, not only to humanity at large but to each and every nation, and who will guide the future evolution of nationalism again into channels of international peace and justice. Perhaps it cannot be done. But it is certainly worth the most serious effort.

For Americans, to whom this book is particularly addressed by special reason of the fact that its author is one of them, it may be pertinent to say a few last words in respect of the problem of national education. We Americans must give immediate and close thought to our own American nationalism and to our own American education. We have at the present time too many beams in our eyes to qualify us to pluck moats out of European eyes. We have a good deal of cant and even more of unpardonable self-deception. We boast of our schools, our intelligence, our wealth, our leisure, our great free press, our service and our altruism. We talk about peace more than any other nation.

Yet, in fact, integral nationalism is far advanced among us. We are peculiarly intolerant of any domestic dissent, of all foreigners and minorities in our midst. We are

CONCLUSION

peculiarly gullible, peculiarly ignorant, peculiarly emotional. While talking about the wickedness of others and our own good intentions, we despise and abuse the League of Nations and distrust most international undertakings; we go in for the biggest navy afloat—our pet form of militarism; we erect our tariff barriers higher than anyone else; we press forward imperialism and unblushingly deny to Latin Americans what we claim for ourselves; and we put reservations, formal or mental, to almost every international engagement which we make.

Much has been said in this volume of the formulation and acceptance of nationalist doctrines in England, Germany, France, and Italy and of the influence of nationalizing tendencies in these countries on the rest of the world. Similar doctrines have been formulated and accepted in the United States, and now and henceforth, with the United States a far greater force for good or for ill in the world than ever before, the influence of our nationalist evolution will be more and more extensive and penetrating. It is for thoughtful Americans, *par excellence,* to turn their attention to schools, publications, and societies within the United States and to endeavor to make them agencies of a nationalism that shall be humanitarian and truly enlightened. Within the United States must Americans seek the answers to the major questions whether international education is confined by the very nature of things to a comparatively small minority, whether present popular disillusionment about war will prove permanent, and whether the masses in a national state can be educated in internationalism and for peace as well as in nationalism and for war.

INDEX OF NAMES

A

Alexander I, Tsar, 100, 110, 113, 117-118.
Alfieri, 87 n.
Annunzio, D', 216-217, 218, 221
Ashley, 276 n.
Austin, 158, 159.

B

Bacon, 169.
Bainville, 204.
Barère, 47-49, 50, 53, 54, 58, 60, 62-63, 64-65, 67, 68, 70 n., 76-77, 78, 79, 82, 290.
Barra, 55.
Barrès, 168, 184-202, 203, 204, 205, 211, 213, 215, 216, 217, 218, 222, 290.
Bastiat, 158, 243.
Baudeau, 241 n.
Beaumarchais, 184.
Bebel, 256.
Bentham, 5, 11, 39, 120-134, 136, 138, 142, 144, 157, 164, 170, 290, 301.
Bernhardi, 102 n.
Bernstein, 260.
Besse, 204.
Beyle. See Stendhal.
Bismarck, 214, 223, 226, 248, 272, 278-280, 285.
Blackstone, 92.

Blanc, 265.
Bluntschli, 158.
Boileau, 218.
Bolingbroke, 17-22, 24, 27, 33, 34, 41, 42, 56-57, 86, 87, 89, 90, 92, 127, 241, 290-291, 298, 301.
Bonald, 88, 95-100, 101, 109, 111, 116, 178, 180, 184, 221, 290, 298, 301.
Bonaparte, Louis Napoleon. See *Napoleon III*.
Bonaparte, Napoleon. See *Napoleon I*.
Bossuet, 98.
Bouche, 201.
Boulanger, 186, 188, 197, 198.
Bourget, 204.
Brentano, 276 n.
Briand, 164, 210 n., 314.
Bright, 158, 242, 281.
Brissot, 45.
Bucher, 276 n.
Buffon, 98.
Burke, 88-95, 97, 101, 109, 111, 123, 126, 178, 180, 184, 221, 263 n., 290, 298, 301.
Byron, 138.

C

Canning, 159, 247.
Capet, 210.

Carnot, 49-50, 54, 56, 58, 60, 290, 301.
Casimir-Périer, 158.
Castelbajac, 115.
Castlereagh, 113, 133.
Cavour, 154, 158, 159, 243, 246.
Cervantes, 184.
Chamberlain, Austen, 281.
Chamberlain, H. S., 223.
Charles, Archduke, 104, 113.
Chateaubriand, 109, 181 *n.*
Chaumette, 46.
Clootz, 39.
Cobden, 158, 242, 243.
Comte, 168-173, 174, 185, 188, 202, 205, 206, 209, 213 *n.*, 222, 289.
Condorcet, 62, 229.
Corridoni, 217-218.
Couthon, 47.
Crispi, 285.
Croce, 214, 218.
Cunningham, 276 *n.*

D

Dante, 152, 214, 220.
Danton, 46.
Daudet, Léon, 204.
Defoe, 184.
Déroulède, 188, 197.
Descartes, 169.
Desmoulins, 46.
Dillon, Mlle., 140.
Dimier, 204.
Disraeli, 267 *n.*, 285.
Dreyfus, 187, 203.
Dupont de Nemours, 241 *n.*
Durkheim, 213 *n.*

E

Elizabeth, Queen, 7, 20, 86.
Engels, 251-253, 257.

F

Faucher, 158, 243.
Fénélon, 98.
Ferry, 285.
Fichte, 87 *n.*, 101, 154, 223, 263-266, 277, 290.
Fourier, 249.
France, Anatole, 203.
Frederick the Great, 171.

G

Gagern, 158.
Galileo, 169.
Garibaldi, 154, 158.
Gentile, 214-215.
Gerlach, L. von, 223.
Gervinus, 158.
Gibbon, 88.
Gioberti, 215-216.
Gladstone, 159, 247.
Grégoire, 66.
Grote, 158.
Grotius, 5, 7, 11.
Guizot, 139-147, 151, 158, 243, 290.

H

Hamilton, 268.
Hansemann, 158.
Hastings, 89.
Hébert, 46, 74-75.

INDEX OF NAMES

Hegel, 87 *n*., 154, 173, 185, 213-215, 223, 251, 255, 257, 263, 289.
Held, 276 *n*.
Henry IV, of France, 100, 210.
Henry VIII, of England, 86.
Herder, 17, 27-34, 41, 42, 56-57, 87, 92, 101-102, 263, 290, 301, 308.
Hildebrand, 274 *n*.
Hitler, 223, 308.
Hobbes, 124, 172.
Homer, 1.
Hugo, 138, 158.
Humboldt, W. von, 134.

J

Jeanne d'Arc, 98, 210.
Jefferson, 228.
Johnson, Samuel, 88.
Joliclerc, 56 *n*.

K

Kant, 28, 206, 263.
Kingsley, 266-267, 277.
Knies, 274 *n*.
Korais, 158.
Kossuth, 158.

L

Laffitte, 158.
Lasker, 158.
Lassalle, 255, 256, 258, 265, 272.
Lassere, 204.
Laveleye, 158.
Ledru-Rollin, 158.

Le Goffic, 204.
Leibnitz, 100.
Lemaître, 204.
Liebknecht, 255.
Lieven, Countess of, 140, 142.
List, 267-272, 277, 290.
Lloyd George, 281.
Locke, 23, 86.
Louis IX, 98.
Louis XIV, 58, 61, 183, 210.
Louis XVI, 40.
Louis XVIII, 50, 114-115, 140, 141, 142.
Louis Napoleon. *See Napoleon III.*
Louis Philippe, 49, 141, 243.
Luther, 28.

M

MacDonald, 164-165, 281.
Machiavelli, 214.
Macmahon, 203.
Maistre, de, 109.
Malthus, 242.
Marat, 46, 80.
Marcus Aurelius, 9.
Marx, 250-255, 257-262, 272, 289, 296.
Maurras, 165, 168, 184, 202-212, 213, 215, 217, 218, 222, 230, 287, 290, 308.
Mazzini, 138, 139, 151-157, 158, 213, 215, 216, 217, 225-226, 257, 290, 308.
McKinley, 285.
M'Culloch, 158.
Mendelssohn, Dorothea, 102-104.

[325]

INDEX OF NAMES

Metternich, 116-119, 140, 152, 160.
Meulan, Mlle., 140.
Mevissen, 158.
Michelet, 147 n., 158.
Mill, James, 158, 242.
Mill, John Stuart, 133 n., 158.
Milton, 23, 86.
Mirabeau, 48, 61, 71.
Mistral, 203.
Montalembert, 109.
Montesquieu, Léon, 204.
Moses, 25.
Müller, 223.
Mussolini, 166, 213, 220-221, 223-224, 230, 290, 308, 309.

N

Napoleon I, 49, 50, 51, 60, 63, 75, 81-83, 85, 87, 105, 110, 113, 116, 133, 134, 135, 139, 143, 147, 155, 197, 220, 263, 267.
Napoleon III, 159, 174, 211, 243.
Nelson, 113.
Nietzsche, 185, 186, 189, 216, 219, 223, 289.
Novalis, 102 n.

O

O'Connell, 158.
Owen, 249.

P

Paine, 39.
Palacky, 158, 294.
Palmerston, 159.
Pascal, Georges de, 204.
Peters, 284-285.
Pétion, 45.
Pitt, 89, 113, 133.
Pius XI, 210 n.
Place, 158.
Prince-Smith, 158, 243.
Proudhon, 250, 255, 257.

Q

Quesnay, 241 n.

R

Racine, 98.
Rehberg, 263 n.
Renan, 181 n., 185, 196, 202.
Ricardo, 242.
Robespierre, 44, 47, 48, 74-75, 80, 81.
Rodbertus, 265, 272-274, 277.
Roland, 45.
Roosevelt, 285.
Roscher, 274, 277.
Rossi, 158, 243.
Rotteck, 147.
Rousseau, 17, 22-27, 33, 34, 40, 42, 45, 47, 51-52, 56, 67, 87, 90, 96, 102, 123, 124, 170, 241, 263, 290, 308.
Russell, 227-228.

S

Sainte-Beuve, 202.
Saint-John, Henry. *See* Bolingbroke.

[326]

INDEX OF NAMES

Saint-Just, 47.
Sanctis, De, 214.
Say, 243.
Schäffle, 276 *n.*
Schlegel, A. W., 101.
Schlegel, F. von, 88, 101-109, 110, 111, 116, 178, 181, 290, 298.
Schleiermacher, 102 *n.*
Schmerling, 158.
Schmoller, 276 *n.*
Schopenhauer, 185, **223**.
Senior, 158, 242.
Shakespeare, 102.
Siéyès, 48, 71.
Smith, Adam, 134, 241, 243, 245, 275.
Sombart, 276 *n.*
Sorel, 213, 217, 218, **261**.
Spaventa, 214.
Stein, 134, 243.
Stendhal, 55 *n.*
Stocks, J. L., 231 *n.*
Stresemann, 314.

T

Tacitus, 1.
Taine, 168, 173-184, 185, 186, 188, 196, 202, 213 *n.*, 222.
Talleyrand, 62, 71.
Tennyson, 244.
Thiers, 159, 198.
Thompson, William, **228**.
Tieck, 102 *n.*
Toynbee, 276 *n.*
Treitschke, 223.

V

Vaugeois, 204.
Vergniaud, 45.
Vico, 214-215.
Victoria, Queen, 266.
Villeneuve-Bargemont, 267 *n.*, 277.
Voltaire, 70, 89.

W

Wagner, Adolf, 272, 275-277.
Wagner, Richard, 223.
Welcker, 139, 147-151, 158, 290.
Wellington, 113.
William I, 280.
Wilson, 164.